Working the Planning Table

Negotiating Democratically for Adult, Continuing, and Workplace Education

Ronald M. Cervero
Arthur L. Wilson

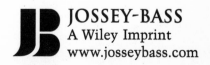

JOSSEY-BASS
A Wiley Imprint
www.josseybass.com

Published by Jossey-Bass
A Wiley Imprint
989 Market Street, San Francisco, CA 94103-1741   www.josseybass.com

Jossey-Bass books and products are available through most bookstores. To contact Jossey-Bass directly call our Customer Care Department within the U.S. at 800-956-7739, outside the U.S. at 317-572-3986, or fax 317-572-4002.

Jossey-Bass also publishes its books in a variety of electronic formats. Some content that appears in print may not be available in electronic books.

Library of Congress Cataloging-in-Publication Data

Cervero, Ronald M.
  Working the planning table : negotiating democratically for adult, continuing, and workplace education / Ronald M. Cervero, Arthur L. Wilson.
    p. cm.
  Includes bibliographical references and index.
  ISBN-13 978-0-7879-6206-7 (alk. paper)
  ISBN-10 0-7879-6206-6 (alk. paper)
  1. Adult education—Planning. 2. Continuing education—Planning. 3. Education, Cooperative—Planning. I. Wilson, Arthur L., 1950- II. Title.
  LC5219.C43 2005
  374.12—dc22
                                        2005021722

Printed in the United States of America
FIRST EDITION
HB Printing   10 9 8 7 6 5 4 3 2 1

Contents

Preface

In *Planning Responsibly for Adult Education: A Guide to Negotiating Power and Interests* (1994a), we offered an understanding of planning grounded in the everyday realities faced by people responsible for educational programs. The book offered an approach that highlighted the politics of the social and organizational settings in educational planning. Our theory has since influenced many other books and articles about program planning (Caffarella, 2002; Donaldson & Kozoll, 1999; Sork, 2000). More important, many practitioners have found that this framework provides both the language to discuss and the strategies to address critical issues in planning educational programs (Cervero & Wilson, 1996). Since the publication of the 1994 edition, we have done a great deal of research and writing that has further developed this approach to planning (Cervero & Wilson, 1998; Cervero, Wilson, & Associates, 2001; Wilson & Cervero, 1996, 1997), and we have developed a variety of materials that can be used by planners in their everyday practice. We have worked with other people to develop refinements of and applications for the theory in various contexts, including higher education (Hendricks, 1996; Kleiber, 1996), women's education (Scott & Schmitt-Boshnick, 1996), state educational policy (Maruatona & Cervero, 2004), corporate education (Mabry & Wilson, 2001; Rees, Cervero, Moshi, & Wilson, 1997), literacy education (Drennon & Cervero, 2002; Sandlin & Cervero,

2003), religious education (Burns & Cervero, 2004; Guthrie & Cervero, 2001), HIV/AIDS education (Archie-Booker, Cervero, & Langone, 1999; Sessions & Cervero, 2001), community development (Carter, 1996; McDonald, 1996; Mills, Cervero, Langone, & Wilson, 1995), public heath education (Umble, Cervero, & Langone, 2001), and continuing medical education (Maclean, 1997).

We started the theory's development with a question that many adult education planning theorists thought they had already answered: What do planners do? From 1994 until now, our answer to that question has remained the same: planners exercise power to negotiate interests, and in doing so they should nurture an ethical commitment to substantively democratic participation. The claim that planners negotiate interests in relations of power has led us steadily toward the question that drives this book: Program planning for what? In framing education as the struggle for knowledge and power in society (Cervero & Wilson, 2001), we have argued that educators are knowledge and power brokers in this struggle. So why does planning matter? Because planners offer educational programs that produce educational and political outcomes that benefit some people more than others. The key questions, then, are who benefits and, more important, who should benefit from these educational programs—and what kind of difference should the programs make? In answering these questions, we take the stance that planners need an ethical commitment to democratic planning, a political analysis that anticipates threats to and opportunities for enacting this commitment, and negotiation strategies tied to this commitment and analysis to improve the lives of individuals, the functioning of organizations, and the health of communities.

Why does the field need another book that focuses on the politics and ethics of educational planning? Whereas the 1994 book provided a vocabulary and a lens to see the social, political, and ethical realities facing planners, this book uses that lens to connect the technical and political decisions that people make at the planning table. There are two major differences between the presentations of the theory in the two books: (1) the planning table metaphor now provides the centerpiece for the theory, and (2) the practical decisions and technical strategies about needs, objectives, instructional design, administration, and evaluation are now connected to the real-world contexts in which power, interests, ethical commitments, and negotiation strategies are part of everyday life.

Purpose and Organization of the Book

This book offers a theory that accounts for planners' lived experience and provides a guide for their practical action in developing educational programs. The theory has been formed out of studies and observation of planners' experience over the past fifteen years as they developed programs in social and organizational contexts. These lived experiences have highlighted the fundamentally social character of planning and focused attention where decisions are truly made about educational programs—at "the planning table." We use three planning stories to illustrate how dimensions of the planning table (power, interests, ethical commitment, and negotiation) are central to planners' everyday work. Our theoretical claims come alive in the stories of these planners, which can effectively teach others about how to respond to the realities of practice. These stories dramatically illustrate a key point of the book: the technical work of planning is also always political.

The theoretical justifications for that claim are presented in Part One. Chapter One provides an overview of the theory and introduces the three planning stories. Chapter Two presents an extended version of all three planning stories. Chapter Three explains the planning table metaphor and its key dimensions (power, interests, ethical commitment, and negotiation). It ends with an explanation of why an ethical commitment to substantively democratic planning provides a guide to practical action. In Part Two, Chapters Four through Eight explain and illustrate how people work the planning table to negotiate educational and political outcomes for multiple stakeholders. These chapters are organized around the planning tasks for a program's needs assessment (Chapter Four); educational, management, and political objectives (Chapter Five); instructional design and implementation (Chapter Six); administrative organization and operation (Chapter Seven); and formal and informal evaluation (Chapter Eight). We begin each chapter with a summary of the guidance other planning texts have offered on the task. We do this to recover the many important insights and provide resources for the technical strategies useful for each task. Each chapter then offers four principles that provide practical guidance about how to complete the tasks in the face of social and organizational power relationships. The fourth principle in each chapter shows how planners can enact an ethical commitment to substantively democratic planning when negotiating the specific task. In Chapter Nine, we explore the central question of the book: Why does planning matter? We propose an image of educational planners as leaders who are strategic organizers of education in the struggle for knowledge and power. We discuss this image within the traditions of adult education planning, leadership, and administration theory. We end on a personal note with a discussion about why we used planning stories as a central feature of this book, how we teach planning, and why learning from planning experience is so crucial to becoming good planners.

Audience

We have written *Working the Planning Table* to provide a guide for planners who develop educational programs that make a difference in the world. The primary audience is anyone who has some responsibility for planning education for adults in social or organizational settings. These roles and settings include, but are not limited to leaders and continuing educators in community colleges and higher education, human resource and organizational development specialists in business and government, labor and union educators, social movement activists, instructional developers for distance education, adult literacy educators, community educators and organizers, and educators in professional associations. The second audience we hope to reach comprises people pursuing advanced degrees in the fields of adult, continuing, higher, and workplace education as well as our colleagues who teach planning courses in these graduate programs. We hope that in the luxury of advanced study these people can take the time out to reflect and then act on the theory we offer in this book. We believe that by seeing what's really going on at the table, planners are more likely to offer programs that can increase people's life chances, improve the functioning of the organizations where people work, and strengthen the communities in which they live. Informed by a decade of experience and research, this new book, we hope, offers a more mature, practical, and user-friendly version of the theory.

Acknowledgments

This book is the culmination of a project that we began in 1989, so it is impossible to recognize all of the people who have shaped it. We received many constructive suggestions about *Planning Responsibly for Adult Education* that helped us see which concepts helped people make sense of their experience and where the theory fell short. These came from hundreds of students in our classes and the people in our presentations and workshops in North America, Malaysia, Africa, and Europe over the past twelve years. We greatly appreciate the many people who have conducted research using the theory and showed us new ways to understand the issues of power, interests, negotiation, and democratic planning. Almost all of these people are referenced earlier in this Preface, and we encourage you to read their work. A special note of thanks is due to Tom Sork for continuing to push us to make our ideas clearer, especially in relation to the forms of negotiation. The Practitioner Inquiry story came alive through Cassie Drennon's willingness to resurrect her experiences, so we owe her a great debt of gratitude.

Two graduate assistants, Kate Monghan and Kit Ng, were very helpful in formatting and editorial work on the manuscript. Finally, we really appreciate the advice given us by Tom Heaney, Tara Fenwick, and an anonymous reviewer as we were at the final stage of producing the manuscript. They helped to validate most of our work and identified some inconsistencies and omissions.

February 2005
Athens, Georgia   Ronald M. Cervero
Ithaca, New York   Arthur L. Wilson

Part I

Working the Planning Table
A Theory for Practice

Ralph Tyler was right, but only partly, when he offered guidance to educational planners in his classic 1949 curriculum manual. Tyler (1949, p. 1) identified four central questions that educational planners should address:

1. What educational purposes should the school seek to attain?
2. What educational experiences can be provided that are likely to attain these purposes?
3. How can these educational experiences be effectively organized [to attain the purposes]?
4. How can we determine whether these purposes are being attained?

Developing objectives, selecting content, organizing learning experiences, and evaluating results—this is the part that Tyler clearly got right in offering guidance. These four planning questions, representing a robust tradition in curriculum and instruction for nearly a hundred years (Petrina, 2004; Walker, 2003), have been central to nearly all subsequent theoretical formulations (Reid, 1979; Schubert, 1986; Schwab, 1969). This classical view likewise has had many proponents in American adult education, as indicated very early by Bryson (1936) and Knowles (1950), confirmed in the 1980s by Sork and Buskey's (1986) and Sork and Caffarella's (1989) reviews of planning theory, and recently reconfirmed by Sork (2000) and Sork and Newman (2004). Sork and Caffarella (p. 234) expanded Tyler's four curriculum questions into six planning steps that "illustrate the most common planning logic found in the literature" of adult education: "(1) analyze planning context and client system, (2) assess needs, (3) develop program objectives, (4) formulate instructional plan, (5) formulate administrative plan, and (6) design a program evaluation plan." Brookfield (1986, p. 233) termed such planning steps the "sequential institutional model," a direct invocation of Tylerian systems logic and procedure. Planners have to be not only cognizant of the steps in the classical models but also technically skilled in their procedures, which Sork and Newman (p. 96) liken to "the production of a piece of theatre in which if everything goes well, ideas, people, and resources coalesce." Thus, there are compelling reasons to draw upon the insights of this viewpoint. What Tyler's and other models do not get right, however, is how planners should address these questions in practice. Although these models organize attention to important aspects of planning, they offer limited guidance in the real places where real people struggle to plan real programs.

In Part One, we introduce a theory that provides such guidance for planners organized around the metaphor of "working the planning table." We also present three planning stories that will illuminate the theory throughout the book: "Practitioner Inquiry for Adult Literacy Teachers," "Continuing Education in the Society for Valuation Professions," and "Management Education at the Phoenix Company." We open Chapter One with vignettes from each story to embody the "planning table" metaphor. The remainder of Chapter One provides a rationale for the theory: working the planning table matters because educational programs produced there have educational and political outcomes for multiple stakeholders. Chapter Two provides an extended version of each planning story that includes organizational charts, program schedules, and planning calendars and documents. Chapter Three provides a full articulation of the theory, describing its key concepts and showing how the theory can guide practical action.

We use shorthand phrases throughout the book for two concepts central to the planning table metaphor. First, the phrase *social and organizational* refers to two dimensions of power that structure social life more generally. These two dimensions include both socially based power relations, such as race, class, gender, and sexual orientation, as well as organizationally based power relations, such as hierarchical position. Second, although democracy is a highly contested concept with multiple meanings, we use the term *democratic planning* in a very specific way throughout the book. As explained in Chapter Three, the ethical commitment to "substantively democratic planning" is undertaken in the face of structured inequalities created by social and organizational power relationships. By using this phrase, we define the need for stakeholders to have a "substantive" role in making decisions about educational programs at the planning table. Our theory recognizes that structured inequalities not only keep people away from the planning table, but also generally allow a "token" rather than a "substantive" representation for those people with little power who are present at the table.

The lengthy accounts of each planning story in Chapter Two offer key images and analytic themes and a sense of our position on each story. At the end of Chapter Nine, we offer an explanation about the value of stories and their extensive use throughout the book. Although all three stories actually happened, we used two different methods to develop them. We wrote the Phoenix story for the 1994 book by observing planning meetings at the company and debriefing the planners (Pete and Joan) after each meeting. Pseudonyms are used to mask the company name, its type of business (referred to only as a "service" business), and the planners. In contrast to telling that story as outside observers, we made a conscious decision to tell the other two stories as autobiographies of our own planning. All of the events and activities that Arthur describes in the Society for Valuation Professions actually happened, although to protect its anonymity we are not using the society's real name. Likewise, the story that Ron and Cassandra Drennon tell of the Practitioner Inquiry program happened in Georgia.

Although the stories' human dynamics illuminate the theory, they present a very limited range of the forms education can take and who its planners are. We use the term *planners* to refer to a family of roles that have responsibility for social interventions with an educational outcome in any social or organizational setting, such as learners, teachers, program planners, social activists, community organizers, instructional designers, human resource development directors, organizational developers, managers, leaders, and policy analysts. The planner can be an individual (an adult literacy teacher), an informal group (a corporation's task force), or an institutional leadership (a community agency's board of directors). In our view, then, "A planner can be anyone, anywhere, anytime" (Hooper, 1992, p. 53). As these examples show, "education" takes many forms, and organizations that offer formal educational programs also embrace a multitude of alternative formats, such as mentorship, learning communities, e-learning web forums, individualized computer-based modules, guided practice, scaffolding, action learning, and cross-functional projects. The audiences for these programs can range from a single person (an executive coach's client) to millions of people (a television show).

Chapter 1

Seeing What Matters

Education as a Struggle for Knowledge and Power

Real people plan real programs in real places to produce adult education. Experienced educators understand what it takes to work effectively with other people in social and organizational settings to produce educational programs for adults. These educators typically have particular ways of "seeing" (that is, understanding) the conditions in which they work and how to get the work done. Even though educators often recognize the contingencies, dilemmas, ambiguities, challenges, and opportunities of working with other people to plan programs, most adult education planning theory has not taken these into account. Over the decades, the gamut of rational decision-making models, linear and feedback procedural task systems, and general planning theories have not produced working understandings of the context in which people plan programs. Most planning theory, with its lack of attention to context and its pervasive focus on planning steps, is only partially helpful in focusing attention on what matters in planning programs. These planning steps frame practice as an iterative series of activities that begins with needs-assessments, includes educational design, and concludes with evaluation. In contrast, we frame planning practice as a social activity of negotiating interests in relationships of power (Cervero & Wilson, 1994a). To better understand power, interests, and the practical action of negotiation, we have focused on the "people work" of planning (Wilson & Cervero, 1996). This work happens in complex, messy settings in which people gather at planning tables to make decisions about the educational objectives and the social and political objectives of educational programs.

In the first part of this chapter we introduce three planning stories that illustrate where educators do the work that matters: at the planning table. In the second part we introduce the major theme of the book: planners work to produce educational outcomes and, simultaneously, social and political outcomes for multiple stakeholders. In the last part, we discuss the historical development of our theory and its relationship to other educational planning theories.

Seeing What Matters I
The Planning Table

Each of the following vignettes introduces an actual planning story that shows the everyday life of educators making decisions about programs in social and organizational contexts. Each vignette is followed by the identification of the planning tables. We use the term *planning table* as a metaphor to focus attention on what matters in educational planning: namely, the fact that people make judgments with others in social contexts about specific program features. The many variants of this metaphor speak to issues of power, participation, and decision making across all areas of social life. The variants include references to people "sitting at the table," "who was (or was not) at the table," what people "bring to the table," and putting issues "on the table." The planning table can be either a physical one where people meet to make decisions or a metaphorical one where people make decisions with others on the telephone, in hallways, or privately in offices.

Management Education at the Phoenix Company

We tell this story as researchers who investigated the planning practices of people at the Phoenix Company, which was first reported in our 1994 book. This incident introduces Pete, a vice president, and his early struggles to understand and manage the power relations as he was attempting to change the company's organizational culture.

The Phoenix Company is a service-oriented business that has conducted an annual management education program for the past ten years. The president, Mr. Jones, along with his top management team of vice presidents, has used this program to review the past year's efforts and present plans for the coming year to the middle management of the Phoenix Company. Over the past two years, however, an organizational struggle has emerged about the focus and type of activities used for this program.

As vice president for human resources, Pete has been one of the primary planners of the program. The program was typically held as a two-day retreat at a site away from the company, in which the executives made "informational presentations" announcing plans, projects, and goals for the coming year. Pete has been trying to work with Mr. Jones to include interactive and experiential learning activities in the retreat to make it more focused on organizational development.

Pete told this story of planning the program with Mr. Jones and Brad, the executive vice president. Pete had wanted to develop a retreat program in the spring that was more interactive than previous programs, "but the president was not ready to do it . . . he said that he might want to do it in the fall, but I never heard from him again." At about this same time, Pete was embroiled in a contentious relationship with Brad, who perceived that Pete was trying to undermine his authority. In the summer, this situation erupted into a serious confrontation between the two, at which time Pete was also informed that Mr. Jones expected him to hold the annual retreat in one month's time. Pete recalled that at that moment he felt as if he were standing on the deck of "a sinking ship":

> We [Pete and Brad] got into a couple of real shouting matches in the budget preparation that I didn't understand. Apparently, the executive VP believed I was trying to undermine his

authority and that I was questioning his judgment in an inappropriate way. He really got upset about it. We continued to have disagreements on into the summer, and that's when he shook his finger in my face one day in July and said, "Goddammit, where is our retreat, Pete? The boss said he wants to have a retreat; I just talked to him last night, and he wonders why you haven't planned it. His understanding was that you were going to do one in August, and he wants to know why you haven't got it together." That's exactly what he said in front of a whole group of people when I had not even heard the word *retreat* in the last sixty days . . . much less been given the mandate to do it.

When Pete tried to explain the circumstances to Mr. Jones, the president "was very critical." Pete knew Brad "had done a real good job of letting [Mr. Jones] hear his side of it before I ever got there" and, consequently, felt "like a lamb taken to the slaughter." So Pete pulled together the program using Harvard Business School cases as directed by Brad, secured the site, and hired an outside consultant from a local university to facilitate the program. As Pete recounted his planning, he said: "In some ways it was really good, but I was still in this real struggle because I threw it together at the last minute, I planned it under pressure, I didn't go to the right person for direction. So I really did a lot of reflecting on why I had screwed up and why I had gotten blamed for not doing a good job." However, Pete felt that the program "ended up being a real success, very positive." This was due, in large measure, to the fact that Mr. Jones himself was very positive about what had happened and publicly commended Pete at the end of the program.

Planning tables abound in this story. The initial table is structured by the traditions and protocols in which people have planned previous retreats; the decisions made and protocols established at those tables are the ones Pete is attempting to change. A second table lies in the informal conversations Pete has had with the president in trying to persuade him to endorse a more experiential, interactive retreat format. The most obvious planning table is the literal one in the budget meetings. The "shouting matches" at this table further the deteriorating relationship Pete has with Brad. The open conflict at this table bleeds into another planning table in which the vice president does "a good job of letting [Mr. Jones] hear his side of the story" so that Pete felt "like a lamb taken to the slaughter" for not doing the planning for the retreat.

The slaughter metaphor is perhaps not overstated, for it represents Pete's sense of how power is being exercised at these various planning tables. The metaphor points directly to the people-work of planning in complex organizational settings. Although important activities of planning programs are clearly being tended to (decisions are being made about where the retreat will be held, what the curriculum will be, how it will be facilitated), the people making decisions at these planning tables are also embroiled in power struggles over whose educational vision for the retreats will prevail. This planning is about more than collecting data to be used in a needs-assessment; it is also about who has the power to determine the features of the educational program. This opening scenario shows that Pete's initial efforts to alter the function and purpose of the retreat flounder because he "threw it together at the last minute . . . planned it under pressure . . . didn't go to the right person for direction." Pete may be managing some parts of planning properly, but he certainly struggled with managing the people-work. Whose educational vision will prevail as the planning begins for the next retreat?

Continuing Education in the Society for Valuation Professions

This planning story, told in the first person by Arthur Wilson, is about the development of a new continuing education program for a professional society. Arthur describes his first meeting with the Society's president, who explains to Arthur how he should understand the reasons for the Society's new educational program. This

*meeting takes place at that ubiquitous planning venue in adult
education: the restaurant table.*

It was my first day "at the office." I'd only been there once before
to interview for a position as director of education for the Society for
Valuation Professions (SVP), a professional association for testing and
certifying the technical expertise of property valuators. When I entered
the office suite, briefcase and trench coat in hand, I wasn't entirely
sure they were expecting me, as I was asked to sit in the reception
area for some time while the receptionist went looking for the executive director.

I had only met the director during the interview. We had talked
then for about an hour, in which I recounted my adult education
experience—mostly adult literacy teaching and professional development for literacy educators—while trying to disguise my lack of
"corporate" experience. I was also trying to find out what this job—
vaguely described as "helping this group do adult education"—was
about.

I learned that the director had been in the position only a few
months himself—the reason he could shed little light on what the
issues were. Neither of us had any professional experience as valuators either. The little I learned in this meeting was not greatly
increased in the subsequent phone call offering the position. Three
weeks later I found myself in new clothes in a new city in a new job
as I heard the executive director's voice from down the hall. Greeting
me warmly, he said, "Let's go see your office." Winding through the
maze of suites, we got there and he indicated for me to put my coat
and case down. He then said, "You might want to get something to
take notes with. You're going to meet the president." Almost before
I had a chance, literally, to hang up my coat, I was about to meet
SVP's president—a major architect in reorienting the focus of this
organization and the person who, as I soon would learn, was going
to "brief me about how things are."

The director and I went next door to a conference hotel restaurant where the president was eating breakfast. He had just taken the

early shuttle from the city where he worked as a senior manager in a major accounting firm; he would be returning on the afternoon flight. As we joined him (we wouldn't leave the table for several hours, two meals, and countless cigarettes and cups of coffee later), I noticed on the floor next to him a bulging case marked "SVP," crammed with papers, folders, and notebooks. The president said he had come to town on my first day to welcome me and to help me "learn who was important" and "what our plans are."

As the president talked, his SVP case grew smaller as a stack of documents—lists of names, committee memos, meeting minutes, Society resolutions, educational marketing brochures and appraisal programs of study from competitor societies, even organizational train-the-trainer manuals—grew in front of me. I tried, gamely, to ask questions, to talk educationally, to inquire about objectives, instructors, courses. But that was not why I was there. Never, in what I had thought would be a program development discussion, did we talk about education other than as a "product we have to deliver to members if the Society is to survive." Never was it discussed what the education was really about or how it was going to get done, just that they were going to do it. What we did talk about—or rather what I was told—was the recent history and circumstances that had led to the organization's taking on something it had historically shunned.

Here is what the president wanted to be sure I understood as I began the work of assisting the creation of their new educational program: the newly created director's position was part of an organizational identity change—an attempt to reconfigure the Society's relationship with its members, with the occupation it represented, and with the public it served. Part of that transformation included doing something the association had officially said for decades it would not do: becoming a teaching society to provide entry-level professional education for aspiring and novice valuators. Teaching was something other organizations did, not the Society for Valuation Professions. In the words of one of its presidents, this Society was different because it was "multi-disciplinary . . . the only Society that tests and certifies professionals who appraise all types of tangible and intangible, real and personal property." As echoed by the chair of the Education Committee, "SVP has traditionally been a testing and certifying association. Its mission . . . has been to provide public testimony of the practicing appraiser's competence in his or her chosen specialty. This testifying process is substantiated by a rigorous system of examination and appraisal practice review." Thus the organizational function was to "certify" the expertise of established valuators rather than train new ones. The president's and chair's words represented a dominant Society mantra that had long stood as an organizational definer of its identity and purpose. If applicants successfully completed the Society's technical expertise examinations, such candidates could then append the Society's initials to their professional identity in the way that RN, JD, AIA, MD, and PhD are appended in other occupations. People's professional identities were constituted by such "designations"; the designations could make significant differences in professional standing, capacity to generate income, or even whether or not the profession could be practiced. What the president emphatically wanted to be sure I understood was how crucial a successful continuing professional education program was, not just to the Society's makeover but also to how that makeover would alter the relationships with its members (the appraisal profession) and their clients (the general public).

One of the last things the president gave me was a list of names and telephone numbers. Most names were of people he had briefed me about during the long morning and early afternoon; he now charged me to "talk to them right away." I later realized I was, in effect, being given the names of those who were "on the right side"— those working to change the Society's traditional stance against providing education for its members. Before I even knew I was on a side, I'd been given allies. What I was learning that day was that there were serious issues at stake, so much so that the president of the association felt compelled to get to me first—before anyone else, even the director—to explain how I "should see things."

There are two planning tables represented in the opening scenes of this story. First is the one around which the director and Arthur gather to discuss the new education director's position—the executive director's desk. That meeting and subsequent telephone call were productive for beginning to establish working administrative relationships necessary to implement the Society's goals. But because both the executive director and the education director were new to the organization and neither were appraisers, the meetings at this table were relatively unproductive for understanding the Society's goals, plans, or conditions in which they would be enacted—hence the urgency of the restaurant meeting.

The second table at the restaurant meeting with the Society's president was clearly significant because it conveyed what the president thought was at risk and what needed to change. The president was using his power as president to make sure Arthur got the "right" message right from the start. As at the Phoenix Company, this story demonstrates that the political work of planning (in this case, constructing and organizing alliances) is just as important as designing curricula, training teachers, and evaluating outcomes. The latter were almost never mentioned in this initial encounter, although Arthur made efforts to bring them to the table. These alliances would embody and construct the new educational vision for the organization, reshaping its relationship with the membership as well as with the consumers of its professional services and the public in general. As in the Phoenix Company story, then, Arthur's educational planning is not just about the participants' educational outcomes, but also about strategic positioning of the Society in its profession. We should see this intersection of educational and political outcomes as routine—not extraordinary—in program planning. Historically, the organization's membership had typically shunned any role the Society could have had in formally educating neophyte practitioners in their profession, preferring a gatekeeping role of determining access to the profession's senior ranks. That stance now needed to change because of professional, economic, and legislative pressures. As we'll show in Chapter Two, the educational program was the means through which the mission and practice of this organization would change—but not without resistance. How crucial would the educational program be in changing the organization? Would the Society survive? Like the Phoenix Company story, the SVP story represents a site in which stakeholders in a social and organizational context vie for control to enact a particular educational vision.

Practitioner Inquiry for Adult Literacy Teachers

This planning story is about a staff development program that Cassandra (Cassie) Drennon and Ronald Cervero worked on together for adult literacy teachers. The incident described in this section is told by Cassie, who was facilitating a workshop for these literacy teachers. The situation and circumstances Cassie describes illustrate another ubiquitous planning table: the classroom itself. [Note: We wrote this section and the Practitioner Inquiry section in Chapter Two in collaboration with Cassandra Drennon.]

It was midafternoon on Friday at the local conference hotel where a group of twenty-four adult literacy teachers were nearing the end of a two-day retreat for the Practitioner Inquiry (PI) program. In the spirit of the collaborative intent of "practitioner inquiry," the goal for this retreat—the second of four retreats planned for the yearlong program—was for teachers to design a research project pertaining to teaching and learning that they would carry out with learners in their classrooms. So far, all activities we had planned for the retreat had gone smoothly.

On this particular afternoon, we had split the participants into two groups of twelve for the purpose of generating data collection strategies through a brainstorming process. In each of two meeting rooms, teachers clustered around three or four round tables. The procedure was for teachers to take turns sharing with the group the action they intended to take in their classroom (such as implementing a new strategy for teaching reading or instituting a new attendance incentive program) and the research questions they wanted to pursue. Then the rest of the group brainstormed different ways data could be collected in order to answer the questions. A participant from each group had volunteered to lead the discussion and to record the ideas generated during the brainstorming on a flip chart. I sat among the participants and contributed ideas along with them during the brainstorming process. The process was going smoothly until Jean explained the background of her project to the group.

Jean's research project grew out of an initial concern that the young men she was preparing for the GED were living in what she perceived to be a "cultural black hole." As a consequence, she had explained during various activities throughout the retreat, the young men she was teaching needed to be more knowledgeable about life outside of their small community. Jean's colleagues, however, had suggested she was failing to appreciate the rich culture of the region in which she was working and the distinctive local knowledge of the people there. Based on the encouragement from her fellow researchers, Jean had decided to try to "hook" the students' interest in learning by first developing curriculum from their local interests—such as hunting and fishing. She thought she might gradually add content to the curriculum about national and world events that she felt the students needed to understand.

As part of her presentation to the group during the brainstorming exercises, Jean began explaining what life was like for out-of-school youth in her community who came to GED classes. She offered descriptions of their dress and slang terms they used to categorize one another according to social groups. One of the terms she threw out was *wigger.* Sonya, an African American woman sitting at an adjacent table, asked, "What is a wigger?" and Jean responded matter-of-factly, "White n——."

When Jean uttered the term *white n——*, I felt my breath taken away. I looked at Sonya, who had asked the question. She had turned to Lois, the discussion facilitator positioned at the flip chart—another

African American woman. The two women made eye contact and then Lois said something like, "Oh I've heard of that. I saw a documentary on that." Then she went right on facilitating the discussion about data collection.

As the group leader, I did not know what to do. I looked around the room to see how other people were feeling. Some people were looking at the floor. Some people had no noticeable reaction. Lois had so quickly moved ahead with the conversation that I guess inside of me I was saying, "Great. I'm glad that's over." At the same time I knew something destructive had just occurred. I felt bothered by what had just happened, and then, I hate to say it, but I also felt relieved that the conversation was moving on.

At the end of each inquiry retreat, we had participants fill out a critical incident questionnaire to identify moments that might have been particularly troublesome or, on the other hand, particularly effective in terms of achieving the goals of the retreat. None of the participants mentioned the incident with Jean on those questionnaires, and nobody said anything to us about it immediately after the retreat. But on the following Wednesday I received an e-mail from Sonya. She started by saying that she had enjoyed the retreat and had gotten a lot out of it. She went on to write, "Jean's white n—— comment had no place in what we were trying to accomplish." She wrote, "I made no comment on the evaluation because I needed time to think about how I felt about the comment. I didn't say anything about it because I didn't want to disrupt the session. I didn't think any response would have benefited our purpose. But," she wrote, "having had time to think about it, and my own values and beliefs, I still feel the same way . . . OFFENDED." Sonya did not ask anything of me specifically. She just signed this e-mail message and I was left wondering what in the world to do next.

It is not uncommon in traditional planning theory to assume or even assert (Boone, Safrit, & Jones, 2002) that planning is something done before educational activities begin. Indeed, as Cassie indicates in her depiction, "all activities we had planned for the retreat had gone smoothly," which would tend to confirm this view. Yet an extremely disruptive incident occurred that threatened to undermine how smoothly the planning and retreat had developed to that point. Experienced educators know that no matter how well the activities are "preplanned," the exigencies of the situation often present opportunities as well as dilemmas that require ongoing adjustments as the activities occur. The fabled "teachable moment" is a reminder of this frequent occurrence, to which we might add its counter, the "lost opportunity." One way to see this planning phenomenon is that teaching and learning processes at actual learning sites also constitute a planning table.

There are several planning tables in this story. First, decisions are made as the wigger incident unfolds in the learning site. Cassie bravely admits her paralysis, saying her "breath was taken away." Even with Sonya potentially challenging the insensitivity of the remark, Lois goes "right on facilitating" the activity. Cassie chooses not to intervene after ascertaining what she took to be the mood of the group yet knowing something destructive had just occurred. Other decisions occur when the participants choose not to report the incident on the evaluations. Finally, Sonya does decide to respond and Cassie is left "wondering what in the world to do next."

Even though the planning for the session had gone well, its enactment required an ongoing series of judgments about what to do in the real time of classroom activity. These decisions are made not only during the activity itself but subsequent to it as well, and each affects the process and the consequence of educational activity itself. Nor does the incident occur in isolation. Indeed, even though the planning has gone smoothly and represents a particular participatory ethic about organizing knowledge and practice, a powerful social force—racism—intrudes. Like the other two stories, then, the story of Cassie's planning is not only about participants' learning, but also about reproducing or challenging the political system of racism. Was the incident as destructive as Cassie feared? What will the consequences be?

Seeing What Matters II

What's Going On at the Planning Table

People at physical and metaphorical planning tables plan educational programs. In introducing the three planning stories that are used throughout the book, we identified the planning tables around which people have made decisions about educational programs. There is nothing particularly extraordinary about what is happening in these programs; rather, it is their everydayness that makes them useful for understanding the nuances of working with people in social and organizational contexts. Indeed, what people do in practical situations at these planning tables depends, in part, on how they see what's going on. Most important, the dynamics of the social and organizational context shape educators' practical action. The educator's perspective on these dynamics matters at each of the multiple planning tables for an educational program. Can she see who benefits and who loses from her actions at the table? If not, the planner is likely to be blindsided by the actions of others, as Pete was by the executive vice president. In the Phoenix Company story, a struggle for power was played out through the planning of the program, and that struggle determined, in part, how needs were defined, what was taught and learned, and who benefited from the program.

Pete's experience points directly to the part of practice that many theories ignore: practical action requires planners to see that educational programs benefit many people in many ways. By assuming that programs are only about educational outcomes such as increased knowledge, most planning theories ask people to see with one eye closed. In contrast, the three planning stories illustrate the driving insights around which we structure this book. In order to see what's going on at the table, planners need to pay attention to the educational *and* the social and political outcomes that people seek to achieve from educational programs. Further, planners need to see that while these outcomes can be distinguished in theory, in practice they are utterly interdependent. As Pete engages in practical action at the table, he simultaneously develops the program's educational features (purpose, curriculum, instructional formats) and—just as important—seeks to strengthen the power and visibility of the human resources office. Likewise, in the SVP story, Arthur goes into a meeting with questions about how best to organize the educational program, whereas the president of the Society is most concerned with changing the strategic position of the Society in the valuation profession and creating a new income stream for the Society. In the PI story, as the planners develop educational activities consistent with their participatory education vision, they are called also to address the power relations structured by race in society. These stories illustrate the need for adult educators to plan with both eyes open in working the planning table, thus seeing both the educational as well as the social and political outcomes resulting from the program.

These stories demonstrate that in the struggle for the distribution of knowledge and power in social and organizational contexts, educational programs are not a neutral activity. This view calls for a relational analysis that takes seriously the idea that education does not stand outside the unequal relations of power that more generally structure social life; rather, educational programs not only are structured by these relations, but also play a role in reproducing or changing them. The heart of this relational analysis is the fact that "education represents both a struggle for meaning and a struggle over power relations. Thus, education becomes a central terrain where power and politics operate out of the lived culture of individuals and groups situated in asymmetrical social and political positions" (Mohanty, 1994, p. 147). Planners' work, then, embodies the struggle for knowledge and power as it is embedded in wider forces that structure social and organizational life (Cervero & Wilson,

2001). More specifically, planners operate at the intersection of these struggles and structural forces in their practice, seeking to provide programs that simultaneously produce both educational outcomes and social and political outcomes for multiple stakeholders. Even though balancing both sets of outcomes can be difficult, planners can neither "step outside" such conditions nor be neutral about who should benefit. This relational view therefore requires that planners ask that timeless political question about their efforts: Who benefits? Necessarily tied to this political question is the ethical one: Who *should* benefit? To assume neutrality in educational planning is disingenuous at best. More important, such political naïveté, whether feigned or real, allows others' social vision and political agendas about who should benefit from educational programs to prevail.

In the remainder of the book, we draw upon these planning stories to exemplify the connections among the technical, political, and ethical dimensions of planning (Caffarella, 2002; Cervero & Wilson, 1994a; Sork, 2000; Sork & Newman, 2004). We conclude Chapter One by locating our approach to planning in the theoretical discussions that have occurred over the past several decades. We discuss how our theory has evolved since we began with the question: What do educational planners *really do* when they plan programs for adults?

Seeing What Matters III

Planning Theory and Beyond

We have planned hundreds of educational programs for adults over the past thirty years, including community-based adult literacy programs; hospital-based continuing education courses for nurses and physicians; professional development workshops for literacy, community college, and extension educators; antiracism workshops for university faculty members; and graduate courses in adult education. These programs were serious attempts to improve the lives of people, the organizations in which they worked, and the communities in which they lived. The models that were supposed to guide us did not really account for the realities of working with other people in planning these programs. As faculty members responsible for teaching about planning to practicing educators, we felt a sense of unease that soon became public. How could we teach, and therefore endorse, planning theories that did not even account for our own experience? We had to rely on a literature base that fell profoundly short of making sense of what really mattered in developing educational programs. In 1989 we began to put a name to what really happens and what really matters in planning educational programs.

There was no shortage of program planning models to draw on, as Sork and Buskey (1986) demonstrated in their review of ninety-three program planning models that had been published from 1950 through 1983. They pointed out that since the 1949 publication of "Tyler's *Basic Principles of Curriculum and Instruction,* in which he outlined a decision-making framework that continues to undergird many approaches to programming, a substantial literature has developed" (p. 86). The problem was that although many options were available, there were no true choices. Despite these multiple variations, Tyler's classical planning logic was both universal and unassailable in every single model (Sork & Buskey, 1986; Wilson & Cervero, 1997): assess needs, construct objectives, develop content, choose instructional methods, and evaluate learning. Tylerian-like theory continues to proliferate today not just in education but in nearly all other planning disciplines as well (Forester, 1989, 1999; Friedman, 1987; Hooper, 1992). From our experience, these theories were not able to see, nor address, all that mattered. The problem has been that most theories have only attended to the dimensions of good planning that address educational agendas (such as developing objectives and evaluating outcomes). Even though adult educators have long acknowledged planning's political challenges and ethical dilemmas (Boyle, 1981; Brookfield, 1986; Clark, 1958; Griffith, 1978; Newman, 1994), for over fifty years the literature has been unable to account *theoretically* for these issues. Planning theory has focused on processes used to develop educational outcomes, while it has ignored the social and political outcomes that also result from educational programs. So we kept asking: Where is the real world in these models? What about the messy social and organizational contexts in which people do this work? We found some comfort in Houle's (1972) insightful assumptions, which suggest that any effort to plan "must be centered as far as possible upon realities, not upon forms or abstractions" (p. 32). Caffarella (1988) had a similar insight in presenting the first version of her own model, fashioned after Tyler's: "Developing training programs rarely works in a completely logical fashion . . . the more persons that you add to the planning process, the less logical the process tends to be" (p. 36). Caffarella is correct: when educators find themselves in situations in which people are not involved in planning educational programs, the models reviewed by Sork and Buskey (1986) might be excellent guides to practical action.

Our questioning built on others' insights that these models do not account for what happens when people plan educational programs (Boyle, 1981; Brookfield, 1986; Sandmann, 1993). Boyle (1981) found that "a rational model is rarely, if ever, achieved in the practical world of planning with people" (p. 42). Sork and Caffarella (1989) agreed that "anyone who claims that a planning model accurately represents how planning occurs in practice . . . has a naïve understanding of what planning involves" (p. 234). Brookfield (1986) concluded that the models do not provide effective guides to practical action, leading practitioners to develop their own "context-specific theories-in-use" (p. 259). Sork and Caffarella went even further, asking that new theories be developed that account for the importance of context. Thus, for decades planning theorists have argued that the context for planning matters. Houle's (1972) two-part planning system—identifying an educational situation and addressing his decision points—is perhaps one of the more powerful presentations of the importance of context. Sork and

Caffarella noted that the "exigencies" of practice might be so complex as to make planning theory irrelevant. Not only was this an explicit recognition that context matters, but their observation also confirms the inability of planning theory to articulate any particular understanding of how context works. Many theories over the decades have included some version of the planning step "to analyze the context" (Boone, 1992; Sork, 2000; Sork & Caffarella, 1989; Sork & Newman, 2004). But too often the exhortation stops there. There has been little discussion in the literature about how to understand the social and political dimensions of the context (Sork, 2000; Wilson & Cervero, 1997). Our initial work sought to characterize the political contexts of planning as negotiating interests in relations of power (Cervero & Wilson, 1994a, 1994b; Cervero & Wilson, 1995). We sought to identify the conditions that planners experience, but that existing theory does not help them to see.

Developing theory to account for the realities of educators' contexts already had a robust tradition in the K–12 curriculum literature (Reid, 1979; Walker, 1971, 2003), beginning with Schwab's classic, "The Practical: A Language for Curriculum" (1969). We entered this ongoing questioning of planning models with a desire to produce a theory that could both account for what educators face in their organizational and social settings and serve as a guide to practical action (Cervero & Wilson, 1994a, 1994b; Wilson & Cervero, 1995; Forester, 1989). Foley (1999; see also Apple, 1996) echoes these two criteria, saying that educators have a need for theory "that both explains and enables action" (p. 130). In developing our theory, we took the position that people would not really apply theory to practice. A more accurate understanding is that theory organizes attention to possibilities of action: "theories do not solve problems in the world; people do. Nevertheless, good theory . . . can help alert us to problems, remind us of what we care about, or prompt our practical insights into cases we confront" (Forester, 1989, p. 12).

Historical Development of Cervero and Wilson's Planning Theory

To be optimally useful, then, planning theories must both account for what actually happens when people plan educational programs and also provide a guide to practical action. We sought to meet these two criteria by deriving a theory from real-time observations of planning for three educational programs (Cervero & Wilson, 1994a). Based on these stories, we defined planning as a social activity whereby people construct educational programs by negotiating personal, organizational, and social interests in contexts marked by socially structured relations of power. The four concepts that structured the theory (power, interests, negotiation, responsibility) account for the world that educators experience, define their essential action, and prescribe their ethical obligations. As a guide to practical action, our theory identifies the repertoire of technical knowledge and skills, the political analyses, and the normative standard of nurturing substantively democratic planning that educators need to master to be able to plan responsibly (Cervero & Wilson, 1994a, 1994b). Whereas previous planning models focused solely on the educational outcomes, the theory posits that planning practice always has two types of outcomes. As planners negotiate interests in relations of power, they produce educational outcomes and, simultaneously, social and political outcomes by reproducing or changing the social and political relationships that make planning possible (Cervero & Wilson, 1994a, 1994b, 1998).

The four key concepts provided the structure of the theory, and we continued to develop areas of the theory in later publications. We introduced the metaphor of the planning table (Cervero & Wilson, 1998) as a way to locate the theoretical concepts in the real world of planning, saying that "planners routinely negotiate power and interests in terms of whose interests get to the planning table and how those interests shape the program. . . . Determining whose interests get to the planning table . . . is the fundamental ethical question" (Wilson & Cervero, 1996, p. 21). Another major development came in response to Sork's critique (1996) that the theory "did not distinguish between different kinds of negotiations" (p. 84). Based on a suggestion in his critique, we distinguished more clearly between the substantive negotiations about the educational outcomes of the educational program and metanegotiations about social and political relationships involved in planning the program (Cervero & Wilson, 1998). More recently (Cervero & Wilson, 1999, 2001; Wilson & Cervero, 2001, 2003), we have developed our understandings of adult education as a struggle for knowledge and power in society. This political interpretation of practice, which Sork and Newman (2004) describe as moving "beyond the conventional" (p. 112), asks more precisely who benefits from adult education and in what ways. The question of benefits is critical to understanding the practical action of adult educators in terms of its intentions and consequences. Other adult educators have adopted and adapted some of the concepts into their own models and analyses of planning (Hansman & Mott, 2001; Rothwell & Cookson, 1997; Sork, 1997). In the most recent version of her model, Caffarella (2002) has tended to issues arising from people's involvement in planning and has made power and negotiation central to understanding the context for planning. Donaldson and Kozoll (1999) have focused on the issues arising in those situations in which institutional collaboration is a central dynamic. Sork (2000) has elaborated on our description of planners' necessary repertoire of ethical, political, and technical knowledge and skills (Cervero & Wilson, 1994a) to propose a "question-based approach to planning" because he believes "that posing and answering questions will lead to better decisions and therefore better programs" (p. 180).

Who Benefits in the Struggle for Knowledge and Power?

Theory should not be seen as positing some transcendent truth but as providing plausible grounds for politically pitched and ethically illuminated practical action (Harvey, 1996). In seeing educational programs as a terrain in the struggle for knowledge and power, it is practically and ethically essential to ask who benefits and in what ways (Cervero & Wilson, 2001). Education matters because it is about making individual, organizational, and social change, which benefits people educationally, socially, and politically. In acknowledging that planners deliberately intervene in people's lives to make change, theories must address the question of who should benefit from these changes. Because education affects the distribution of knowledge and power, there is no politically or ethically innocent position from which to plan programs (Cervero & Wilson, 1999, 2001). By producing both educational and political benefits, planning practice answers the question about whose interests matter (Wilson & Cervero, 2001). Such action should be directed by an ethical commitment to substantively democratic planning (Cervero & Wilson, 1994a). With this ethical commitment, we align ourselves with others (Hall, 2001; Newman, 1999; Walters, 1996; Youngman, 1996) who maintain that all forms of education offer the practical space for the distribution of knowledge and power that creates hope and the possibility for increasing people's life chances.

To act practically, planners need to understand how social life is organized, have a vision for how education should change the world, and have strategies for achieving this vision (Livingstone, 1983). Chapter Three explains more fully how the theory addresses all three requirements for practical action by offering defining features of social life (power and interests), a vision for educational planning (substantively democratic participation), and negotiation strategies (for consultative, bargaining, and dispute situations). In Chapter Two, we offer a more extensive account of the three planning stories begun in this chapter. These accounts are used to illuminate the presentation of the theory in Chapter Three and its application to specific planning tasks in Chapters Four through Eight.

Chapter 2

Practicing Educational Planning
Three Stories

In Chapter One we used three vignettes to illuminate the planning table as a metaphor that organizes attention to what matters in educational planning. In this chapter we offer a fuller telling of these three planning stories: (1) Practitioner Inquiry for Adult Literacy Teachers, (2) Continuing Education in the Society for Valuation Professions, and (3) Management Education at the Phoenix Company. We use these three stories throughout the remainder of the book to illustrate how educational planners can use our theory to see the social and organizational settings in which they work and see how to act in those settings. For each planning story we describe the social and organizational context in which the educators planned their programs, provide a summary of program planning meetings and other relevant events, and recount what happened after the programs were offered.

Practitioner Inquiry for Adult Literacy Teachers

The Practitioner Inquiry (PI) program was part of a larger project of adult literacy staff development funded by the state department of education and administered through the university. The state department funded all of the literacy programs in the state, employing a thousand teachers. Our university's Department of Adult Education was in its eighth year of administering this staff development project for teachers, the centerpiece of which were daylong workshops offered on a series of Saturdays each spring. As part of my faculty responsibilities, I (Ronald Cervero) had been part of the leadership for this project since its inception. Cassie Drennon became a doctoral student in the department and joined the staff in the project's fourth funding cycle. She had led a PI program in another state before moving, and she suggested that we offer a PI program as part of our staff development project. We developed the proposal, obtaining funding from the state department for our sixth funding cycle. The program was favorably received by teachers, and the state department funded it again in our seventh funding cycle. In our eighth year we enjoyed a sustained and positive relationship with the state department and the literacy programs across the state. The third PI program was one of four components of that year's overall staff development project.

Practitioner Inquiry had been used as an approach to staff development for literacy teachers in a number of states over the previous decade. In contrast to other forms of staff development, PI puts a great deal of authority into the hands of teachers to determine the focus of their own learning (Drennon & Cervero, 2002). We described the program in a recruitment brochure that was mailed in early October to all of the literacy teachers in the state:

> Practitioner inquiry is different from the kind of staff development that most teachers are used to. It is ongoing throughout the year, it offers a high level of support to a relatively small group of teachers, it focuses solely on the concerns that teachers who participate raise about their own practice, and it is about teachers generating valuable knowledge for the adult literacy field. Practitioner inquiry affords both new and experienced teachers the opportunity to explore their own theories about teaching and learning. It also provides teachers with the practical skills, the structure, and the encouragement to

pursue promising ideas in the classroom and to carefully study the results. In this model, teachers are both learners and researchers. Teachers in a practitioner inquiry group learn enormously—not only through their own research projects, but also from the research projects of every other member in the group. And, through brief reports that they write, members of the group contribute their knowledge to others in the broader adult literacy field.

The teachers in the first two PI programs had successfully completed their projects and we developed a publication for each group, *Practitioner Inquiry Briefs*, which summarized the findings and implications for each teacher's research project. The third year of the PI program started out as our most promising year (see Exhibit 2.1). Twenty-eight teachers—a record number—applied to participate, and twenty-four were accepted. Of the twenty-four teachers, eight had participated in the previous year and were returning for a second year. There were twenty women and four men, representing a variety of racial and ethnic groups (six Black, one Hispanic, one Asian, and sixteen White), coming from seventeen different programs located throughout the state. They received the acceptance letters at the end of October and returned a contract agreeing to participate in all four retreats scheduled for the program and to produce a report for the *Practitioner Inquiry Briefs*. In addition to the retreats, our staff provided ongoing support to the teachers via the program's listserv, telephone and fax, and personal site visits.

Summary of Planning Meetings

The three planners for this year's program were Cassie, me, and Dougie Taylor, a woman who had been a participant in the first program and was now a graduate student in the department. Cassie and Dougie were each employed twenty hours a week to plan and facilitate the PI program. They functioned as cofacilitators for the

Exhibit 2.1.   Program Planning Calendar.

10/01–09/30	Year 1	First Practitioner Inquiry program funding cycle
10/01–09/30	Year 2	Second Practitioner Inquiry program funding cycle
October 1	Year 3	Third Practitioner Inquiry program funding cycle begins
October 2		Promotional materials and application packets distributed
November 17–18		First PI retreat held: identify research topics
January 8–9		Second PI retreat held: plan data collection
April 5–6		Scheduled dates for third PI retreat: analyze data (retreat canceled)
April 13		Formal cancellation of third Practitioner Inquiry program
June 14–15		Scheduled dates for fourth PI retreat: present results (canceled)
September 30		Originally scheduled completion of third Practitioner Inquiry funding cycle

program and were the primary planners for each of the four retreats. I was also administratively responsible for this part of the project and served as the liaison with the project manager of the state department, who approved key decisions, such as the content of the recruitment brochure and the *Practitioner Inquiry Briefs*. Because Cassie and Dougie shared an office, much of the planning occurred as an ongoing informal process rather than through a series of formal meetings. Every week or two, however, the three of us would meet to engage in more formal planning. Before the retreats, the meetings were used to critique the emerging retreat agenda, possible instructional activities, and policy issues (such as how to handle a participant who was going to miss a portion of the retreat). Immediately following each retreat, we used the meetings to debrief on what had occurred, with an eye toward the next retreat.

We faced two particular challenges this year because of our two-year history with the program. First, in contrast to the first two years, the number of participating teachers had doubled, to twenty-four, and some of them were participating for a second year. Thus, although we had been successful with many of the program's features in the previous two years, we had to rethink many of these activities due to the size of the group and the teachers' varied levels of knowledge and experience regarding the PI approach to staff development. Second, given our belief in the importance of modeling the principle of learner involvement on which the program rested, we continued to struggle with how to substantively involve the teachers in planning. This struggle was made more complex by virtue of the increased size of the group, because planning decisions were continually being reviewed with the teachers both prior to and during each retreat. For instance, we decided to create a rotating participant advisory group to help plan each retreat. We targeted returning members for the first retreat's advisory group. In order to establish the advisory groups for the remainder of the year, we planned to explain the opportunity at our first retreat and then post a sign-up sheet for those who would be interested.

Planning for Retreat 1

Our goals for the first retreat were to establish a sense of community with the group, to orient the teachers to the process of practitioner inquiry, and to help each teacher identify a researchable practice-based problem. We made several planning decisions in order to begin developing a sense of community in the group. First, we planned to begin the first retreat (see Exhibit 2.2) with a Group

Exhibit 2.2.   Practitioner Inquiry Project: Retreat 1 Agenda.

Monday, November 16–Downtown Hotel

1:00–1:15	Greetings, logistics, and announcements	
1:15–2:20	*Group Resume activity*	Getting to know each other
2:20–2:45	Goals and overview of today's session	
2:45–3:00	Break	
3:00–3:30	*Penny activity*	Some principles of PI Review of the year's timeline
3:30–4:15	*Doubting and Believing activity*	Discussion of preassigned readings
4:15–4:30	More nuts-and-bolts information about the Practitioner Inquiry project	
4:30–5:00	*Excitement and Concerns activity*	Small group informal discussions with experienced group members
5:00–6:00	Social gathering and cash bar	
6:00–6:45	Buffet dinner	
6:45–7:45	*Project Idea Sharing activity*	Half the group briefly shares their project ideas with the others

Tuesday, November 17–Rustic Lodge

8:00–8:30	Buffet breakfast at the lodge	
8:30–9:30	*Project Idea Sharing activity*	Half the group briefly shares their project ideas with the others

9:30–10:15	Demonstration of Critical Friends Conversation	Two large groups
10:15–10:30	Break	
10:30–12:00	Critical Friends discussions	Pair work
12:00–12:45	Lunch	
12:45–1:00	Personal reflection or journal writing	Individual work
1:00–1:15	Debriefing the Critical Friends activity	
1:15–2:15	*Concept Mapping activity*	Two large groups Mapping of the research problems
2:30–3:30	Brainstorming alternative ways of looking at the problems	Groups of four
3:30–3:50	Large group debriefing	
3:50–4:30	Closure: Travel vouchers, evaluation forms, e-mail assignment	

Resume activity, in which participants conveyed their collective, rather than individual, strengths and experiences. We also made the decision to disallow late arrivals and early departures in order to communicate the idea of mutual responsibility. Finally, we planned to address the process of community building by being intentional about the formation of small groups. Thus we planned the composition of small groups rather than leaving the groupings to chance. To do this we took into account (1) preexisting relationships between teachers, (2) teachers' previous participation in the PI program, and (3) considerations of race and gender.

We needed to strike a balance between the roles of expert knowledge and indigenous knowledge in the group. We addressed this using a Doubting and Believing activity on the first day, which allowed the group members to critically discuss selections of academic literature about teaching and learning. However, the majority of time at the retreat was allotted for them to share their own theories and practices. To facilitate this, we planned that prior to the retreat they would each write up a "critical incident" (a puzzling classroom situation) and bring it with them for group analysis with the help of "critical friends." Each group member would take a few minutes early in the agenda to explain the classroom situation that they wanted to research. The Project Idea Sharing activities were scheduled for Monday evening and Tuesday morning. We then set aside time during the remainder of Tuesday morning to discuss this critical incident in pairs. In this way, the teachers would help one another, through a brainstorming process, to examine their underlying assumptions about the critical incidents and to consider a range of alternative perspectives. We planned to conclude the retreat by giving an e-mail assignment that would stimulate ongoing conversation about the emerging research projects.

During the planning process, we struggled with how to engage the knowledge and experience of teachers who were participating in the program for a second year without creating a hierarchy that privileged these returning teachers. It was important to us that all participants would engage in the process as colearners. We wanted to ensure that there were many opportunities for new participants in the group to learn about practitioner inquiry directly from their more experienced peers. One way we decided to involve returning members was by setting aside time on Monday for an Excitement and Concerns activity. In this activity, returning members would lead small group discussions with new members of the group about any concerns they wanted to raise.

Retreat 1: November 16–17

Day one of the retreat, which took place at a downtown hotel, played out as we had planned it, with few changes to the agenda. We convened the group at 1:00 P.M. and offered the usual welcoming remarks and logistical details. Everyone seemed engaged during the Group Resume activity that followed. Other key events in the agenda flowed smoothly: the Penny activity was an experiential activity using pennies and magnifying glasses to demonstrate principles of inquiry. The Doubting and Believing activity included a discussion of Stephen Brookfield's chapter entitled "What It Means to Be a Critically Reflective Teacher." The Excitement and Concerns Q&A sessions, led by experienced group members, and individual sharing of research ideas in the Project Sharing activity rounded out the day. As far as we, the facilitators, could tell, the activities accomplished their objectives: participants seemed to be experiencing success.

On the second day of the retreat, we moved the meeting a few miles to a rustic retreat center owned by the university. We had planned the move in advance to afford the group an atmosphere more conducive to reflection and small group conversation— hallmarks of the second day's agenda. Although the plans for the first half of the morning played out as expected, Cassie and Dougie ended up completely reorganizing the afternoon session as they went along.

Before lunch, pairs had been discussing the critical incidents each had written about in preparation for the retreat. The purpose of the paired discussions was for the teachers to begin thinking more deeply about these incidents. They accomplished this with the help of a "critical friend" who posed questions designed to reveal their underlying assumptions and values. In any group, this activity tends to leave the participants feeling less sure of their understanding, as it reveals tensions, contradictions, and ambiguities. By the time the pairs broke for lunch, Cassie and Dougie could sense an increase in the group's anxiety level. Although a Concept Mapping activity had been planned for immediately after lunch, they decided on the spot that the group would be better served through a less intense group activity with leader involvement. They altered the agenda to accommodate two concurrent, rather free-flowing, large group discussions, one led by Dougie and one led by Cassie. Individuals in each group took turns sharing the most interesting ideas they had been exploring with critical friends and their understanding of the assumptions currently guiding their thinking.

Dougie and Cassie concluded the activity by giving the e-mail assignment as planned; they then invited everyone to evaluate the retreat by answering a set of open-ended questions. The evaluations largely reflected our perceptions that the retreat had gone well. They also revealed, to our surprise, that one activity had had the opposite of the intended effect on at least one person. This teacher reported feeling most distanced from what was happening during the Group Resume activity: "UGH! My qualifications, in my view at least, established my place in the pecking order as very low, and did not allow for general life experiences to be taken into account."

Planning for Retreat 2

Since the first retreat had gone as well as it had, there were no unusual issues to take into account as we developed the agenda and activities for the second retreat. Cassie and Dougie continued their ongoing planning and worked with me to review the developing plan. By the end of the first retreat, the teachers had framed their research problems fairly well. Between the first and second retreats their major assignment was to further develop their problems into a specific set of research questions, a task that they successfully accomplished by interacting with other group members and the facilitators using e-mail. Goals for the second retreat were to refine the research questions with guidance from the facilitators, learn about data collection strategies, and propose a design for their research projects. The discussion of research designs requires teachers to have an in-depth understanding of each other's projects. Therefore, the major design decision needed for the Brainstorming Research Designs activity (see Exhibit 2.3) was about whether to separate the full group into two separate groups of twelve teachers each, for both the Thursday afternoon and Friday morning sessions. In the prior two years, we needed only one group because there were only twelve teachers. However, we developed the groups to maximize diversity of research topics, levels of experience with PI, and teacher characteristics (such as work location, gender, and race). Cassie and Dougie told the teachers about this decision when reviewing the agenda with the group during the opening session.

We continued to struggle around the issue of teachers' involvement in the planning process. We found that the idea of a teacher advisory group was not working as planned. Although all twenty-four teachers signed up to advise on one of the remaining three retreats because we had asked them to, Cassie and Dougie's phone meetings with them fell flat. In fact, several individuals said they trusted us completely to plan the sessions without their input. However, Cassie and Dougie were able to substantively involve the teachers in real-time planning during the retreat. For example, at the first retreat in November, one of the participants had raised the question of where we would meet for our final session on June 15. She had wondered if we could meet somewhere that would make it easier for their program directors to attend and be part of the final presentations made by the teachers. We therefore decided to raise this question for discussion at the opening session of the second retreat and to propose that we would plan the June 15 session in detail at the third retreat in April.

Retreat 2: January 7–8

The teachers' written evaluations of the two days were very positive, with many commenting on how much learning had occurred and how much their research projects had developed. One teacher

Exhibit 2.3.   Practitioner Inquiry Project: Retreat 2 Agenda.

Downtown Hotel
Thursday, January 7

1:00–2:00	*Welcome and news sharing*	
	Overview of this retreat	
2:00–3:00	*What makes a "good" research question?*	Large group discussion
	Critiquing the Research Questions activity	Small groups
3:00–3:15	Break	
3:15–4:15	Data Collection activity	Presentation and discussion
4:15–5:15	Brainstorming research designs	Two large groups Three people x 20 minutes each
5:15–5:30	Evening data collection assignment explained	
5:30–8:00	Dinner on your own	
	Data collection activity and readings	Pair work or individual

Friday, January 8

7:30–8:30	Breakfast buffet in the hotel restaurant	
8:30–8:45	*Debrief yesterday*	
8:45–10:00	*Brainstorming research designs*	Two large groups Four people x 20 minutes each
10:00–10:15	Break	
10:15–11:15	Debrief Data Collection activity	Full group
11:15–12:15	Lunch	

12:15–2:00	Brainstorming research projects	Two large groups Four people x 20 minutes each
2:00–3:00	Project planning, create wall poster with timeline	
3:00–3:50	Review gallery of project plans and timelines	
	Reviewers offer praise and friendly advice using stickers	
3:50–4:30	Travel vouchers, evaluation, e-mail assignment, and closing remarks	

commented that "It was all great. Retreat was well planned, very organized . . . I feel very excited about my research project and look forward to hearing other team members' projects." Another said: "It is very nice to make new friends in this PI group, especially those from other parts of the state. It is interesting to hear about the problems and successes from small, rural areas—different from the larger suburban area where I work."

Two incidents occurred during this retreat, however, that would dominate the next month of planning. The first resulted from the decision to split the teachers into two groups for a significant part of the two-day retreat. The outcome of this design feature was that the two groups ended up doing some of the activities differently from each other and therefore had very divergent experiences at the retreat. This was not a problem in itself, except that trying to process the activities as a full group became awkward. For example, Cassie and Dougie had given an assignment in which pairs of people were to make an observation and individually note what they each saw. However, Cassie told the group to write down their observation and Dougie did not. The problem occurred when the assignment was processed in the full group and there was confusion as to whether one group had done things incorrectly. This issue would be carried into the postretreat planning as we considered whether to simply run two autonomous groups or continue with one group for the last two retreats.

The second incident was the "wigger" discussion that occurred in Cassie's group of teachers (described in Chapter One). The other group was unaware of the incident, yet it had a high potential to affect the dynamics in the next retreat. Remarkably, there was virtually no mention of this incident in the full group or on the written evaluations that the teachers completed at the retreat's conclusion. One teacher alluded to the incident, saying: "One practitioner mentioned that the feedback at the end of the retreat had validity problems due to the fact the suggestions weren't able to account for the dynamics that were going on in our session. Didn't bother me though!" This comment foreshadowed what would come next in our planning.

Planning for Retreat 3

When Cassie received an e-mail from Sonya on Wednesday, January 13, the teachers were now certainly participating in the planning for the next retreat. Cassie made a note that "when I received this e-mail I realized this [incident] was more significant than I had acknowledged previously. . . . Now I realized that I needed to respond to Sonya and I probably needed to do something constructive about this issue with the whole group." She discussed the situation with Dougie and me, as well as with other trusted colleagues who she felt could offer some perspective on what to do. Cassie then called Sonya the following night. Her notes from the conversation show that Sonya "was sure everyone noticed the incident when it occurred . . . there could have been snappy comebacks made but she chose not to do that because she didn't think it would accomplish anything. Her opinion was that she [Jean] could have found a better way to say what she had to say." In order to develop a course of action, Cassie had another conversation with Sonya and then called Jean on Saturday, January 16, to tell her that Sonya had been offended by her use of the "n——" word. Cassie's notes show that Jean said: "She 'didn't mean anything by it.' She was just explaining something about the boys in her local area. . . . She had mentioned the incident to [a teacher] on the drive home and told her how sorry she was that she had used that word in the session." Jean agreed to call Sonya and apologize. Jean called Cassie on Monday to say that she had left four messages that were not returned and that she was going to write a letter, which she did eight days later. On Thursday, January 21, Jim, who was in Cassie's group at the retreat, called to talk about his project. He then said, "Before we get off the phone there was something else I wanted to bring up." He said that he didn't write it on his evaluation form (that's what Sonya said too), but that he thought "the comments and the attitude of the woman from up north were really inappropriate." On Monday, January 25, Cassie called Sonya, who said that she had talked with two other teachers who were in the group and that "they felt the same way—offended. Michael thinks the group needs to discuss it." Sonya also acknowledged that Jean had called her and that she had not returned the call because she had been collecting her thoughts. She said that she intended to call Jean that night and would call Cassie after that.

On February 8, Cassie again called Sonya, for what would be the final time, to check on her e-mail assignment for her project. Sonya then told her that she had received a letter from Jean. Sonya said that in the letter Jean apologized for making the comment and invited Sonya to call and talk some more about it. Sonya said that she had not yet called her but that she would. While the planning about the incident was playing out, Cassie and Dougie were also discussing the idea of whether or not to have two autonomous groups at the next retreat. Dougie supported this option, but Cassie wanted to keep one group and find ways to avoid some of the problems the two-group design has caused at the second retreat. This was clearly a fundamental issue that would alter the next two retreats and, ultimately, the project. The "wigger" incident bolstered Dougie's case because twelve people had not experienced the incident and did not know about it. However, this fundamental design issue became less important as it became clearer that there might not be a need for another retreat.

The Aftermath

As it turned out, there would be no need to develop another retreat agenda. While we were deep in the process of working through the issues raised at the January retreat, the future of the entire program was being challenged. On February 5, our funding agency called to give verbal notice that two other components of the overall grant would be canceled. A letter from the agency on February 11 indicated that "no further expenditures are allowable under this contract" and that we would need to develop a new proposal if we wanted the PI program to continue because the "existing contract does not call for contract amendments." There had been absolutely no prior indication that there were any problems with the overall project—we had been blindsided. In fact, we were never informed about what, if any, problems caused the funding agency to cancel the other two components of the overall grant. The agency did tell us that they wanted to continue funding the PI program and one other component of the grant. We furiously developed a new funding proposal to continue the PI program and submitted it on February 24. The remaining two retreats were scheduled, as in the original proposal, for April 5–6 and June 14–15. We now began to worry that the cancellation of the the PI program could potentially be the collateral damage from the cancellation of the other two components of the grant. Nevertheless, we continued to plan the activities for the April retreat.

Meanwhile, Jean and Sonya, who had not seen each other since January 9, continued to communicate sporadically through e-mail and letters about the incident. In mid-March they found themselves at the annual state conference for literacy teachers. They sought each other out and had lunch together during the second day of the four-day conference. Later that afternoon, Jean and Sonya spoke to Cassie at separate times. Both teachers told a consistent story: each had come to understand how the other viewed the situation and had forgiven the pain they had caused the other. They were enthusiastic to raise this issue for the group at the next retreat in April because of the opportunity for learning that it provided. Unfortunately, Jean and Sonya never had the chance to meet the group again.

As the days passed in March with no approval for the new proposal, we began to strategize alternative dates and activities that would allow teachers to continue their projects. When we did not receive approval by the end of March, we informed the teachers that the April 5–6 retreat would be rescheduled for a later date. We also began discussions to decide if and when we would need to abandon the program. On April 13, our university project officer sent a letter to the funding agency withdrawing our proposal, saying: "With the departure of key staff members recently and the compressed timeline from now to the expected completion date of the proposal, we will not be able to carry out the Practitioner Inquiry component." Cassie and Dougie then called each of the twenty-four teachers to tell them that the program had been canceled. They offered to help the teachers complete their projects, but indicated that we would not be able to meet again as a group.

Continuing Education in the Society for Valuation Professions

At the time that I (Arthur Wilson) was hired as the education director, the Society for Valuation Professions was a professional association with about five thousand national and international members. Nearly all the members were located in the United States, and there were small numbers from approximately fifteen other countries.

The Society's purpose is to provide testing and certification of valuation expertise. The organization was formed in the early 1950s from the merger of two other valuation societies that had formed in the 1930s. As the president who spearheaded the educational reinvention of SVP remarked in the 50th Anniversary Commemorative Edition of the Society's professional journal, "Those founding fathers recognized the need for a set of principles and ethical practices that would become the bedrock of SVP's professionalism. Our present *Principles of Appraisal Practice and Code of Ethics* is the result of their work, and states the standards of conduct to which all members must subscribe. That document sets out the appraiser's obligation to his client and to the public, including the requirement that he [sic] attain and maintain appraisal competency." This represents the genesis of the testing and certification identity of the organization. Thus the organizational mission was then (and still remains) to create "professionalism" among its members through promoting general valuation principles and testing members' professional competence.

Professional societies often have two organizational hierarchies: one for the members (see Figure 2.1) and one for the headquarters administrative staff (see Figure 2.2). The organizational chart for SVP members represents a typical structure of authority and responsibility in voluntary associations. For this organization, it also reflects a succession model in that secretaries and treasurers could be in line to become vice presidents. Senior vice presidents would be chosen from the vice presidents. Following their terms as senior vice presidents meant that they would then usually serve for one year as president and then another year as "past president." Because voluntary associations are often susceptible to policy inconsistency, this succession order helped to structure leadership and policy continuity into organizational governance, which is why the president was so intent on my learning the "players" at our initial meeting. Given the agreements the presidents entered into with one another in order to stay in the succession line, this president knew that he had not one year but three years to work on the changes he and others envisioned. The selected committees listed on the organizational chart in Figure 2.1 are the ones who were most directly involved in designing and implementing SVP's new educational system. A significant amount of the Society's policy was developed at the committee level and then "recommended" as resolutions for the regional governors and executive leadership to endorse or vote upon formally at their biannual legislative meetings.

As a subset of the larger organization, the headquarters staff (see Figure 2.2) functioned to provide administrative assistance to the general membership (dues, testing, certification, conferences, and public relations), the Society's multiple committees, the board of governors, and its executive leadership. The staff consisted of a few professionals and a cadre of clerical managers. The public relations director and I each had professional training and experience in our respective responsibilities. The executive director was a retired U.S.

Figure 2.1.   SVP Governing Structure.

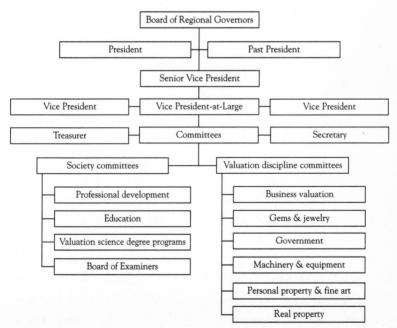

Figure 2.2.   SVP International Headquarters Organizational Chart.

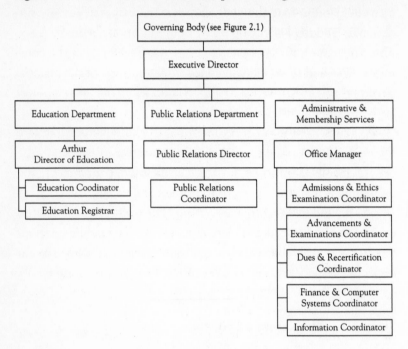

military officer. The Education Department was staffed with only one person—me, as the director—for its first year, which is the focus of this case. The education coordinator was added at the beginning of the second year and the registrar later that year.

SVP: Professional Identity and Market Control

Throughout its history, the Society had focused on the usual things occupational organizations do: soliciting members, holding conferences, devising and policing professional standards, managing public relations, representing member interests in state and national legislatures, and testing and certifying members. A unique feature of this organization in comparison with other appraisal societies, other than its historical disavowal of teaching responsibilities, was its multidisciplinary constitution: "our founding fathers recognized the common principles and theory that underlie all appraisal work, and their vision was not limited to any single discipline." Other organizations typically focused on one type of property valuation, such as real estate. With its focus on general valuation principles employed in the appraisal of multiple types of property, SVP constituted its organizational identity—and thus the professional identity of its members—differently from that of other organizations. Historically this multidisciplinary definition had sustained SVP's efforts to continue as a viable organization. Longtime members were fond of calling themselves the "Cadillac society," a metaphor referring to their perceived and selective superiority to other appraisal organizations because of their multidisciplinary focus and general valuation principles.

When I became its education director, SVP was grappling with two major organizational problems. First, there was a membership problem. The SVP professional designation—the entitlement of appending "SVP" to one's name upon successful testing—did not have market strength comparable to competing designations from certain other organizations in some disciplines. This meant that for some disciplines certain designations from other organizations were financially more remunerative; other SVP disciplines had no competing designations. Because of its multidisciplinary focus and its depiction of appraisal work as a *valuation science* of general principles, SVP tended to attract that subset of the overall valuation profession interested in constructing and promoting itself as a more traditional profession based on academic preparation and scientific principles; other societies tended to focus more on appraisal procedures. In terms of member recruitment, which affected organizational financial prosperity and legislative lobbying power, single-discipline valuation societies tended to fare better. Second, at the time of this case, other than member dues, Society publications, regional and national "seminars," and annual conferences, there were no other organizational products that could generate dollars to finance its activities. Other appraisal associations did provide initial preparation and continuing education courses. By promoting its multidisciplinary identity and focus on professionalism, SVP depended upon recruiting its members by their "testing in" after getting their education from other societies, corporate training systems, or academic degrees. During the time of my involvement with SVP, it had become quite apparent across the profession of managing voluntary associations that dues and conferences alone could not provide sufficient income streams to maintain occupational societies, and SVP was clearly a poster example.

Both of these problems were wrapped up in an even larger issue: the lack of a publicly recognizable or accorded professional identity. As the chair of one of SVP's discipline committees put it, "Overall appraisal is still in the pioneering stage . . . [yet] all types of appraisal are moving in the direction of true professionalism . . . [in time] in order to succeed professionally, an appraiser will have to have a degree in valuation sciences." This chairperson asserted that the key issue in terms of organizational focus on professionalism and education is that "in response to public demands, appraisers will probably adopt standards and self-policing in the manner now practiced by accountants and lawyers." It is no coincidence that the discipline chair invoked comparisons to accountants and lawyers. Many of the SVP members who were instrumental in developing the new educational system were also keenly driven to acquire public recognition not as a trade occupation but as a profession. Thus a major role of this organization was the construction and promulgation of "professional" valuator identity and practice, hence the hallmark invocations of scientific principles and ethical standards. As another discipline chair described the concern: "The identification and valuation of personal [and other kinds of] property is considered by some to be an art; by others, an applied science. Such interpretations, though cause for lively debate, seem to have identical foundations and goals: professionalism." I would be remiss not to note the constant use of the word "professionalism" by many of the actors in this story. Doubtless most meant the use of the word to refer to the "proper" behavior of individual valuators—hence the abiding organizational concern with ethics and knowing the "principles of appraisal."

But these invocations of professionalism also have to be read as a serious occupational concern with professionalization (Cervero, 1988; Larson, 1977; Wilson, 1993). The professional identity of valuators at the time of this planning story was not well established. There was little public understanding or even knowledge about what valuing meant compared with what we publicly presume to know about lawyers or doctors. Many members of valuation societies were keenly aware of this lack of public identity. Their professional identity was actually headed toward a crisis during my tenure with the SVP. Not only was there little public understanding of valuation work—prompting the societies' large public relations and pro bono efforts—but also there was at this time congressional legislative and regulatory pressure for a national uniform licensing of valuators. If uniform licensing were to become a reality and if the various appraisal associations could have their designations enacted as part of licensing, that in turn would drive recruitment and thus association financing. Further, these ongoing professionalization issues were exacerbated by a national economic crisis in which various kinds of property valuators were deeply implicated. This crisis eventually cost the U.S. public billions of dollars and produced intense state and congressional scrutiny of and attempts to control the occupation. One indicator of professional identity is self-policing; typically, trades are externally regulated by states.

These major national problems were creating intense pressures to respond. Consequently, in addition to enhancing a society's competition for membership and professional business, education programs of these societies became even more important in establishing a professional identity that could withstand public scrutiny. SVP's historical reluctance to provide formal education had weakened both its ability to recruit members and its members' ability to compete in their respective professional markets. That stance had poorly positioned the association for responding to increasing public demands for external regulation. These pressures drove the organization to redefine its historical position. Not providing education to entry-level Society members could effectively bring about the demise of the Society, or so a significant subset of SVP members was beginning to believe. The newly imagined but not yet named SVP education program was thus a direct response to these internal and external organizational problems. This is what the president had come to tell me on my first day of work and why so little of our discussion was actually about education itself or what we traditionally assume to be educational talk. Indeed, the stakes were high and there was a need for allies.

Director of Education—Role and Identity

I noted earlier that my own professional identity was also tied up in this case. My first meeting with the president provides certain insights: education was a "product" that I was to help "produce"; there were enormous internal and external pressures requiring response; and finally, in SVP's view, professional education should focus on the adoption of prescribed ethical principles, the acquisition of scientifically established general principles, and the ability to execute proper technical procedures. This common underestimation of professional practice dominates much of continuing professional education (Cervero, 1988; Nowlen, 1988). At this time the dominant position in adult education, which I unreflectively represented then, was to see education as process and educators as facilitators. Educational work, as I understood it then, had to do with learning theories, instructional methods, writing objectives, program planning, logistics, and publicity management. The president and I were clearly not talking about the same thing. It is no wonder that I was a bit overwhelmed by the president's portrayal: this was not educational talk, but something else that I did not have words for then.

What will become evident as I now turn to sketching some key events is how the Society's expectations for what "the educator" would do became an ongoing challenge for me. From the beginning, the organization tended to see me as a manager of the technical implementation of their decisions, whereas I tried to position myself as a professional educator with specific expertise they lacked. In many ways, we had the same problem: lack of a well-understood professional identity. Over time, I came to a deep appreciation of their professional identity issues because they paralleled mine; the organization never acquired the same appreciation for me. My first meeting with the Professional Development Committee (PDC), barely two months into the job, shows how these large organizational issues and my role as an adult educator began to develop in the construction of this new educational program: SVP's *Fundamentals of Valuation*.

Summary of Planning Meetings

Exhibit 2.4 provides a calendar of key events in the development of SVP's new educational program. The conditions facing the Society, as I've explained, had been developing for several years. The scale and impending impacts of that situation were what the president was so determined to focus my attention on that first day of work. Before and during my first year with the organization, the Society had begun to respond in very specific ways. First was the ongoing campaign within the organization itself to redirect the Society's position on providing education. That campaign's initial successes led to my being hired shortly after the new executive director had been "brought on board" (military language dominated organizational talk). An acting director (in actuality the organization's retained attorney who had managed mostly in absentia) had been in place for two years prior to the arrival of the new executive director, who was hired in July following the board of governors' approval of his hiring, given at the annual meeting in June. At that same meeting the board of governors established a new committee to organize and implement its new educational program: the Professional Development Committee (PDC), chaired by the newly inaugurated president (who subsequently briefed me on my first day). The chair of

Exhibit 2.4.   Society for Valuation Professions Program Planning and Implementation.

Year 1

July 1	New Executive Director of SVP hired
August 10–11	First Professional Development Committee (PDC) meeting
October 7	SVP Director of Education hired
December 6–7	Second PDC meeting
January 17–19	Board of Governors interim meeting
March 8–9	First SVP Course Development and Instructor Training Workshop
April 3–6	First presentation of Phase I courses: Fundamentals of Valuation
May	Phase I course and instructor evaluations
June 23–29	Society Annual Conference: PDC & Education Committee meetings
	First annual education report to PDC and Board of Governors

Year 2

October 8–12	Second presentation of Phase I courses: Fundamentals of Valuation
December 10–14	First presentation of Phase II courses: Fundamentals of Valuation
January 8–11	Board of Governors interim meeting
February 5–8	Third presentation of Phase I courses: Fundamentals of Valuation
April 2–5	Second presentation of Phase II courses: Fundamentals of Valuation
June 22–27	Society Annual Conference: PDC & Education Committee meetings
	Second annual education report to PDC and Board of Governors

Note: By the end of the third year of program development, all four levels of valuation courses for five disciplines had been developed and presented at least once and were in scheduling rotation in multiple sites in the United States. Instructor training and course development continued regularly on a discipline-by-discipline basis either at headquarters or at annual and interim meetings.

SVP's Education Committee put it this way: "Within the past two years . . . the Society has begun to take a more active role in establishing a complete educational system for its members. Beginning with the establishment of the Professional Development Committee, [we have been making] progress toward its goal of establishing a thorough system of professional development for its members . . . a clear educational career path." With that mandate the PDC met in August to begin developing that "clear educational career path." At this first meeting, the executive director was charged with finding a new director of education. He hired me in October. The organizational structure and personnel were now in place to begin the serious business of "establishing a thorough system of professional development" for the Society's members.

December: Second PDC Meeting

Professional Development Committee meetings typically represented a relentless work ethic. Meetings, which could occur in any major city in the United States, would often begin at 8 A.M. and continue through to 6 P.M. Committee members worked through lunch together, met again collectively for dinner, often finished the night with many informal conversations, then started up again at 8:00 the next morning. This PDC meeting, the first I attended as director of education, was no different, and the talk was all educational business for the entire two days of the meeting. The meeting minutes indicate the scale of discussion: "The meeting began with status reports from the various discipline and other committee chairpersons. These included information on each discipline's progress with course development, textbook acquisition, syllabus construction, examination review, and various advanced seminar offerings."

A number of program decisions were made at this meeting, several of which would be presented as resolutions to the upcoming board of governors' meeting in January. Among them was a formal statement of the "system of professional development" the committee was charged with developing:

The mission of the Professional Development Committee has been to develop a clearly defined series of procedures and courses that lead from candidate to senior member designation. This conception of SVP professional development now exists. It is important to note that the committee now distinguishes two essential types of SVP programs: academically accredited *courses* (of 3 to 5 days) [these courses represented the "new" part of the educational system] available to current and entering candidates (as well as non-members) to help them gain the necessary educational preparation to pass the ethics, general valuation theory, and technical expertise exams. Advanced technical *seminars* (1 to 2 days) [several of these already existed] will also be available for the continued professional development of designated members. . . . SVP courses will be oriented towards the beginning appraiser while seminars will be topically dedicated to the seasoned practitioner.

My charge was to provide support for the courses, which were the major concern of the PDC. Individual discipline committees managed the advanced seminars. The PDC went on to develop the details of this system in terms of specific discipline courses, course duration, grading, tuition, instructor salaries and expenses, and numerous other program and logistical matters: "The consensus of the committee was to recommend this course development plan to the board of governors. All committee members were also asked to take opportunities to begin disseminating the education plan information to local governors in order to facilitate its formal adoption." This last recommendation showed how far this organization had come in reconstituting itself in response to member and public demands. It also showed that continued progress was not assured: formal resolutions still required legislative approval, which required lobbying the regional governors for support.

Several items emerged from this general resolution that would need resolving in future meetings. One was a "special committee request" that "all discipline committees submit project budgets to develop both the long and short-term goals of their course programs . . . in order to prepare for the budget meetings" at the next board of governors meeting in January. Financing for the new educational system had yet to be worked out at the organizational level. Other decisions required my immediate attention. First, the PDC—and in effect the organization—committed to presenting five discipline courses in April of the coming year. Although I had some notion of what that would entail, it would become increasingly clear to me that the members of this committee had not yet realized the scale of what they were pledging themselves to do. Another committee decision was to conduct an "instructor training clinic" in March. Many of the committee members had experience working in large corporations in which instructor training was typically part of management education (two of the documents the president had given me at our first meeting were corporate instructor training manuals) or experience in other societies that required instructor training prior to teaching society courses. So the idea of preparing instructors for courses was not foreign to this committee.

Although I had not been asked to specifically do so for this meeting, I had prepared a brief handout of the rationale for why instructor training was essential to the program's success and "a listing of potential content areas for an instructor training course." I was trying to establish a place for myself in program development by bringing to the table something I had yet to hear much discussion about. When the discussion arose in the meeting, I volunteered my presentation, which was met with a respectful but quizzical reception: instructor training seemed to mean to them ensuring that instructors knew the "correct" discipline content knowledge and how to use media technology, whereas I was talking about *adult* education in terms of course objectives, learning theory, instructional methods, matching methods with objectives, and evaluation, as well as something that would subsequently become a major issue: experiential and interactive approaches to learning. I remember thinking then that I was just trying to bring my educational expertise to their educational problem. I later realized that by introducing a set of issues of which they were largely unaware, I managed to acquire the permission to address them.

As a result of this meeting, I now had an instructor training clinic to run in March in addition to implementing five separate discipline courses in April. As the meeting was breaking up, the president remarked, "Now you know what we're going to do. You've got your work cut out for you." Doing that work—even agreeing about what that work was—represented a persistent conflict. Nearly every assignment I was asked to take on during the meeting, except for instructor training, had to do with logistical and management implementation tasks including arranging course sites, organizing instructor travel and lodging, developing publicity, collecting fees, and reproducing course materials. The tension was between my view of myself as an educator who supposedly knew something useful about how adults learn and the committee's view of me as a logistics manager. Learning, however, was not yet nor would it ever really be on the Society's program development radar. Although the Society appeared to be on its way to resolving, at least internally, some of its identity questions, mine were just beginning: Was I just a meeting planner or could I be an educator?

January: Board of Governors Interim Meeting

The PDC decided at its December meeting to present to the board of governors its overall two-tiered education system as a formal resolution for the Society to adopt and enact. As the chair of the Education Committee indicated in one report, "SVP is establishing a foundation for the Candidate, through a series of clearly defined steps, to gain the essential education leading to a designation in SVP. The Society's in-place annual seminars and new avenues being developed for the tested/certified practitioner will help broaden the experience and expertise of the professionally qualified appraiser. The total program will, therefore, enhance the professionalization of appraisal practice by providing the structured body of knowledge requisite for defining it as a profession." The chair of the PDC added: "One prime objective is to reach non-member appraisers through our education and other support programs, and encourage them to participate in achieving professional certification and designation." The successful adoption of resolutions representing these major policy and practice changes in the Society's history just four months after the PDC's first meeting and just six months after the inauguration of the president, who was directing these efforts, illustrates just how quickly the association was responding to conditions.

Not everything progressed smoothly, though. As I indicated earlier, one of the internal issues was the need to generate additional streams of income, which SVP expected the new education program to do. That expectation, however, did not address the issue of how to finance the construction of the program itself. SVP certainly was not insolvent at this time, but it was not "swimming in cash" as some of the other organizations supposedly were; it had few resources to underwrite the scale of the education program now being envisioned. For example, hiring the executive director was "within" the board's previously passed budget. My position as the director of education, however, was not included in the previous budget, even though I had already been hired. At the January meeting the board had to endorse funding my position retrospectively. This question opened up the unaddressed issue of how to fund the new education program. The problem was directly expressed in terms of adding two new staff members in less than six months with no new increases in income. Budget issues did not get resolved at this meeting, but I did get my first lesson in how to "cook the books." During budget committee discussions, one committee member demanded, "Well, how much is this program going to cost?" The PDC chair snapped, "150K," which was just a made-up number to quiet the questioner. No one had projected costs and they had no data or program experience with which to do so. After this somewhat vitriolic confrontation in the budget session, a hastily arranged compromise included creating an "education course income" category in the budget to offset the projected costs of implementing the courses. The budget now "balanced." The members decided that if the program were to cost this much, they would expect the program to operate initially only at a cost-recovery level, with the expectation that it would soon generate surplus funds for the association. Even though these projected costs and income were arbitrarily created, I learned a quick lesson about how serious the finances were and how the strengthening but shallow support for the program could easily be undermined by program financial losses.

A second incident reflected on my developing role in the organization. I had fared moderately well at the December PDC meeting. I learned much more about the conditions facing the organization. I began to get a sense of what I was to do, introduced the idea of adult education, became acquainted with many of the names on the president's list, and developed some important working relationships with several key committee members who would prove to be continuing allies throughout my tenure at SVP. However, as noted above, the budget issue had cast a pall over the growing support for the program—and my formal introduction to the board of governors did not help. The president and the PDC had already checked me out; the interim meeting was used to "present" me to the board. Although I was unaware of it, introducing me was an agenda item during one of the board's general sessions. The president introduced me as the "new education director" with "a science degree in education." Suddenly there I was, standing at the open end of a large U-shaped array of some twenty-five Society governors and executive leaders.

After the president's welcome and introduction, one governor rather innocently asked what I thought I could do for the organization. The PDC had not asked this question, instead presuming I

would be providing essentially logistical assistance. Now, at this crucial moment, I got the right question but had no idea how to answer
it. This became and still remains one of my most embarrassing public moments as an adult educator. When the governor asked the
question, a flush of fear ran through me as my mind frantically
scrambled to respond. I remember clearly thinking, *I've read Mal-
colm Knowles; I know the answer to this question. I know what adult
educators are supposed to do.* But I also clearly remembered the PDC's
earlier reaction to my instructor training recommendations; they
had only a vague idea of what I was talking about. So, what do I say?
Of course, all this was happening in two or three heartbeats and I
had to respond, so I stammered, "Evaluation—I can help evaluate
your programs. Good programs require evaluation and no one has
talked about doing that yet." I am still surprised to this day that they
did not fire me immediately and take away my airplane ticket home.
I had missed a crucial opportunity to take a public stand on what I
should be doing for the organization.

March: Course Development and Instructor Training Workshop

The PDC minutes of its December meeting reported that "An
instructor training clinic is being planned for March. This workshop, in addition to adult education methodology, will focus on
preparing the projected April discipline courses and exams in a standardized manner that will allow academic accrediting." At the
December PDC meeting I had asked for course outlines, instructors,
and marketing suggestions. I did not receive any of these in time for
the January governor's interim meeting. At that meeting I repeated
my requests, adding requests for course objectives and participant
benefits. Not only did I need such responses for marketing, but I was
also acquiring evidence that the course designers and instructors
had not started to actually prepare the courses. This was cause for
concern, of course, but I was also learning that, although they were
earnestly dedicated, many of the designers and instructors were vol-
unteering their time. For the volunteers, the time spent on SVP was

not typically billable to clients; to put it bluntly, for some members time spent on SVP meant a real loss of income. Thus SVP obligations usually were taken care of at the last minute in airports and on weekends. Unfortunately, marketing could not wait until the last moment nor could designing three eight-hour days of instruction for five separate discipline courses. In early February I sent out a memo saying "the major focus" of the workshop is "to finalize discipline course formats . . . and organizational arrangements for the April courses . . . to investigate and share your various adult education experiences and teaching methods." Once again, I asked for program content information. Enclosed with the memo was a short reading on "preparing to teach adults" and a list of "principles of adult education."

The workshop unfolded more or less as planned. Approximately thirty SVP members attended. This included four to five from each of the five disciplines preparing courses for April as well as several other PDC and Education Committee members. The first day was spent mostly in discipline work groups preparing course syllabi for the April program. Similar to the president in my first meeting with him, the various discipline committees did not really realize what it would take to put three full days of instruction together. Because I had been unable to get course objectives before this workshop, I asked course designers to develop them at this meeting along with specific day-by-day course content outlines. Attempting to construct these first-level courses revealed an ongoing program development issue: the lack of agreement on what should be in the courses. Yet by the end of the day, even though much was still undecided and under debate, all but one group had at least developed a tentative content outline for the three-day program. As was their norm, they continued working informally into the evening over dinner and afterward. We reviewed and shared plans the next morning, partly to keep the work moving and partly to reinforce their sense of themselves as a multidisciplinary profession sharing similar valuation principles (almost always expressed more rhetorically than actually).

The last part of the workshop was a sharing of teaching practices. A number of the participants with previous appraisal teaching experience shared "teaching tips" that, as is usual with adults, proved motivational for neophytes and confirmatory for the experienced. I learned that there were some potentially good instructors. I also learned that no one was really thinking about these courses as having much to do with learning. Nor, for that matter, were they prepared to think about how to do adult education systematically; they thought teaching consisted mainly of telling people what you know. Although I continued my attempts to keep adult education on the table—I had managed to focus this workshop on relevant adult education issues and tasks—most of my work continued to be focused on program logistics and implementation.

Fundamentals of Valuation: Phase I and Beyond

Five discipline courses were presented in April at a local university through its continuing education department. Courses began on a Thursday morning and concluded on Saturday evening with an examination (subsequent programs ran for three and a half days, with an exam for each course on Sunday morning). More than one hundred participants completed these first courses; some courses were oversubscribed, with more than thirty, while others had fewer than ten. The program also included SVP's first formal presentation of "valuation theory" as the bedrock of professional valuation practice. This presentation was delivered by a professor with whom SVP had contracted to write a text on valuation theory and who directed a valuation sciences degree program (this aspect of the programs continued to be problematic throughout my tenure).

It seemed to me at the time that there were more than the normal number of site problems. For example, one building in which we had classes was having its exterior sandblasted; on another day there was a bomb scare. Overall, however, the program seemed to go well—at least as reported in the various evaluation forms returned by the course instructors, designers, and participants. I shared in the initial enthusiasm until I did a financial review—the program had lost $7,000! As I began a systematic review of the instructor, course, and program evaluations in May, I could also see that some important educational dimensions of the program needed to be addressed before the next scheduled offering. Meanwhile, logistical and coordination demands continued to increase.

Epilogue

The remainder of the planning calendar (see Exhibit 2.4) consisted mainly of the Year 2 development cycle and showed the expansion arc of the program. During my three years with SVP, we added new courses and sites constantly. By the time I left, we had developed four courses for each of five disciplines and were offering programs in every month except December. Enrollment demand continued to increase, with programs averaging 125 to 150 participants each. After the first program, all programs recovered their costs and generated modest net profits. From this initial modest success, the SVP education offering has grown to exceed the expectations of the program originators. Today the organization has become quite vibrant. During my involvement its total annual budget was something less than $1 million. Now the budget is several million, much of which is attributable to this major reorientation from a testing to a teaching Society. Once run by a staff of twelve with only one person dedicated to education, the organization now employs more than thirty, half of whom work on education. The Society has quite effectively turned its education program into a major profit center. I will lay claim to contributing to its initial efforts to get started, but I have had no responsibility for its subsequent successes. Recall, however, the president's words to me on my first day: education was a product that the Society had to sell to members and nonmembers in order to survive financially. As far as that goes, I think he was right; history has proved this true. The question of what constituted "good" continuing professional education, however, emerged early and continued throughout my time there. My role as an educator never became as important as my role as a manager did. Financial interests always dominated program development.

Management Education at the Phoenix Company

Pete, whom we first met in Chapter One, is one of five vice presidents of a 1,280-employee service-oriented business, the Phoenix Company. Considered a cheerful and gregarious person, Pete manages the human resources division, which comprises several operational departments: personnel, employee health, employee safety, customer service, volunteers, and educational services (see Figure 2.3). A ten-year employee, Pete strongly believes it is his responsibility to push for training that reshapes the organizational culture. Although Pete enjoys a fair amount of latitude in determining what the organizational needs are for management education, his previous efforts to use the annual retreat to change the organizational culture using experiential activities have failed. However, the need to have an annual management retreat and the company president's concern over ineffective departmental meetings coincide to offer Pete the opportunity for which he has been waiting.

Joan, Pete's partner in planning the retreat and the manager of a department in his division, is very familiar with the corporate climate at Phoenix. She has a good relationship with Mr. Jones and interacts well with other employees. Joan shares with Pete a commitment to improve communication within the company. Recently rehired after working eighteen months for another company, Joan had previously worked compatibly with Pete for several years. Joan sees herself as having a "driver personality," so she is more impatient than Pete with the slow pace of change in the corporate culture at Phoenix.

Figure 2.3.   Phoenix Company Organizational Structure.

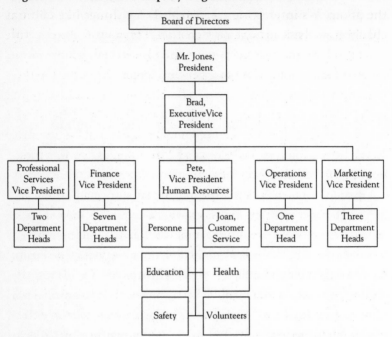

Note: Sixty-five line supervisors report to nineteen department heads.

Because the circumstances surrounding the planning of the previous retreat almost resulted in a disaster for Pete (as detailed in Chapter One), avoiding a similar situation is uppermost in his mind. This time, Pete plans to be in control of what is going on, beginning with keeping Mr. Jones well informed about what he and Joan are doing. To this end, he breaks the normal chain of command by communicating directly with the president—bypassing Brad, the executive vice president. Even though Pete is in a much better position this time around, the memory of the previous retreat compels him to be diligent not only in keeping Mr. Jones apprised of what he and Joan are doing, but also in cultivating support for the retreat among other key vice presidents. Describing the way in which he has learned to work within the system at Phoenix, Pete explains that it is "through practice, just through experience with the group. It's interesting . . . generally for things like cultural changing and basic management changes, I try to work directly with the president and just keep everyone else kind of informed . . . because I know if I can get one person's agreement at the top then I trust my judgment enough to know that everyone else can live with it. But if I open it up, it will be just a dogfight." Pete is indirectly revealing that a lack of open communication is part of the organizational culture at Phoenix and that working politically is a necessity for getting one's job done.

A couple of months into planning the retreat, Pete hired George as an outside consultant for his expertise in facilitating corporate groups. George was a well-known and successful leadership consultant in the city in which the Phoenix Company is located; he is considered an expert group facilitator. Pete and Joan hired George because they believe the program will be better received if someone outside Phoenix facilitates it. Pete, Joan, and George are all under a great deal of pressure to produce a program that is not only a "first" in the company's history (by using experiential learning to address an organizational problem), but one that effectively meets its stated objectives and results in a favorable response from the participants. Knowing what transpired last time around, it is not surprising that Pete was extremely sensitive to the organizational culture and wants to do everything he could to get participants in the proper frame of mind for the retreat and to keep them in that mind-set during the retreat.

Compounding the complexities of planning the retreat, Pete and George have conflicting ideas about what the main focus of the program should be and how learning should be facilitated. George was committed to using the retreat to promote participatory management, whereas Pete was focused on making communication flow more smoothly from top to bottom in the organization. As far as participatory management was concerned, Pete thought top managers would claim that they believe in it and practice it. "But in actuality," he added, "their tendency is to be quite directive, sometimes to the point of making decisions, omitting people who need to be involved." Given the apparent prevalence of a top-down approach to management at the Phoenix Company (see Figure 2.3), Pete thought managers might feel threatened if participatory decision making was "really talked about a lot" at the retreat.

Summary of Planning Meetings

In each of the six formal planning meetings (see Exhibit 2.5) that Pete and Joan held with either Mr. Jones or George, incidents occurred that had a direct bearing on how the planners constructed the retreat program. On January 2, Pete and Joan initiated the first meeting with Mr. Jones to "test the waters" and, as they said, "get the go-ahead" to begin planning that year's retreat. Joan remembered that "we talked about ideas, he gave us some direction." One of the things they discussed was "better communication from the department director level up and down." Mr. Jones was particularly concerned about this organizational problem because, as Pete explains, the president "has this monthly meeting with hourly employees and they keep telling him over and over again that we don't know what's going on, our supervisor doesn't answer our questions, they criticize other departments in a department meeting and they never get follow-up." Pete also remembered that it was "his [Mr. Jones's] idea that we focus on the department meeting." At this first planning meeting, the decision was made to have a retreat and to focus the program on management training—more specifically, on communication at the department head level.

Pete and Joan planned their strategy for the meetings with Mr. Jones very carefully: "We did a lot of talking and planning between these meetings to see where we wanted to take the discussion and what we wanted to accomplish." At the second meeting on January 17—held, as Pete says, to get "a little more permission to go ahead"—they discussed matters such as time, place, and participants, as well as their proposed broad objectives of the program (see Exhibit 2.6).

Exhibit 2.5.   Program Planning Calendar—Phoenix Company.

Timeline of Events

September, Year 1	Most recent company management retreat
September, Year 2	Joan rehired
January 2	Pete and Joan's first meeting with Mr. Jones to discuss retreat
January 17	Second meeting with Mr. Jones
February 13	Third meeting with Mr. Jones
February 21	Memorandum sent to program participants announcing retreat purpose and dates
March 7	Pete and Joan's first meeting with George, the outside consultant
March 21	Second meeting with George
April 6	Memorandum sent to retreat participants with agenda for final retreat
April 27	Third meeting with George
May 3–4	Phoenix Company retreat

Although Pete and Joan wrote up the objectives as a proposal, no formal document was presented to Mr. Jones. Rather, as Pete said, their tentative program objectives and logistics talking points were used as a "guideline, a check sheet." In preparation for this second meeting with Mr. Jones, Pete had also informally surveyed key vice presidents to gauge their reactions to what he and Joan planned to propose to the president. As Pete recalled, "I try to learn from my mistakes and I learned that there are some political players on the vice president team, that it is good to go and just run ideas by them and warm them up to what's going on—if they're not involved. So I went by and talked to three vice presidents about this whole idea."

Exhibit 2.6.   Pete and Joan's Management Retreat Proposed Objectives.

- To improve department heads' and supervisors' perceptions of how they communicate and how they come across to their staff

- To give each individual an opportunity to lead a group and to receive feedback on her or his effectiveness

- To reinforce the value of good communication for managers

- To provide an opportunity for team building within the management group

---

From one vice president Pete "got a definite green light to include mid-level managers." From others he got either supportive or differing opinions about scheduling and other logistics on the "check sheet." The result of this background work was that Pete met with the president with a limited set of choices—and Pete knew which options the vice presidents would support, should the president consult them. Pete reported, "The meeting was terrific. He loved all of our ideas. We got everything we wanted. Everything." Pete, Joan, and the president confirmed that the retreat purpose would be department communications, and they decided that the retreat would be held in the spring, on a Thursday and Friday, at an out-of-town resort, and would include top and mid-level managers.

Continuing their strategy, Pete and Joan went into the February 13 meeting with more options they could live with, to give Mr. Jones "a chance to choose." For instance, although several consultants were proposed, getting Mr. Jones to approve the hiring of George proved to be surprisingly simple. Pete and Joan knew that George "had a positive relationship" with Mr. Jones. As Pete recalls, "We were diplomatic in presenting [hiring George] to him. We said we've interviewed some people and we've really looked at the needs and we've selected George." Mr. Jones accepted their decision unquestioningly. Pete was also able to obtain Mr. Jones's buy-in for the Executive Adventure portion of the retreat, which is an outdoor team-building exercise that would be the focus on the first day of the retreat. Joan made what Pete described as "our best sales pitch." It helped that Joan knew Mr. Jones's secretary had recently participated in a similar exercise and that she had spoken highly of it to her boss. As Joan says, "He had some firsthand knowledge from someone other than us that that was a good program. And didn't even question us on that."

What neither Pete nor Joan could predict, however, is whether Mr. Jones will participate in the outdoor team-building exercise. Pete felt that the "personal risk" would be too high: "He [Mr. Jones] is not particularly interactive or relaxed being part of a group. In fact, a typical behavior that he will have at a retreat is to pull his chair out of a group and sit over in another part of the room as an observer." Because Joan so strongly believed that this type of exercise "immediately breaks down so many barriers," she replied that she would ask him to participate, "very casual, lighthearted, when the moment is right."

Although they had not gone into specifics about what participants will actually do in the Executive Adventure exercise or any of the other group work planned for the second day of the retreat, Joan believed that Mr. Jones "knew that we're going to do whatever it takes to be successful." Pete was more pragmatic in that he continued to mention that he was giving not only the president but also the other vice presidents a "little bird's-eye view" of what is going to occur. In doing this, he was informing participants early on not only about the exciting features of the program, but also about what was expected of them. Before the first meeting with George, then, Pete and Joan—in close consultation with Mr. Jones—decided on the program objectives and the general outline of the events for the retreat. With these decisions made, Pete and Joan sent out a memo to all potential participants on February 21. During the following three meetings, Pete and Joan, with George, worked out the learning activities for the second day of the retreat and tied both days of the retreat program together.

On March 7, Pete and Joan met at the Phoenix Company with George for the first time. In this meeting two different but related exchanges illustrated the emerging conflict between Pete and George about the purpose of the retreat. Pete began the meeting by reviewing the preliminary program objectives (see Exhibit 2.6) to help George understand that the retreat will focus on issues of "communication, team working, and those kinds of things." As Pete concluded his synopsis of possible activities for the second day of the retreat, George responded, "OK. Let me clarify again . . . the people who are there see the need and the value for these particular activities in terms of the objectives. Have they bought into the fact that, hey, we need some guidance and updating on how to conduct good meetings?" To Joan's response of "I don't know," George continued for some time expressing his concern about including participant input, until Pete felt he had to reiterate the purpose of the retreat as he, Joan, and the president had determined it. In explaining the purpose of one of the educational exercises planned for the second day of the retreat, Pete said, "we feel like we want to provide a skill-building opportunity on how to conduct a meeting, and this comes directly from Mr. Jones [who is] saying that the information is not getting down to the lower levels of the company." Pete went on to give specific instances in which managers have inadequately communicated with employees in departmental meetings. For example, he told George that he had had a meeting "today with sixty dietary people who had a department meeting last Monday and nobody said a word or asked a question. So what does that tell you? It tells me that their department manager has not set an environment where people feel comfortable questioning and commenting." He also stressed that Mr. Jones was quite unhappy about the communication breakdown between managers and employees: "I think that's a real hole and I think Mr. Jones has identified that one of our objectives is one of our agenda items." These exchanges began the struggle between Pete and George over the purpose of the retreat.

The meeting continued with George trying to understand the real purpose of the retreat. Finally the heart of the difference in their two approaches to the program emerged. George interpreted Pete's interest in communication and team building as Pete's desire to promote participatory management in the company: "One of the questions that I have is the feeling on the part of the company that this is participatory management and this is something that has become part of our culture in our department. Or is it something else?" Pete responded by clearly communicating to George that the retreat would be about team building, not participatory management, saying: "I don't think we're as participative as we like to think we are. I think the heart of a good meeting is in the approachability that people feel comfortable in raising their hands and I don't think that our managers set the climate for people to raise their hands." Thus, Pete reiterated the central purpose: fixing the communication problem in department meetings so employees do not take their complaints to their meetings with Mr. Jones.

At their second meeting at the Phoenix Company on March 21, George came back with a number of suggestions for activities to be used on the second day of the retreat that could help meet the four stated objectives (see Exhibit 2.6). He proposed using a "desert survival exercise" to build on the first day's Executive Adventure exercise focused on improving team building:

> Now this is just an idea, but I was trying again to apply it to the objective of working together as a team, particularly supporting others, leading in a positive manner, working cooperatively, that in order to survive we have to work cooperatively and support each other, have to listen to other people's ideas and they may be incorrect but we're going to analyze that later, and why did someone with an incorrect solution or idea, why did his or her idea prevail, why did they listen to you when you said we should save this rather than what I want.

Although Pete and Joan were a bit hesitant about using the desert survival exercise, the planners worked out a timetable for the two days so that on April 6 Pete and Joan were able to send the seventy-two participants a memo with the final retreat agenda (see Exhibit 2.7). In the memo, they noted that "An exciting program is planned which will focus on team building within our group and strengthening communication at all levels within the company."

Although it was an amicable meeting, with the planners making many instructional decisions, George again brought up his concern about participant input into decision making. He suggested surveying the participants about the quality of their department meeting. The three planners decided against it because, as Joan noted, "I'm not sure how honest people would really be on a little survey they know is going to be mailed in to somebody." In place of the survey, Pete suggested sending to participants "an article with our objectives so that really they would be thinking that way" when they arrive at the retreat.

The final planning meeting before the actual retreat on May 3 and 4 was held on April 27 at George's university office. It's important to remember that before George became involved in the planning, Pete and Joan, in consultation with Mr. Jones, had established the substance of the objectives (see Exhibit 2.6) for the Friday morning portion of the retreat. The actual wording of the objectives, but not their intended outcomes, continued to change several times during the planning. These objectives had guided the continuing discussions about what would be the best activities to accomplish them. In the previous meetings, the planners had discussed using the desert survival exercise, the departmental meeting exercise, and the table topic exercise during lunch. However, the planners were not completely settled on whether these would be the best exercises to address the objectives. Therefore, a major purpose of the final planning meeting was to make the final decisions about which activities to use so that they could be ready for the rapidly approaching retreat.

The meeting started with Pete, Joan, and George discussing how to conduct the desert survival exercise and the department meeting exercise. They focused on how to select and organize the groups, when to hand out the survival exercise instructions and department meeting scenarios, and who should process the different aspects of the exercises. As they decided about what to do, the continuing tension about the purpose of the retreat, evident in their earlier meetings, arose again. It began when Pete expressed his concern that the exercises needed to have "a real-world connection" and that they, the planners, had "to hammer away at what makes it real." This, for Pete, was "what's going to be different" about this retreat: the department meeting exercise would address "real issues" in the company. George assured Pete that the desert survival exercise would also help meet that objective because participants will have the chance to evaluate department management leadership and help promote participatory management. Because Pete's purpose was not to criticize management but to help them by "providing skill-building exercises" to facilitate the flow of information through the company, he had to finally confront George: "No, George, this retreat is not about participatory management. We can't use this retreat to criticize leadership skills." George quickly but with some embarrassment responded, "Oh . . . OK." The issue of participatory management disappeared from the discussion as the planners quickly decided the technical matters of how to implement the exercises.

The Management Education Retreat and Beyond

In spite of complex organizational relationships and differences of opinion among the program planners, the annual retreat (see Exhibit 2.7) held by the Phoenix Company finally, as Joan observed, "fell into place." A two-day program held at an out-of-town resort facility, the retreat provided an opportunity for top- and mid-level managers in the company to get to know each other better and to participate as a group in team building and other learning exercises.

Exhibit 2.7. Phoenix Company Management Retreat Agenda.

Thursday, May 3

12:00–1:00	Lunch at retreat site
1:00–1:15	Welcome, overview, and purpose of the retreat *(Pete)*
1:15–5:15	Outdoor Adventure exercise
5:15–7:00	Free time
7:00–until	Outdoor barbeque and social time

Friday, May 4

7:00–8:00	Breakfast buffet
8:30–8:45	Overview and purpose of morning activities *(Pete)*
8:45–10:00	Departmental Meetings–Disaster or Success? *(George)*
10:00–10:15	Break
10:15–11:15	Desert Survival exercise *(George)*
11:15–12:15	Departmental Meetings exercise *(Pete and George)*
12:15–1:15	Lunch
1:15–1:30	Summary and wrap-up *(Joan)*
	Closing comments *(Mr. Jones)*

Of the seventy-two managers invited, sixty-two attended the retreat, including Mr. Jones.

The retreat agenda began with lunch on the first Thursday in May. After lunch, all the managers, including Mr. Jones, were assigned to preselected groups of thirteen to participate in team-building exercises designed to strengthen interpersonal relationships. These outdoor exercises were developed and led by an Executive Adventure firm. Dinner and preplanned social activities rounded out the day's events. The first activity on Friday morning was a workshop entitled "Departmental Meetings–Disaster or Success?" Participants in small groups identified characteristics of successful and unsuccessful meetings. George used the identified characteristics as the basis for a full group discussion about how to conduct effective meetings. After a break, the next activity was the desert survival exercise. Again, participants were divided into small groups, this time to make decisions about how their group might survive being lost in the desert. In debriefing participants after the exercise, George stressed the importance of communicating as a team member. For the third and last exercise, on departmental meetings, participants were asked to role-play scenarios based on actual problems the company was facing, such as implementing the new smoking policy and addressing the shortage of available employee parking. George also facilitated the full group discussion that followed, the goal of which was to help participants learn to deal with difficult questions asked in meetings. The retreat ended just after lunch on Friday with a wrap-up given by Joan and closing remarks made by Mr. Jones. Based on the results of the evaluation forms completed by forty-three of the participants at the end of the program, both Thursday and Friday sessions were well received. The informal feedback was also positive. Even Brad—the once-problematic executive vice president—made a point of calling Pete the Monday after the retreat to say (as Pete recalls) "how well it went and how he enjoyed it and how people [at Phoenix] . . . came up to him and started a conversation that he had never said any-thing but hello to before the retreat." Mr. Jones also told Pete that they had done an "excellent job."

Conclusion

These three planning stories exemplify the necessary political work all planners must negotiate in doing even the most mundane planning task or procedure. As we did in the first chapter and will throughout the rest of the book, we use the stories to show how the common tasks of educational planning—ranging from needs-assessment through evaluation—have political as well as educational outcomes. The stories show the confluence and effect of power, interests, negotiation, and ethical commitment when planners work their planning tables. In telling these stories, we recognize that we have selectively constructed them to bring a specific interpretation to the messy, negotiated action of actual planning practice. We return to this point in Chapter Nine, in which we explain why we have used the planning stories in this book, how we have learned from the stories, and how we have used them in our teaching.

Chapter 3

Negotiating Democratically for Educational and Political Outcomes

In his famous announcement of "the practical," Schwab declared that the "classical" field of curriculum and instruction—the most dominant influence on adult education planning theory—was "moribund, unable by its present methods and principles to continue its work" (1969, p. 586). In introducing the deliberative tradition (Walker, 1971) as a way to understand what planners actually do, Schwab charged theorists to focus on "choice and action" that would lead to "defensible decisions" (1969, p. 587). Although the deliberative tradition brings us appreciably closer to what planners actually do, questions of political and ethical action are only marginally addressed (Walker, 1990, 2003). Nonetheless, the political consequences of educational planning have long been recognized, as evidenced early in the twentieth century by the curriculum theorists who asked, for example, "Dare the School Build a New Social Order?" (Counts, 1932). The most recent manifestation of a critical tradition emerged in the 1970s, with the analysis of schooling curricula as political texts (Pinar & Bowers, 1992). This tradition asked whose knowledge counts in determining the educational and political outcomes of schooling (Apple, 1979; Pinar, 1974; Schubert, 1986). Pinar and Bowers (1992, p. 187) note that although the "apolitical blindspot of the traditional field has been now corrected," there have been "limited suggestions offered by advocates to inspire classroom practice" (p. 183). Other theorists have noted similar deficiencies in adult education theories (Newman, 1999; Walters, 1996; Youngman, 1996).

It is no revelation to announce the prevalence and importance of organizational politics in everyday life. In describing "organizations as political systems," Morgan (1986) "captures an aspect of organization that has escaped us up to now" (p. 141). In Morgan's view, effective organizational work requires understanding conflict, analyzing interests, and exercising power, which he identifies as having as least fourteen sources. Although Bolman and Deal lament that "it is disturbing to see political forces corrupting decision making" (1997, p. 162), they depict organizations "as alive and screaming political arenas that host a complex web of individual and group interests" in which "scarce resources and enduring differences give conflict a central role in organizational dynamics and make power the most important resource" (p. 163). They argue that their "political frame emphasizes that organizational goals are set not by fiat at the top but through an ongoing process of negotiation among the key players" (p. 165). Thus, ignoring the reality of organizational politics forces educators to plan with one eye closed—or worse, it may be like trying to cross a crowded intersection with both eyes closed (Forester, 1989).

Seeing that programs have both educational and political outcomes is not new either (Heaney, 1996). Adult educators have noted the "politics" of planning educational programs in social and organizational settings as early as the 1950s. Although recognized, such insights have received little theoretical attention. Consequently, no practical understanding of the politics of planning has emerged, other than to note that the "people-work" of planning represents a hindrance to rational planning procedures such as those enumerated by the Tyler Rationale. As every review for nearly twenty years has demonstrated (Cervero & Wilson, 1994a; Sork, 2000; Sork & Buskey, 1986; Sork & Caffarella, 1989; Sork & Newman, 2004; Wilson & Cervero, 1997), classical planning theory has dominated adult educators' theoretical efforts to understand

and improve planning practice. These theories have promoted an idealized and decontextualized view of rational decision making rather than a situated understanding of human action.

Such a dominant view has not gone unchallenged. In the early 1990s we began building on the analyses of the curriculum field and other planning disciplines to work out a "guide to negotiating power and interests" in planning (Cervero & Wilson, 1994a). Although numerous theorists continue to present adult education planning models blind to political dynamics, Sork's (2000) review of planning theory has challenged these efforts. In supporting our theory (1994a), Sork (2000) argued that in addition to the "technically capable planner," adult educators must also become "politically aware" and "ethically sensitive" planners. Although Sork promotes the necessity of integrating politics and ethics with technical expertise, he argues that we have yet "to reach firm conclusions about what it means to be a politically aware planner" and have not provided "much help in clarifying what it means to be an ethically sensitive planner" (2000, p. 178). Others have built upon our theory. In the most recent edition of her planning manual, for example, Caffarella (2002) has integrated political and ethical insights into her model. Donaldson and Kozoll have argued that collaborative planning is "truly a social activity" in which "different interests and relations of power are also present, as is their negotiation" (1999, p. 135). In our recent work (Cervero, Wilson, & Associates, 2001), we have been more explicit in defining adult education as the struggle for knowledge and power.

Decades ago Simon's (1955, 1956, 1957) notion of "bounded rationality" challenged the rationality models in management theory, such as those that underpin classical curriculum models. Clearly antecedent to the deliberative tradition in curriculum planning (Houle, 1972; Schwab, 1969; Walker, 1971), Simon's bounded rationality recognized the interactive dynamics of people working in social and organizational settings. Subsequent efforts in the critical traditions have added color to the palette of context and action by introducing power and interests (Apple, 1996; Pinar & Bowers, 1992). Despite our efforts and those of others, however, much adult education planning theory continues to provide procedural guides to "practice" while ignoring the mounting insights from other disciplinary investigations. Because such theory is blind to the prevalence and effect of organizational politics, we disagree with Sork's (2000, p. 179) skepticism "about the prospects of developing a theory or model that is suitable" to account for what happens in practice and to provide a guide to practical action. Although sympathetic to Sork's concern, we believe our theory provides explanatory power *and* practical guidance.

Why Planning Tables Matter

In this section we develop the planning table metaphor introduced in Chapter One as the central dynamic of program planning, and we explain why it can both account for people's lived experience and provide a guide to practical action. If program planning cannot be accurately depicted as a sequence of activities that begins with needs-assessment, moves through educational design, and ends with evaluation, then what do planners actually do? In place of the logic used in classical planning models, the starting point of our theory is that "people plan educational programs" (Cervero & Wilson, 1994a, 1996). Unlike the classical planning models, the theory offers an account of people's lived experiences when planning in social and organizational contexts. This starting point highlights the fundamentally social nature of program planning and focuses attention on where decisions are truly made about educational programs—namely, at "the planning table" (Cervero & Wilson, 1998).

Drawing Attention to What Matters

The planning table metaphor draws attention to the fundamental idea that *people make judgments* with others in social and organizational contexts that determine the specific features of an educational program, such as its purpose, content, audience, and format (Cervero & Wilson, 1996). The planning table can be a physical one at which people make decisions about an educational program. More often, however, it is a metaphorical table, accounting for the judgments that people make with others in conversations on telephones, through e-mail and faxes, and sometimes privately in offices, hallways, and restrooms or at social gatherings. People make these judgments about the features of educational programs at multiple, historically developing, and intersecting planning tables. For example, in making decisions about the management education program, Pete and Joan worked at *multiple* planning tables. At one table, with the president, they made decisions about the overall need, purpose, and place for the program. At another table, they worked out the specific features of the educational design with George, the outside facilitator. At other planning tables, Pete had one-on-one meetings with three vice presidents as he sought approval for the key features of the program. The work at these planning tables was *historically developing* in the sense that each discussion crystallized additional judgments about the objectives, the activities, and the leadership for the program. For example, each of the three meetings that Pete and Joan had with the president built on decisions and discussions from the previous meetings. The work at these planning tables was *intersecting* in that Pete's efforts to gain approval from the vice presidents for certain program features provided important information and leverage as he worked the planning table with the president.

Drawing Attention to the Making of Judgments

A second reason for the planning table as an organizing theme is that it draws attention to *when* judgments are made that determine the features of an educational program. The history of the planning table for a program might have begun well before the "formal planning" was initiated. For example, the management education program at the Phoenix Company had been an annual event for several years. Thus, when Pete and Joan entered the president's office for their first planning meeting, their efforts were part of a long-standing set of traditions in the company about how the planning would occur as well as about the purposes and format for this program. These prior judgments about the uses of the annual retreat formed a strong frame around the possibilities for the one being planned. This attention to when judgments are made that determine the features of a program also shows that planning does not stop when a brochure is printed or an instructional design is written down. It is important to recognize that the instructional site itself forms a critical planning table for any educational program. For example, instructors often make judgments about the content during the program, ad hoc decisions are made about changing the design due to suggestions from the learners, mistakes are made by the facilitator in carrying out the design, and unexpected opportunities become available to the group in organizing the curriculum. Although these are generally thought of as "implementation" decisions, this distinction between planning and implementation misses the opportunity to see that learners are *always* at a planning table for any program. Although important judgments prior to the educational activity generally delimit what is possible for the educational agenda, people either support or change these decisions at the planning table with learners. The PI program provides a good example. The agenda for the afternoon of the second day called for a "concept mapping" activity, which had been successful in the previous two PI projects. However, when Cassie and Dougie sensed a rising anxiety among the participants, they decided at lunch to change this activity to a less structured one, allowing the teachers to continue the morning discussion.

Drawing Attention to the Character of Planning

A third reason for the planning table as an organizing theme is that it draws attention to the fundamentally *social and political character* of educational planning. Although some planning models urge educators to pay attention to context (Boone, Safrit, & Jones, 2002;

Caffarella, 2002; Sork, 2000), they do not *locate* where and how political relationships play out in the planning process nor do they show specifically how to plan strategically within these relationships. By noting *where* judgments are made about a program, planning is moved out of the minds of individuals and into socially and politically constructed places (Wilson & Cervero, 2003). Most important, the planning table shows specifically and concretely where power operates to affect educational programs. Thus, the planning tables (both literal and metaphorical) are the central link between the individual person and the political and social structures within which people make judgments about a program's purposes, content, and audiences. In the SVP story, we see precisely how political relationships shaped the judgments about specific features of the *Fundamentals of Valuation* program. The organizational structure at the Society—specifically, the Professional Development Committee—provided the political frame for making decisions about the program. Indeed, the creation of the Professional Development Committee was a concrete political strategy used by the Society to change how decisions were made about education. Thus, membership in this committee mattered because it defined who sat at the planning table. Arthur worked this politically constructed planning table to make the fundamental decisions about the program's purpose, audience, and general outlines of its format. The point is that people work planning tables structured by existing social and political relationships to make the judgments about an educational program's features.

Connecting the Domains of Planning

Finally, the planning table metaphor connects the *technical, political, and ethical domains* of planning (Cervero & Wilson, 1994a, 1994b; Sork, 2000). To have any hope of connecting ethical beliefs, political analyses, and technical skills, we must look to the planning tables where the real work gets done. Virtually all of the theory about planning educational programs separates the technical processes from the political and ethical realities that educators face. Indeed, these two dimensions of education often exist in parallel universes. In one dimension, education plays an important role in the ongoing distribution of knowledge and power in social and organizational contexts (Cervero & Wilson, 2001). The other dimension highlights the technical processes of planning, such as the development of surveys and focus groups to collect data from learners about their needs (Sork & Buskey, 1986; Wilson & Cervero, 1997). Separating these two dimensions of education into issues of ethics and power and issues of technique and practice has failed to give educators the tools and analyses necessary to plan responsibly. This separation produces a missed opportunity to offer practical strategies that educators can use to plan democratically in the face of the power relations that shape what is possible, or even imaginable, in social and organizational contexts. For example, when Pete and Joan discussed with George the idea of surveying people attending the program, they were addressing both technical and political issues. Although it was important to design a technically credible survey, it was equally important to determine how they would use this information to decide about the features of the program. Although people's technical knowledge and skills are critically important in planning (for example, about budgeting and instructional design), these processes are always embedded in political and ethical domains (Cervero & Wilson, 1996). As Forester (1989) so clearly points out: "Once reported or uttered, even the most technical judgment becomes an integral part of the political world; it becomes inescapably political, seeking legitimacy by appealing to the consent of those concerned with the merits of the case" (p. 72). That legitimacy is enacted at the planning tables where decisions are made that determine the features of educational programs.

Dimensions of the Planning Table

This section addresses four key dynamics that operate at the planning tables where educational programs are produced: (1) *power relations* enable and constrain people's access to and capacity to act at the planning table, (2) people represent *interests* at the table, (3) *ethical commitments* define who should be represented at the table, and (4) *negotiation* is the central practical action at the table. These four dynamics are linked to form a definition of program planning as a social activity in which people negotiate with and among interests at planning tables structured by socially organized relations of power. This activity produces programs that have educational and political outcomes for multiple stakeholders.

Power Relations Shape the Planning Table

By defining planning as a social activity, what matters most is which people are at the table deciding the features of an educational program. Planning tables do not simply arise out of people's minds but rather are firmly rooted in ongoing sociopolitical relationships and represent places where power is both produced and used (Wilson & Cervero, 2003). These power relations are fundamentally important because they influence whose interests are represented at the planning table. Power is defined in many different ways, but for our theory it has three important characteristics (Giddens, 1979; Isaac, 1987; Winter, 1996). First, power is a social and relational characteristic, not simply something that people "possess" and use on one another. Second, it is necessary to distinguish between power relations as a structural characteristic and people's exercise of their power, which is an individual activity. Third, although power relations are relatively stable, they are continuously negotiated at planning tables.

Power is the capacity to act, which is distributed to people by virtue of their position and participation in enduring social and organizational relationships (Apple, 1992; Giddens, 1979; Isaac, 1987; Winter, 1996). Recognizing that people have "power" means that they have a certain "capacity" to act, rooted in a specific socially structured relationship; such capacity to act is not simply a consequence of individual attributes. Here is an example of the relational nature of power: when Cassie was planning with Dougie, they had a roughly symmetrical power relationship in contrast to her greater power when she was making decisions with program participants and her lesser power with Ron. Even though she is the same person in each situation, her capacity to act is different because of the socially organized relations in which she is a participant. Another example is the fact that Pete had much less capacity to act at the planning table with the president than at a planning table with the hourly employees at the Phoenix Company. Again, he is obviously the same person at each planning table, but his capacity to act is different based on his organizational role as vice president and his social position as a white male in relation to the others at the table.

Defining power as relational means that it frames all human interactions (Foucault, 1977; Giddens, 1979). Power is not specific to a particular form of relationship, such as the case where one person gets another person to do something she would not otherwise have done. Although this coercive relationship is the most common view of power, it is entirely too restrictive (Isaac, 1987; Wilson & Cervero, 2002; Winter, 1996). Even though many power relationships are highly asymmetrical forms of domination, there are also relationships in which the capacity to act is distributed relatively equally to all people at the table. For example, the six Valuation Discipline committees at the SVP had the same organizationally defined capacity to develop workshops, even though the exercise of that power varied by individuals and individual committees. We agree with Forester (1999), who concludes that "Where some focus on power as structuring and limiting, I take power to be enabling as well, a politically shifting relationship rather than a fixed position or possession" (p. 6; see also Isaac, 1987; Wilson & Cervero, 2002; Winter, 1996). These power relations matter because they shape who has the capacity to be represented at the planning tables where decisions are made about educational programs.

Although power both enables and constrains action, exercising power in concrete situations is always a form of negotiation among the various people involved (Cervero & Wilson, 1994a). Even in asymmetrical power relationships, there is always some form of negotiation in determining who is at the planning table and what happens there. As Giddens (1979, p. 149) argues, "However wide the asymmetrical distribution of resources involved, all power relations manifest autonomy and dependence in both directions." At Phoenix, although Pete clearly was in a subordinate relationship to the president, the organizational structure limited how the president could exercise his power, and it distributed to Pete the capacity for a "variety of modes of leverage, maneuvering, and strategic bargaining" (Isaac, 1987, p. 91). The outcome of people's exercise of power about and at the planning table cannot be predetermined, but is contingent on how people choose to use that power. Although Pete could have exercised his power to bring managers and workers to the planning table, he did not. However, he did exercise his power by hiring a consultant and by getting approval for his plans from the other vice presidents before going to the president. This example acknowledges the existence of preexisting power relationships, while showing that people always face the problem of how to achieve their interests by exercising their power.

The third important characteristic of our theory is that power itself is always being negotiated at the planning table (Cervero & Wilson, 1996, 1998). Although the preexisting structural capacity to act is relatively stable, it is affected by who gets to make decisions at the planning tables for an educational program. As Forester (1989) argues, "Every organizational interaction or practical communication (including the nonverbal) not only produces a result, it also reproduces, strengthening or weakening, the specific social working relationships of those who interact" (p. 71). Forester's observation highlights the point that educational planning always has two outcomes: (1) negotiations at the planning table focus on making decisions about the program's educational features, and (2) these negotiations either maintain or alter the social and political relationships of those who are included and excluded from the planning (Cervero & Wilson, 1998). Planners always *negotiate with* their own power and *negotiate between and among* the political relationships of other people to make judgments about the features and outcomes of an educational program. At the same time, planners also *negotiate about* the political relationships themselves, seeking to reinforce or alter them. People's political relationships are therefore not static, because they are continually acted upon through the negotiation practices themselves. For example, by not having the department managers directly negotiate for their interests in planning the retreat, Pete strengthened the existing power structure in regard to who (namely, executives) could articulate the needs for educational programs. In the SVP story the PDC effectively shifted decision making away from the Education Committee, which had traditionally designed educational programs for the Society, by acquiring authority to design and direct the new educational program. The effect that efforts at planning tables have on social and political relationships themselves, which are crucial for enabling planners to act, is an often overlooked outcome of the planning process.

People's Interests Play Out at the Planning Table

If power relations shape the planning tables and people's capacity to act there, then people seek to achieve their interests as they exercise power at these tables (Cervero & Wilson, 1994a, 1994b). People come to the table with a complex set of interests, which are "predispositions, embracing goals, values, desires, and other orientations and inclinations that lead a person to act in one direction or another" (Morgan, 1997, p. 161). Interests are the motivations and purposes that lead people to act in certain ways when confronted with situations in which they must make a judgment about what to do or say. Those involved in planning educational programs exercise their power in accordance with their own specific interests and the interests of others they represent at the table.

We need to make two important points about how interests play out at the planning table. First, the features of educational programs result from the interests that people negotiate at the planning table.

For example, the features of the management education program were determined by the interests that Mr. Jones, Pete, Joan, and George represented at the planning table. Thus, educational programs are causally related to specific interests of the people who plan them (Cervero & Wilson, 1994a). We can now amplify the theory's starting point, saying that "people with interests plan programs." Second, although programs are causally related to people's interests, there is no sense in which the judgments about specific programmatic features are predetermined. Rather, these outcomes depend on which people are at the planning table, which and whose interests they represent, and how they choose to exercise power at the table. Because of these contingencies, for example, the *Fundamentals of Valuation* program could have had different purposes, objectives, methods, audiences, and locations than the ones actually selected. That it ended up being a three-day meeting to address the topic of *Fundamentals*, was held at a college campus, and included an examination all resulted from the power relations that shaped the planning tables, the interests that people brought to these tables, and the specific negotiations that occurred there.

Of the complex sets of interests that people represent at the planning table, some are related to educational outcomes, whereas others are related to social and political outcomes (Cervero & Wilson, 1998). The SVP leaders used professional development programs not only to educate the members, but also to create a clearer professional identity and add a revenue stream for the Society. The people at the Phoenix Company planning table had interests related to the *educational outcomes* of the program. They hoped that the program would give individuals the knowledge and skill to improve communication in the company as a whole. Thus, the expected educational outcomes include not only participants' knowledge but also their use of this knowledge to benefit the wider group, organization, or community. These same people also brought interests related to *social and political outcomes* to the planning table. By trying to bring learners to the planning table, George hoped not only to be seen as a good consultant so that he might be hired again in the future but also to promote his view that company workers needed to be involved in company decision making through participatory management. As a newly employed director of customer service, Joan hoped to use the program not only to gain more visibility in the company and to more clearly define her role, but also to change organizational patterns of interaction through experiential training activities. Pete's interests in the management education program included improving the status of his human resources office as well as improving communication in the company.

People's interests that are unrelated to educational outcomes are often labeled as "hidden agendas," which many believe should not affect the decisions that are made about educational programs. However, it is politically naïve and practically ineffective to ignore the many outcomes that people seek to achieve in planning educational programs. Indeed, this is one of the fundamental blind spots of almost all planning theories, which assume that programs are only about educational outcomes. Interests related to social and political outcomes cannot be wished away; they are as much a part of the planning process as interests related to educational outcomes. Indeed, the former are often *more* important, as people seek to achieve many diverse political outcomes at the planning table. As Pete worked the planning table to reposition himself and his department, he has to negotiate with George, who wanted to use the program to foster participatory management in the company. Arthur sought to represent learners and promote experiential learning and reflective practice, whereas SVP's leaders sought to use the program to increase membership and influence state and federal legislatures. Cassie and Dougie worked to change whose knowledge mattered in staff development.

Almost always, people at the planning table are representing the interests of others. For example, Arthur saw himself representing the interests of the learners when he negotiated the addition of interactive instructional techniques at the instructor training clinic.

Very often the interests that people bring to the table are contradictory. For example, by intentionally excluding the executive vice president from the planning process, Pete's stated interest of improving communication in the company was outweighed by his personal interest of improving his standing with the president. Thus, the fundamental practical questions about interests at the planning table are, Whose interests are at stake in this program, and what are those interests? By asking these questions, people are able to anticipate, and therefore act, in ways that are both politically astute and practically effective in planning educational programs.

Who Should Be at the Planning Table?

Ethical Commitments in Action

Who sits at the planning table matters because there is a causal relationship among whose interests people represent there, the practical judgments that these people make, and the specific features of educational programs (Cervero & Wilson, 1994a). That educational programs are causally related to people's interests is no superfluous claim, for if program features were not determined by these interests, then what would determine them? Although evidence can, and in many cases should, inform these practical judgments, they are actually made by people seeking to achieve specific outcomes. Even more important, if program features were not produced by people's interests, then why would the programs matter? Educational programs matter because they create possible futures in the lives of people, organizations, and communities. These judgments can only be made based on the ethical commitments that people bring to the planning table about what these possible futures should be and how they can be achieved through education. Ethical commitments are not some metaphysical, disembodied set of principles but rather beliefs about how to act in the world (Flax, 1992; Forester, 1999; West, 1989). These ethical commitments are critical because as any experienced planner knows, "Hundreds of practical judgments must be made, but the labels of 'neutrality' or 'impartiality' hardly inform how those judgments ought to be made in diverse practical situations" (Forester, 1999, p. 190). To fully account for what matters in planning, then, a theory needs to address the ethical commitments that inspire people's actions at the table.

These commitments are played out in decisions about and at the uneven planning tables where people negotiate interests in planning programs. People enact their ethical commitments in practical settings by answering two basic questions: Who should benefit in what ways from educational programs, and whose interests should be represented at the planning tables where judgments are made about educational programs (Cervero & Wilson, 1994a, 2001)? In answering the first question, people's ethical commitments offer a priority order for the political analysis of whose interests are at stake. For example, whereas Mr. Jones might have believed that everyone at the Phoenix Company had a stake in the outcome of the retreat, his primary ethical commitment was to ensure that decisions made at the executive level were effectively communicated downward through the organization. Mr. Jones's beliefs about how to act were at odds with those of George, whose ethical commitment was to develop more participatory forms of management. The second question addresses people's social and political commitments about whose interests matter enough to be represented at the planning table. No evidence could have been used to decide if Pete should have brought representatives of the 1,200 employees to the planning table to identify the retreat's educational objectives. These two sets of ethical commitments, about who should benefit and who should be at the table, are intertwined. For example, Pete's beliefs about a communication problem helped determine the objectives *because* he was also able to determine who should sit (and not sit) at the table to develop objectives.

Ethical commitments are also deeply intertwined with the political relationships in the social and organizational settings where planning occurs. People's ethical commitments are typically enacted in a world of conflicting interests and unequal power relations, pro-ducing the uneven tables at which most planning occurs. This point is vitally important because if "ethical thinking is blind to the world of politics and pragmatism, then ethics, it seems, asks us to be saints and martyrs, not planners" (Forester, 1990, p. 253). Without ethi-cal commitments about who should benefit and who should be at the planning table, those with the most power can exercise it to determine the features of a program and its educational and politi-cal outcomes. People's commitments are also important when adju-dicating among the stakeholders' interests related to educational and political outcomes. These outcomes often present competing choices to people at the planning table. Pete had to decide whose definition of the communication problem would drive the retreat program. Would he base the definition of need on the president's view or would he engage managers who were the learners? Would he take the president's view because it was the right definition of the problem or because it would further his political interest to strengthen the human resources office? Pete's ethical commitment about whose interests matter and his political analysis of the situa-tion framed his actions in planning the retreat.

People Negotiate at the Planning Tables

People undertake many forms of practical action when planning educational programs. One form is discussed by theories that focus on procedural tasks, such as writing a budget, visiting a possible site of instruction, and preparing an end-of-program evaluation survey. Planners often bring technical knowledge and rules of thumb to bear in addressing such tasks (Sork, 1996). For example, Cassie and Dougie knew that with twenty-four participants in this year's pro-gram, they needed to create two groups for many activities in order to facilitate participation. Although the SVP leaders did not expect to lose money, for the first offering of the *Fundamentals* program the registration fee was set lower than the competition's programs to encourage participants to switch their allegiance to the SVP programs. Although such activity is typically thought of only in terms of technique, it also represents how planners bring their power and interests to bear in determining which tasks will be addressed and how.

The form of practical action that really matters is undertaken at the planning tables where people confer, discuss, and argue in making judgments about what to do to produce the important features of the educational program. Negotiation is the overall concept describing these interactions, not because there is always conflict involved but rather because all human interactions are, in part, political. Thus, negotiation is the social activity in which people interact at the planning table in order to reach agreement about what to do in relation to the educational program (Cervero & Wilson, 1994a). What makes such negotiations political is that they are neither neutral nor objective nor even simply technical, but rather represent how planners exercise power to represent their own and others' interests in shaping educational and political outcomes. Situations at the planning table may differ dramatically, from those where there is widespread agreement among people's interests to those where high levels of difference and conflict exist. Following Newman (1994), Baptiste (2000) classifies these "social transactions into one of three groupings . . . depending on the severity of conflict they exhibit" (p. 41) and argues that each situation calls for a different overall approach to negotiation. As people negotiate at the planning table, then, they need to be able to anticipate and read situations so that they can use an approach that matches the situation.

There are some situations at the planning table in which "two or more parties whose common interests outweigh any conflicting ones come together with a view to sharing information and solving problems to their mutual advantage" (Newman, 1994, p. 154). The negotiations undertaken in these situations are *consultations* because people treat each other as allies and friends, trust is high, and everyone works together in a mutually supportive way. The planning that Cassie, Dougie, and Ron undertook for the staff development program is a typical example of a consultation. In these situations the amount of power that people bring to the table is relatively unimportant because everyone has a similar set of interests driving their judgments. Everyone is "on the same page," so there is little or no worry that some may leverage their power to harm others at the table. Rather, decision making about the features of the educational program is a form of problem solving. For example, although the political relationships among Pete, Joan, and Mr. Jones were highly asymmetrical, their common interests far outweighed their conflicting ones. Thus, their negotiations about the management retreat were consultative: friendly, noncoercive, and virtually free of conflict. Out of these consultations, they made judgments about the need, purpose, audience, facilitators, and location of the retreat.

Moving along the continuum, there are situations at the planning table "where two or more parties with both common and conflicting interests come together to talk with a view to reaching agreement" (Newman, 1994, p. 153). The negotiations undertaken in these situations are *bargaining* because it is likely that the final set of agreements about the program will not address everyone's interests. People in situations that call for a bargaining strategy need each other, however, and will seek to find, if not to maximize, areas of common interests. Unlike in consultations, the amount of power that people have at the table now matters. Whose interests finally prevail when bargaining at the planning table is strongly influenced by people's political relationships. In fact, "one party may lose out badly in the negotiation and another may gain considerably" (Newman, 1994, p. 153) based on how people choose to exercise their power. An example of this outcome occurred when Pete and George were bargaining over the purpose of the retreat. Their interests conflicted in that George understood the retreat objective as trying to develop more participatory forms of management. Pete (as a representative of top management) did not share this agenda, and he used his power in this situation to focus the retreat on helping managers run better meetings. In situations that call for bargaining, there are many different strategies, ranging from withholding information and using power to keep items off the agenda to efforts by people at the table to educate others about their interests.

At the other end of the continuum lie those situations marked by a great deal of conflict among people at the planning table. These are situations "in which parties whose conflicting interests outweigh any common ones engage with one another, each with a view to winning—that is, furthering its own interests or gaining ascendancy for its own viewpoint" (Newman, 1994, p. 154). The negotiations undertaken in these situations are *disputes,* which "arise when talks have broken down; when distrust is open and rampant; when the battle lines are drawn, and when opposing sides seek actively, freely, and knowingly to frustrate each other's causes" (Baptiste, 2000, p. 43). In these situations, the amount of power that people bring to the table is vital to both the strategy that needs to be used and the likelihood that a person will achieve her objective. The person who has power in a highly asymmetrical relationship can simply exercise that power in a variety of ways to achieve her interests. In a dispute at the SVP, a governor in a budget meeting demanded to know how this new education program was going to be funded, because there was not a budget line item for Arthur's position or for the program's start-up costs. Because he was the Society president and the PDC chair, the president had the power to respond that the Society was going to offer this program even without any visible means of financial support. However, if a person has little power in an asymmetrical relationship, she will need to counteract that power at the planning table. For example, Pete explicitly kept Brad away from the retreat planning tables. He was able to counteract Brad's power by working directly with the president, who signed off on all decisions for the retreat. Pete's alliance with the president at the planning table was an effective strategy in this dispute.

Negotiating Democratically at the Planning Table

This section builds on the planning table metaphor to address the issue of "how to do planning well in a messy, politicized world" (Forester, 1999, p. 10). It moves from accounting for people's lived experience to providing a guide for practical action based on an ethical commitment to substantively democratic planning.

Negotiating at the Educational and Political Intersection

All planning models offer a guide for planning that addresses key questions of educational needs, objectives, instructional design, and evaluation. As explained in Chapter One, however, these models provide little guidance for the common practical situations in which people pursue outcomes at the planning table related to their social and political interests. Indeed, these other interests are generally considered to be "noise" that impedes good planning. Yet, any guide to practical action must address the complete picture at the planning table, including the multiple outcomes that people seek to achieve as well as the social and political relationships that make planning possible. Thus, any guide to responsible planning "requires attention to both the substantive issues at hand and the relationships that link the parties who care about those issues" (Forester, 1999, p. 65).

People responsible for planning educational programs are at the nexus of two evolving sets of negotiations (Cervero & Wilson, 1994b, 1998). Thus they need "to develop the double vision that students of negotiation consider second nature: the ability to pay attention not only as narrower 'technicians' to the 'substance at hand' (what we are negotiating about), but also to the 'relationships between parties' (how we are negotiating this)" (Forester, 1999, p. 89). The "substance at hand" in educational planning involves the actual features of the educational program necessary to produce educational outcomes. Planners must always stay aware of many important substantive issues, such as the educational need, the audience, the market for the program, and the program evaluation. At the same time, they must pay attention to the "relationships between parties," focusing on social and political relationships among people both at the planning table and not at the table and the multiple outcomes that people seek to achieve there. Recognizing opportunities and resolving the dilemmas and contradictions arising from the intersection of these two sets of negotiations is the fundamental political and ethical problem of educational planning (Cervero & Wilson, 1998). While planners must necessarily address political relationships at this intersection, an ethical commitment to substantively democratic planning prevents the stress on politics from degenerating into a "disempowering relativism" (Hart, 1992, p. 157) in which "might makes right."

Committing Ethically to Substantively Democratic Planning

As these two sets of negotiations intersect at the table, planners enact an ethical commitment about who should be at the table and who should benefit from the educational program. Our vision of good planning is based on an ethical commitment to nurturing substantively democratic planning across both levels of negotiations (Cervero & Wilson, 1994a, 1994b). At the level of substantive negotiations, this commitment should produce programs that enlarge rather than restrict people's life chances. At the level of negotiations about people's social and political relationships, planners should focus on the democratic construction of the planning table. Youngman's (1996) advice that there is always a space to work out an ethical commitment to substantive democratic planning cuts across both levels: "Adult educators work in a wide variety of situations, ranging from institutions of the state to organizations of civil society. Their scope for a critical practice varies accordingly. However, it is our contention that spaces can be found in all situations if adult educators are clear about their social goals and how these can be embodied in their day-to-day activities" (p. 4). These spaces exist in negotiating about either a program's substantive features or the social and political relationships at the planning table.

An ethical commitment to substantively democratic planning means that all people who are affected by an educational program should "be involved in the deliberation of what is important" (Apple, 1992, p. 11). As Frankel (1977) says of Dewey's democratic vision, "Democracy is a procedure for melding and balancing human interests. The process need not be conducted, and at its best is not conducted, without regard for truth and facts. . . . Its controlling purpose is collective action, not the accreditation of propositions as true" (p. 20). Thus, a democratizing process means simply that real choices about what collective action to take for the educational program will be put before people at the planning table. By arguing for an ethical commitment to substantively democratic planning, we explicitly align our theory with an intellectual-practical tradition in American education that "rests on a recognition of the importance of a fully political and educative notion of democracy that recaptures the collective struggle by citizens to build institutions in participatory ways" (Carlson & Apple, 1998, p. 9). This tradition builds on both Dewey's vision for democratic forms of education and more recent attempts to reinterpret this vision in a way that recognizes the threats to democratic education posed by the asymmetrical power relationships embedded in existing social, racial, cultural, political, and economic systems (Apple, 1990; Collins, 1991; West, 1989).

The ethical commitment to substantively democratic planning is not an abstract one, because as Apple (1990) points out, "Democracy is not a slogan to be called upon when the 'real business' of our society is over, but a constitutive principle that must be integrated into all of our daily lives" (p. xvi). Substantively democratic planning is to be distinguished from the techniques of formal democracy, such as voting. In educational planning terms, formal democracy might mean arranging people's chairs in a circle around a friendly planning table and asking them what they want to learn.

However, imagine what would happen if the hourly worker, manager, and venture capitalist were placed around the planning table and treated as equals under the guise of equal opportunity. In situations of conflicting interests, this would ensure that those who have the most power would see their interests manifested in the educational program. Substantive democracy insists on the recognition that systems of power and privilege do not stop at the doors of the social and organizational contexts in which programs are offered (Cervero & Wilson, 2001). People's efforts at the planning table should be guided by the principle of "pragmatics with vision" (Forester, 1993, p. 39), which stresses the need to hold firm in democratic values, matching planning strategies to social and political relationships to nurture that commitment.

The principle of "pragmatics with vision" requires planners to recognize that in nurturing democratic planning, different situations call for different forms of negotiation (Cervero & Wilson, 1994a; Forester, 1989). The same action could nurture democratic planning in one situation and thwart it in another. For example, although both sets of negotiations are often mutually supportive in consultative situations, planners will encounter bargaining situations in which there are trade-offs across these two levels of negotiations. Worse yet, they can encounter dispute situations in which there are even more restrictive strategies that can be used to enact democratic planning at either level. Many of the planning activities for the staff development program were undertaken in consultative situations, in which the planners and learners often refashioned the instructional design of the retreats to meet changing needs. However, the wigger incident clearly presented a bargaining situation in which getting people to talk with one another was a major struggle. In contrast to these situations, if Pete and Joan had brought managers and other employees to meet with Mr. Jones about the program, a substantively democratic planning process would have resulted only if the Phoenix Company presented a consultative situation in which the interests were consensual and political relationships symmetrical. Because the situation was not consultative, the program would probably have been the same in all respects because of the enormous amount of power the president had in the situation. Thus, Pete and Joan would have had to recognize that they faced a bargaining situation at the planning table before they could use a negotiation strategy that would enfranchise the interests of all stakeholders in constructing the program. In the SVP story, initially Arthur was the only one to raise the question of learner needs, and he did so in a consultative fashion, assuming that his being hired as an educator meant that the Society would draw upon that expertise. Because the members of the PDC felt they understood what aspiring valuators needed to learn, they designed curricula and courses representing what they thought would best enhance the professional status of their association and its members. Arthur misread these political relationships and had relatively little power in the organization; therefore, he was unable to promote learner involvement.

These examples illustrate that people need not only an ethical commitment, but also a commitment that is linked with a political analysis, because "good intentions when blind to the context of action can lead directly to bad results" (Forester, 1990, p. 253). However, saying that planners need to negotiate at both levels and take account of the context does not solve the problems of planning. Rather, to say that program planning is political should begin the discussion, not end it. As Forester argues (1999), "No realistic discussion of planning is possible without taking power into account in several forms. If we are to analyze power as a political, and thus alterable, reality rather than as an unchangeable metaphysical ether, let us stop rediscovering and instead assess practically, comparatively, and prescriptively what different actors can do about it" (p. 9). To that end, we propose that planners should work the planning table to produce both educational and political outcomes by using negotiation strategies that honor "democratic deliberations rather than restrict them" (Forester, 1999, p. 9).

Conclusion

We have used Part One to show how planners' perspectives shape their practical action. Throughout much of the last century one perspective in particular, the "classical viewpoint" (Cervero & Wilson, 1994a; Schubert, 1986), has dominated the way we have theoretically understood and practically imagined the work of planning. That viewpoint, representing theoreticians' attempts to address what they have considered as "practical" questions, has indeed helped focus planners' attention on important aspects of their work. Nevertheless, one of the great limitations of this viewpoint has been its failure to understand the nature of practical action in real settings.

We offer a different perspective that puts people at the center of planning action. Working the planning table is at the heart of our theoretical claims about what matters when people plan educational programs in social and organizational contexts. These contexts are structured by power relations and provide the ground on which planners negotiate interests to produce both educational and political outcomes. In the face of power, we continually argue for the ethical commitment to nurture a substantively democratic process when planning programs. This understanding of people acting in context not only accounts for planners' experiences but also provides the best opportunity to produce educational programs that enlarge people's life chances in the real world.

Part II

Working the Planning Table

The Theory in Practice

In Part Two we use Sork and Caffarella (1989) as a way to organize the educational tasks that planners undertake, but we fill in the gap of how to complete those tasks in the real world. We provide three observations to explain how we draw upon—but move beyond—the classical planning models.

First, we recognize that most adult education planning theories offer prescriptions and procedures for analyzing the planning context (Beals, Blount, Powers, & Johnson, 1966; Boone, Safrit, & Jones, 2002; Boyle, 1981; Caffarella, 1994, 2002; Houle, 1972, 1996; Knowles, 1970, 1980; Sork, 2000; Sork & Newman, 2004). For example, the first step in Sork and Caffarella's (1989) model is to analyze the planning context and client system. We do not, however, analyze the context in a separate chapter in Part Two because all five of the chapters concerned with negotiation address planning action in context. Thus, there is no time or place in which planners are not both affected by and affecting the context in their work. So, we examine the last five steps in Sork and Caffarella's model, but we do so using the theoretical perspective introduced in Part One.

Second, most classical planning theories focus on technical prescriptions for addressing each step in the models. Although we recognize that technical strategies for addressing planning steps (such as how to construct a survey to assess needs) are important and necessary, we use Part Two to show that the technical work of planning is always embedded in the political world: "What should be learned? How should it be organized? These seemingly simple questions are deceivingly political" (Petrina, 2004, p. 81). Just as with the context question, there is no time or place in which planners are not also working political relationships in performing technical procedures. Contrary to much traditional theory, which envisions a facilitative, neutral (albeit professional) planner, our theory puts planning procedures into the practical world of social and organizational power relations. Thus, we hope to pull the political out of the hallway and the ethical out of the mythical.

Third, following on Houle's (1972, 1996) model (supported by Caffarella [2002] and others), we address the steps in a linear order even though the realities of planning practice preclude the logic of sequentially ordered steps. As Sork and Caffarella (1989) explain, "although the practice of planning rarely follows a linear pattern in which decisions related to one step are made before decisions about the next are considered, the process can best be understood in a stepwise fashion whereby the logic of one step proceeding or following another step is explained" (p. 234). We draw upon the classical framework not to confirm its logic but to show how real planners confront the challenges of planning every time they sit down at a planning table.

Chapters Four through Eight are each organized around a set of four guidelines (listed below) that provide specific insights and practical guidance about how to carry out that task in the face of the daily opportunities, conflicts, challenges, and dilemmas that confront educators of adults. To create these themes, we ask, Whose interests are at stake and whose really matter? Who benefits from the program and who does not in terms of educational and political outcomes? How do power relationships shape action at the planning table? What are the threats or inducements to substantively democratic planning? What does substantively democratic planning look like in this situation and what negotiation strategies would promote that ethical commitment?

Negotiating the Program's Needs-Assessment

1. Decide Whose Interests Matter and Assess Their Needs
2. Connect Stakeholders' Needs to the Historical and Social Context
3. Anticipate How Power Relations Frame the Needs-Assessment
4. Democratically Negotiate Needs

Negotiating the Program's Educational, Management, and Political Objectives

1. Prioritize Educational, Management, and Political Objectives
2. Negotiate Objectives Before and During the Program
3. Anticipate How Power Relations Frame the Negotiation of Objectives
4. Democratically Negotiate Objectives

Negotiating the Program's Instructional Design and Implementation

1. Manage the Politics of Selecting and Organizing Content
2. Manage the Politics of Selecting Formats and Instructional Techniques
3. Manage the Politics of Selecting and Preparing Instructional Leaders
4. Democratically Negotiate the Instructional Design and Implementation

Negotiating the Program's Administrative Organization and Operation

1. Finance the Message
2. Market the Message
3. Use Program Location to Work the Message
4. Democratically Administer Programs

Negotiating the Program's Formal and Informal Evaluation

1. Evaluate Programs Based on Educational, Management, and Political Objectives

2. Manage the Politics of Evidence and Criteria

3. Anticipate How Power Relations Frame Program Evaluation

4. Democratically Evaluate Program Objectives

Chapter 4

Negotiating the Program's Needs-Assessment

Needs-assessment is one of the most discussed but least well-understood terms in the program planning literature (Sork, 2001). Despite allegations of ambiguity, the confusion is more imagined than real, because there is an enduring, standard understanding of educational needs-assessment. Needs are defined as a discrepancy between learners' current state of knowledge, performance, or attitude and some desired state; empirical evidence must be collected to verify this discrepancy or "gap," and the needs-assessment process must be conducted as the first step in program planning (Apps, 1985; Boone, Safrit, & Jones, 2002; Bryson, 1936; Caffarella, 2002; Griffith, 1978; Knowles, 1950, 1980; Knox, 2002; Mazmanian, 1980; Monette, 1977; Queeney, 1995; Sork, 2001; Sork & Caffarella, 1989). Despite being at odds with the practice of many effective planners, this has been the dominant model for understanding the place of needs-assessment in program planning. The disjuncture between this discrepancy view of needs-assessment and actual planning practice led Sork (2000) to conclude "we have positioned 'needs assessment' as a universal fix, which it clearly is not" (p. 182).

The standard interpretation of needs-assessment actually fails quite spectacularly when scrutinized. For example, just as Griffith (1978) once noted that "meeting the needs of learners" had become "the most persistent shibboleth in the rhetoric of adult education program planning" (p. 382), we would echo the same for the persistent claim that needs-assessment should always be based on collecting empirical evidence. Contrary to this claim, many successful programs are produced without planners having collected evidence to document needs (Cervero & Wilson, 1996; Mazmanian, 1980; Mills, Cervero, Langone, & Wilson, 1995; Pennington & Green, 1976). The disjuncture between the prescription to collect evidence and the practical realities of planning programs has become increasingly apparent in the theoretical literature (Brackhaus, 1984; Caffarella, 2002; Queeney, 1995; Sork, 1998): "Many highly successful programs have had no needs assessment . . . although there is a plethora of prescriptive needs assessment models, few are ever applied in practice" (Pearce, 1998, p. 258). Needs-assessment also may actually "have little to do with programs being successful" (Caffarella, 2002, p. 115; Sork, 2000). Further, the prescriptive literature typically focuses only on the needs of learners (Caffarella, 2002; Pearce, 1998), as if their needs were the only ones that mattered, while ignoring the educational and political needs that other stakeholders have.

Although the standard interpretation typically presents needs-assessment as a value-neutral, technical activity of "measuring" needs, many theorists have pointed out that determining needs requires normative standards to define "desired" states (Apps, 1985; Brackhaus, 1984; Brookfield, 1986; Caffarella, 2002; Davidson, 1995; Griffin, 1983; Griffith, 1978; Mattimore-Knudson, 1983; Monette, 1977; Pearce, 1998; Sork & Caffarella, 1989). Apps (1985) captures this critical insight: "It is clear from the continuing education literature that educators of adults believe it is important to do a needs assessment . . . and that procedures are available for carrying out the process. But . . . is the process as straightforward and value-free as the various procedures suggest? . . . to determine the desired or ideal part of the need equation is not an empirical matter . . . [it is] a normative process" (p. 173). The practical response to determining "the desired" is the "felt needs" approach to planning, in which planners attempt to absolve themselves of any responsibility by having the learners themselves ascertain their own needs (Brookfield, 1986; Griffin, 1983; Griffith, 1978): "There seems to exist in adult education a fear of unmasking the value choices underlying adult educational practice" as if it were possible to release educators from "the ethical burdens involved in determining educational aims" (Monette, 1979, p. 87). Adult educators have noted that "even if planners want to avoid the burden of making value choices, it is impossible for them to maintain a neutral stance" (Apps, 1985, p. 175). Further, the concept of need itself "is strictly incapable of neutrality" (Griffin, 1983, p. 72) because "needs are not absolute but relative to moral values and cultural beliefs" (p. 74).

Because of this normative dimension, needs-assessment also has been recognized as fundamentally a political activity, not just a procedural one (Brackhaus, 1984; Brookfield, 1986; Davidson, 1995; Griffith, 1978; Monette, 1977; Pearce, 1998). Griffith (1978) connects values and politics by claiming that "adult educators have found it useful to treat the needs-assessment aspect of program planning as a political process without describing it in those terms," a process he characterizes as "building a consensus . . . on the selection and ranking of educational needs" by all those who "have value positions which enable them to define needs" (p. 393). Brackhaus (1984) points out that the "most important problems confronting administrators when conducting needs assessment are political, in that individuals and groups often attempt to influence which needs will be addressed" (p. 236). Monette (1977) uses the metaphor that educators "must direct the traffic of values and ideas" when "choosing among conflicting or contradictory needs" (p. 123). Boone, Safrit, and Jones (2002) claim that planners need to "collaborate" with various representatives of stakeholders to reach "consensus" on identified needs, a role "not too different from that of astute political leaders" (p. 147). Thus, the process is "inherently political" (Griffith, 1978, p. 393) because adult educators are "continually faced with choosing among conflicting priorities"

(Brookfield, 1986, p. 165) and contending with interested parties attempting to influence those choices (Pearce, 1998). This "political" interpretation includes the recognition that learners' needs are not the only ones that matter. Various stakeholders besides learners also have needs that they expect programs to address. Because there are more needs than any program can realistically hope to address (Caffarella, 2002), planners are responsible for negotiating choices among them.

With the awareness of these ethical and political dimensions of assessing needs, the discussion in the literature more or less stalls. Recognizing that needs-assessment is a normative and political activity, however, should start rather than end the conversation. The standard view of needs-assessment as scientifically collecting evidence to measure needs fails to account for the ways in which planners' value judgments and political skills influence how needs are assessed (Brookfield, 1986; Griffith, 1978; Monette, 1977). As Davidson (1995) has noted, however, theorists have been "unable to accomplish more than increasing awareness of how power relations [and, we would add, values] govern needs-making activity" (p. 186). Even though the standard view has been challenged by critics who understand planners as value-oriented, active political agents in the construction of needs, these insights exist without placing these agents in contexts defined by socially organized and historically developing power relations. Such power relations enable and constrain planners' political work in determining needs. Davidson's focus on the adult educator as "needs-maker" provides a valuable insight into the political practice of needs-assessment. Because needs are neither self-evident nor "discovered" planners and other stakeholders must construct them. By making "visible the array of communicative activities and structural forces that situate needs as educational needs," Davidson (1995, p. 190) shows how the "textualized" forms of programs—that is, their written, publicly presented manifestations—have been "cleansed of the messy, interactive, negotiated reality" (p. 190) in which the needs were constructed. This is where our approach begins: not with imagined orderly and sequenced needs-assessment procedures that produce succinctly written learning objectives, glossy advertisements, fancy binders, and polished program presentations, but with real planners representing value-laden interests, working messy planning tables to negotiate people's needs in socially organized relations of power. This chapter provides four guidelines for acting in this messy, negotiated practice of constructing needs.

Decide Whose Interests Matter and Assess Their Needs

Planners should understand that multiple interests intersect in the planning of any program and that all stakeholders have educational and political needs derived from their interests. Planners always assess what those needs are, whether or not they collect empirical evidence as a basis for that assessment. These observations contradict the standard understanding that restricts needs-assessment to collecting evidence to determine learners' educational needs (Boone, Safrit, & Jones, 2002; Galbraith, Cisco, & Guglielmino, 1997; Knowles, 1950, 1970; Kowalski, 1988; London, 1960; Queeney, 1995). The practical mistake that planners often make is to assume that needs-assessment and the collection of evidence are the same thing—they are not. Rather, planners conduct a needs-assessment for every program by considering stakeholders' interests and making judgments about the stakeholders' educational and political needs (Brackhaus, 1984; Davidson, 1995; Houle, 1972, 1996; Mazmanian, 1980; Monette, 1979; Pearce, 1998; Pennington & Green, 1976). As Houle (1996) points out, needs-assessments are essentially judgments, because "the impulse to learn or teach may arise from almost any source" (p. 61). Then "a decision is made to proceed. The decision may be taken for granted, it may be rapidly reached, or it may emerge slowly as judgment is brought to bear" (p. 62). Although these judgments can be informed by evidence, no form of evidence can ever determine a need; only people can determine a need. Amplifying this insight about needs-assessment resulting from people's judgments (Reid, 1979; Schubert, 1986; Walker, 1971, 1990, 2003), researchers have shown how planners themselves are often a major source for a program's needs-assessment (Cervero & Wilson, 1996; Mazmanian, 1980; Mills, Cervero, Langone, & Wilson, 1995; Pennington & Green, 1976). Understanding the judgmental nature of needs-assessment identifies planners as actively constructing needs rather than simply collecting evidence about needs. Although it is possible, and generally desirable, to collect evidence about stakeholders' needs, planners make judgments about stakeholders' needs regardless of whether or not evidence was collected to inform these judgments.

In determining whose interests matter in assessing needs, planners should first identify stakeholders who will be in a position to affect or be affected by the program, then ascertain their interests, and finally make judgments about their needs in relation to their interests. As the literature advises, these judgments can be informed by many types of evidence produced by formal data collection methods (environmental scanning, participant surveys, focus groups, previous program evaluations). More often, however, judgments about whose interests matter and the translation of those interests into program needs result from multiple informal and communicative activities (planners' observations, experiences, and relationships; impromptu hallway conversations; fortuitous or deliberate stakeholder interactions or interventions; organizational, regulatory, or social mandates). The planners in our three planning stories used many forms of evidence and communicative activities to determine whose interests mattered and to make their judgments about the stakeholders' educational and political needs.

In the SVP story, the president was a leader of a coalition that included the Professional Development Committee (PDC), the chairs and many members of the discipline committees, the Education Committee, and the organizers of the valuation science degree program. All the members of this coalition shared the interest in changing SVP into a teaching society. Because of the experiences and perceptions these planners had about how the changing external environment was affecting the Society, they made a judgment that translated their overall interest into the educational and political need for a neophyte-to-senior education system. This system would meet the Society's need to compete favorably with other appraisal organizations for new members, to develop new funding streams for the organization, and to position the Society to provide education if uniform licensing became a reality.

In the PI story, because of Cassie, Dougie, and Ron's shared interest in changing standard university-practitioner research relationships, they made judgments about their participants' educational needs based on their experiences with prior PI projects, their interactions with the funding agency, and their knowledge of adult literacy education. Using those experiences, observations, and interactions, they translated their interests into the political need that adult literacy practitioners should be directly involved in creating knowledge that would improve their practice.

In deciding whose interests matter, planners should bring as many different stakeholders as possible to the table to assess educational needs. The three cases illustrate varying examples of who included which stakeholders and how they assessed needs. In the SVP story, the first level of the *Fundamentals of Valuation* program included plenary sessions in which a professor of philosophy lectured on general valuation theory. The valuation course designers made judgments about this educational need based on their practical experience with other appraisers, their professional training in allied disciplines, and the espoused organizational philosophy that novice valuators needed to know general theories of valuation to practice professionally. In the SVP case there were fewer actual stakeholders at the table because the planners themselves represented the program participants, the board of governors, and the Society's membership, as well as the public. In the PI case, because of the high consensus of interests, many of the judgments about needs were conducted informally. For example, Ron routinely maintained contact with the state funding agents to apprise them of the PI project's progress and to stay informed about the agency's evolving needs that might be addressed through the project. Cassie and Dougie made explicit efforts to include learners in assessing their own needs both before and during the program. In this case the planners chose to include many of the actual stakeholders at the planning table. The Phoenix case illustrates a contrary example of *restricted* stakeholder participation in assessing needs. Using evidence from their experiences in the Phoenix Company, Pete, Joan, and Mr. Jones all agreed that retreat participants needed to learn how to work more effectively as a team and to develop more effective communication strategies for conveying management directives to employees. That judgment was based on restricting stakeholder input, because Pete was concerned that if the needs-assessment included the other vice presidents, the traditional participants, or the newly included line managers, it would turn into a "dogfight."

Another practical mistake that planners make is to assume that their assessments should focus only on the educational needs of learners. Such a presumption often has dire consequences because planners should also assess political needs. Although political assessments are rarely openly discussed or evidenced using formal research methods, they are always essential for planning programs. For example, Pete restricted access to the planning table not just so only he, Joan, and the president could determine the educational need but also because by restricting the access of other stakeholders Pete furthered the interest of improving his political relationship with the president. The planners in the PI story had an interest in changing the standard university relationship between researchers and practitioners. The traditional dominant understanding of that relationship is that professional practice is not possible without university-based, rigorously produced scientific knowledge and that such university-produced knowledge and theory has to be acquired prior to engaging in practice (Larson, 1977; Schon, 1983); the SVP story also represents this understanding of professional practice. Cassie, Dougie, and Ron did not subscribe to this particular understanding of the relationship of theory and practice, and they designed workshops that enabled practitioners to become researchers of their own practice in order to produce knowledge about their work; as the recruitment brochure stated, "teachers are both learners and researchers." Cassie's experiences in another state, Ron and Cassie's experiences in the two previous PI projects, and Dougie's participation in a prior PI program validated their construction of this educational need designed to alter relations of power. The planners' interest in maintaining positive relationships with the funding agency was also a constant concern. For example, Ron saw the PI program as continuing and expanding a productive relationship with the state funding agency that had continued for eight years. This institutional relationship with the state provided both good visibility for Ron's department to recruit graduate students and the funds to support them. When the state funding support for the third year of the PI program was abruptly rescinded with no explanation in the middle of the year, it indicated a major disruption in their productive working relationship. Ron was never able to ascertain why the funds were pulled, but he was forcibly reminded of which institution was able to exercise more power in determining which programs would continue and which would not.

Educational planners should also be aware that interests related to political needs often are as important as educational needs, if not more so. At the Phoenix Company, for example, Pete was clear about his own interest in using the retreat to change the perception at the company of the human resources department's value. Key to changing that perception was Pete's "working directly with the president." In order to advance this political interest, Pete made

decisions about educational needs for the retreat in close consultation with the president. When George challenged the educational
need and how it was decided upon, Pete countered that the assessment of the retreat's educational needs came "directly from the president," thereby restricting George and the retreat participants
themselves from providing evidence about those needs. Although
Pete planned the retreat to change the organizational culture, his
primary interest was to transform his political relationship with the
president. This political interest had more influence on many subsequent decisions about the retreat than did the educational need
to address a communication problem at the Phoenix Company.

In the SVP story, the political needs-assessment was conducted
as part of the competition with other appraisal organizations for
members as well as the struggle with state and federal regulators over
who would control the appraisal profession. In addition to this larger
societal planning table, there were political needs-assessments similar to everyday ones in the Phoenix and PI stories. Arthur's first-
day meeting with the SVP president is a good example. Arthur
thought he was meeting with the president to discuss the Society's
educational needs. By not allowing Arthur much room in the
conversation, the president made it clear that he believed that the
Society's political and financial needs were more important. By controlling the conversation, the president underscored what the organizational and political consequences would be if SVP did not
change its educational policy. The political importance of the meeting lay in the president's making sure Arthur became allied with the
pro-education coalition in the Society in order for their new educational program to address these organizational and political problems. Program success was defined in political rather than
educational terms: success meant getting SVP to adopt a new organizational mission and product.

None of the planners in the three cases collected scientifically
derived evidence in the manner prescribed by the standard literature to inform their judgments about educational and political

needs. Nonetheless, the planners in each story "documented" the needs-assessment based on their experiences, histories, reflections, and political relationships. Hidden though they often may be, interests and their manifestation through educational and political needs are vitally important to a program's success. Planners' judgments about whose interests matter and what their needs are constitute the needs-assessment. This is why it is essential to recognize that every program has had a needs-assessment, whether or not evidence was collected.

Connect Stakeholders' Needs to the Historical and Social Context

Theories of needs-assessment suggest that planners should be skilled facilitators who execute procedures to collect evidence. These theories tell planners that if they follow the proper measurement procedures, the information they "collect" will determine the needs for the program. As just illustrated, needs-assessment is really a process in which planners make value-based and politically astute judgments that can be informed by evidence. Those theorists who recognize these deliberative, political dimensions of needs-assessment tend to represent an interpretation of planning as individual action: "The decision about proceeding is essentially a matter of subjective judgment" (Houle, 1996, p. 178). This view understands that planners are not faceless facilitators but real people whose interests are central to determining needs. But these planners are not yet embedded in the socially structured and historically evolving power relations in which they work. Research has confirmed that context matters in planning (Cervero & Wilson, 1996; Mazmanian, 1980; Pennington & Green, 1976), so the inclusion of a "context step" is typical in many planning models (Boone, Safrit, & Jones, 2002; Caffarella, 2002; Houle, 1972, 1996; Sork, 2000; Sork & Caffarella, 1989). But these planning models with context steps do not well describe how real people plan programs in socially organized and historically evolving conditions. As Davidson (1995) argues, in socially and historically situating the construction of needs, needs are not self-evident nor do they emerge fully formed on program brochures. Planners are "needs makers" who construct (not discover) needs through interpersonal communicative activity— talking, presenting, consulting, cajoling, bargaining, arguing, disputing—"performed within the context and constraints of organizations . . . [which] have historically developed features that come under the influence of larger social structures" (1995, p. 183). In this section we illustrate how planners' needs making emerges historically from their communicative activities within the structural conditions of their organizations and the larger society. Planners must make these connections if they are to negotiate the needs-assessment democratically.

The SVP story provides a good example of the effect that social and historical forces and structures have on needs making. Arthur's ideas of the needs-assessment differed dramatically from those of the president, who was clearly thinking with a macro view of the Society's competitive relationships with other appraisal societies for members as well as the impending imposition of external regulatory forces. The president saw the needs for the program as connected to the survival of SVP as well as the appraisal profession itself. Whether SVP and the appraisal profession survived was also connected to a spiraling national economic crisis that the appraisal profession had helped to produce. Even if Arthur had pressed the president in their initial meeting about assessing the needs of individual learners, the president likely would have responded that these needs did not matter if there were no organization or profession left for that individual to belong to. Assessing individuals' needs simply was not a question that made much sense, given the historical and structural forces affecting the Society. And those forces—pending regulatory acts, continuing economic crisis, highly competitive association relationships—did not just emerge spontaneously or in isolation from each other as SVP began to reimage itself as a teaching society. SVP leaders believed they could respond to these growing crises through professional education that addressed ethical, theoretical, and procedural issues in appraisal practice. For example, since its founding from the merger of two appraisal organizations decades earlier, SVP had promoted appraisal ethics as a foundation of its professional identity. The planners utilized their organization's historical strength to help create a new professional identity—an identity that they believed would likely transcend the historical and social forces with which the Society was contending.

For those who might see the SVP case as an anomaly, it should be noted that the heart of the conflict between Pete and George over the purpose of the Phoenix retreat was not simply a matter of miscommunication or the inability of two people to agree. Through their negotiations they acted out different historically located understandings of how to manage organizations. Organizational development theories often promote team building as a way to make organizations work more smoothly. Because Pete and George had different professional positions and interests, they interpreted team building differently. George's abiding interest was to promote participatory decision making, and he saw an opportunity in the Phoenix retreat to promote this democratic value. The quest to provide more opportunities to participate in decision making in organizations that routinely resist such efforts is a chronic challenge in a nominally democratic but rabidly capitalistic culture (Forester, 1989). Pete, who did not necessarily personally disagree with George's participatory values, thwarted George's attempts to introduce participatory management because Pete's political interest in improving his working relationship with the president and the company was more important than including more people in organizational decision making. George saw the team-building efforts of the retreat as potentially enfranchising Phoenix employees, whereas Pete's interest was in making the organizational power hierarchy work more effectively, which was consistent with the president's interests. Pete therefore interpreted team building as having less to do with decision making and more with implementing management directives unambiguously. Pete and George's conflict over defining the educational need manifested ongoing conflicts in organizational management and the larger society. Planners must consider these connections if they are to identify the interests and assess the needs that programs might address.

The Phoenix retreat also provides a good example of Davidson's (1995) argument that planners "define needs as educational through historically developed communicative activity" (p. 194). Historically, the president had used company retreats in the yearly budgeting process to disseminate management directives for departments' goals and objectives. The previous retreat marked a departure because of its focus on organizational development, but it began disastrously because of Pete's communicative practices. He was embroiled in conflicts with the executive vice president and had failed to stay aware of what the president expected him to do: "That's when he [the executive vice president] shook his finger in my face and said, 'Goddammit, where is our retreat, Pete? The boss . . . wonders why you haven't planned it' when I had not heard the word 'retreat' in the last sixty days." That retreat, although hastily planned, was ultimately successful because it provided Pete with "more permission" to continue developing his leadership in changing organizational culture. So the needs for the retreat have to be placed within the organizational history of the changing nature of the retreats as well as Pete's struggles to redefine his own and his department's political relations with the president and other vice presidents.

The history of how Pete, Joan, and the president constructed an organizational problem as an educational need further demonstrates the historically emerging, communicative nature of needs making. One interpretation could suggest that the need to improve communication was determined early in the planning and remained stable throughout planning. Although accurate chronologically, such an interpretation disguises the sometimes consensual, sometimes conflictual communicative activity that determined how an organizational problem came to be defined as an educational need and how the planners documented their perceptions of the need. For example, Mr. Jones, Pete, and Joan each had different experiences in the organization over time that led each one to interpret the organizational problem as poor communication skills and lack of teamwork. Mr. Jones had monthly meetings with hourly employees who told him that their managers were not informing them about important company policies. In her role as director of customer service, Joan had numerous conversations with people throughout the organization about how cooperation across departments was difficult. As vice president for human resources, Pete represented the company in legal disputes with employees failing to follow company or regulatory policies, often because they were unaware of those policies. So when Pete and Joan decided it was "time to go see the president," the three planners were already in considerable agreement about what the primary organizational problem was because each had evidence of what they considered to be the problem— poor communication. Thus, they easily reached consensus that "communication, team building, and that sort of thing" would help improve the company's communication practices and thereby reduce disruption in the company.

This historically evolving, communicative consensual assessment of need was subsequently challenged by George. In the March 7 meeting he asked whether the participants knew why they were coming to the retreat, and in the March 21 meeting he asked whether they could send a survey to the participants asking them "about the quality of their department meetings." George continued to challenge the definition of need because by not involving the participants in assessing their educational needs the retreat did not address his interests in promoting participatory decision making: "Let me clarify . . . the people who are there see the need and the value for these activities in terms of the objectives." George continued questioning the educational need until the final planning meeting, when Pete confronted George to tell him that the retreat would focus not on participatory decision making but on communicating company directives. Although the educational need was consensually constructed early in the planning, it remained a constant point of communicative, historically evolving activity throughout the planning. As Forester (1989) reminds us, talk matters. The educational need was constructed communicatively and emerged historically through the various interactions the four planners had with other people in the company and with each other. Planners failing to understand these communicative, situated interactions will miss opportunities to construct needs democratically.

Even though much of the literature as well as practical wisdom make a distinction between planning programs and implementing them, the negotiation of needs is chronic—and never more so than when instructors finally face learners in educational settings. Indeed, many adult educators would maintain that the sine qua non of practice is the ability to change planned activities as needs emerge in real time (Apps, 1991; Brookfield, 1986; Caffarella, 2002; Knowles, 1980; Knox, 1986). For example, in the PI story the construction of needs represents an evolving, historical, communicative process situated in and embodying structural forces. Cassie brought her experiences with and perceptions of practitioners' needs from her staff development work in another state. Cassie and Dougie had many informal discussions about program needs; then every week or so they had more formal meetings with Ron to discuss and solidify plans. The planners' overall interest in altering the traditional knowledge-production relationships between practitioners and universities, although central to ongoing construction of the program, was, however, deliberately left open to question through the establishment of the rotating advisory group for the PI program. Their willingness to continually reconsider their purposes and activities is exemplified by the specific alterations they made "on the spot" during the second day of the workshop. And the whole development of the PI program itself represented a historically developing movement in professional continuing education theory and practice (Drennon & Cervero, 2002) as well. The program's embodiment of sociostructural forces in needs-assessment is most dramatically represented in the wigger incident. Racism's routine and forceful intrusion into our lives is too often ignored by many and too frequently a reality for many others. In the wigger situation, the inability of the group and the facilitator to deal with the irruption of racism during the second, and what would become the final, PI session required a renegotiation of the needs for part of the third retreat session. Cassie's own self-reflection about what needed to be done, the reluctant but growing input from participants that the group had to publicly come to terms with Jean's comments, and Cassie's ongoing and finally successful attempts over time to get Sonya and Jean to discuss the incident represented the communicative, evolving, structurally situated construction of needs. If there had been a third session, the need to understand and learn from this incident would have been a central one. Planners must recognize this ongoing, communicative construction if they are to negotiate needs-assessments democratically.

As Davidson (1995) says, "Needs are not self-evident" (p. 190), but rather are constructed. Planners and stakeholders are "needs makers" who contribute to the construction of needs with their own assessments (Cervero & Wilson, 1996; Mazmanian, 1980; Pennington & Green, 1976). But this individualistic interpretation of needs construction dangerously misunderstands the real terrain of practice. Although needs-assessment is conducted by individuals, their deliberative conversations are complex communicative negotiations representing historical trajectories situated in organizational contexts and framed within larger social forces.

Anticipate How Power Relations Frame the Needs-Assessment

Bringing up the question of power will typically mute any planning conversation. Even so, many adult educators would agree that planning is inescapably political. This common observation is paradoxical because adult educators have understood needs-assessment activity as political without being able to describe it in such terms (Griffith, 1978). Although the awareness that planners act in political ways to manage the traffic of consensual and competing needs has existed in planning theory for some time, only a few have attempted to present an analysis of power in assessing needs. For example, Rossing and Howard (1994) tell extension educators that they need "knowledge about the existing social power structure" (p. 79) because planners "must necessarily consider and usually relate in some way to power structures and their leaders" (p. 83). In his review of planning theory, Sork describes what he calls the "politically-aware planner" as one who has to become "aware of the role of power, ideology, and interests and how these interact when people work collectively to make decisions about intentions and actions" (2000, p. 177). Planners need to do more than become aware that power relations frame the construction of needs (Davidson, 1995).

Planners must anticipate how power relations frame needs-assessment so they can anticipate whose interests are likely to influence the construction of needs. At SVP Arthur clearly did not anticipate how the power the president exercised could so structure their breakfast conversation to focus on the political needs of the Society as more important than its educational ones. Hence, when trying to understand the educational needs of the Society he became confused. The president clearly had anticipated using power—he *was* the president and he deliberately showed up on Arthur's first day of work—because he wanted to get Arthur politically allied with the pro-education side of the organization from the beginning regardless of whether Arthur understood specific programmatic educational needs. Indeed, getting Arthur into the right camp from the start was crucial to making sure he understood the needs from the pro-educational point of view. In the PI case the planners defined the political needs of the participants by deliberately altering the power relations between university researchers and literacy practitioners so that the participants would need to learn how to conduct their own research. They failed, however, to anticipate that the funding agency would use its power to cancel the program. Pete, during the planning of the previous Phoenix retreat, had failed to anticipate how the executive vice president would use his power to influence the president's perception of Pete's previous planning work in the company. Subsequently, Pete altered his power in the company so that only he, Joan, and the president determined the educational needs for the new retreat.

Stakeholders and planners exercise power at planning tables by making judgments about whose interests matter and which needs programs should address. As planners anticipate how these power relations frame the needs-assessment, they should use these insights to guide practical action at the planning table. Planners must also recognize that they can exercise power less visibly to "act on" the table itself in terms of who gets to sit at the table and what they are able to negotiate there (Cervero & Wilson, 1998). Some planning tables are "flatter" than others because consensual interests can mollify even severe differentials of power. The planning table around which the president, Pete, and Joan gathered is one example. Another mostly flat planning table appears in the PI story: in that situation the planners made explicit efforts to flatten the table and reduce the effect of power by creating as much access to the table as possible. Planners more often find, however, that the planning table is not "flat" in terms of who has the capacity to construct needs for a program. The SVP and Phoenix cases illustrate dramatically unequal tables. Recall Arthur's initial interactions with the PDC and the ongoing renegotiation of Arthur's role as logistics manager into educational planner. Or consider George and Pete's ongoing conflict about whose interests were more important in defining the educational needs of the retreat. Differences in power made significant differences in who got to the tables and what they did there to assess needs. Planners must understand that those who get to the table will bring specific capacities to act and will use that power, however unevenly distributed, to represent their interests in defining needs for the program.

Not everyone has the power to get to the planning table, however, because planners and stakeholders often also use their power to limit (or more democratically, enhance) access to the planning table. For example, understanding how the planners used power to assess the needs is crucial to understanding which needs the Phoenix retreat would ultimately address. Pete, Joan, and the president easily reached consensus on the organizational problem and how they planned the educational program to address that need. Prior to reaching that consensus, Pete exercised power in a number of ways to construct this planning table to increase the likelihood that the planning negotiations would be consensual. First, because of his previous conflict with the executive vice president, Pete went directly to the president for planning this retreat—"I wasn't going to let Brad be a part of this at all." Pete's successful circumvention of the organizational chain of command indicated his changing power relations in the company. On organizational development issues, he could now (but not before) get directly to the president. Second, because Pete believed that including others on the senior leadership team in the discussions at the planning table would turn into "a real dogfight," he constructed the table to include only the president, Joan, and himself. Finally, Pete excluded potential representatives of retreat participants, such as department managers and line supervisors, because he believed he had sufficient evidence for the organizational problem and sufficient power to make the decision in consultation with the president only. "By working directly with the president," only Pete, Joan, and the president sat at the planning table to determine which needs the retreat would address. The construction of that need was a direct manifestation of both Pete's interest in changing his power relations with the president and all three planners' interests in getting the company to operate more smoothly.

While working that planning table, Pete exercised power in other ways to assess needs and plan other program details. Reflecting on "how I screwed up before," Pete did two things to make this table work more smoothly. First, he and Joan went to the second and third meetings with the president with options about who was to attend the retreat, what the objectives would be, where the retreat would occur, and when—choices they knew they could "live with" no matter which ones the president preferred. Second, Pete, in developing those choices, had learned from his previous experience that the president was likely to consult with different vice presidents about specific issues. So prior to presenting choices to the president, he had already talked with the vice presidents to give each one "a little bird's-eye view" of the issues and to get their input on which choices each would support in the event the president did consult with them. Regardless of Pete's personal attributes—which some might depict as sneaky or manipulative and others as crafty or political—only Pete, as a vice president, had the organizational position to exercise power in that way; Joan certainly could not have. So what appears to be a fairly "flat," friendly table of consensual interests was actually constructed that way by Pete's exercise of power. He did so in ways to make sure that only the president, he, and Joan would decide that the educational needs for the retreat were defined as team building and communication.

Power frames not only who sits at the planning table but also what people can do when they get there. The similarities of interests among Pete, Joan, and the president enabled them to easily define the retreat needs, even within asymmetrical power relations. This was not true once George joined the table. Pete had to covertly and then overtly exercise his power several times to keep George's interests in participatory management from influencing what the retreat was about. In the March 7 meeting, when George asked whether the retreat participants knew why they were coming to the retreat, Pete sidestepped George to say that it was not about participating but about communicating clearly. As George demurred, Pete then invoked the power of the president to say that the need to communicate better "comes directly from the president. Sam Jones is saying we're not doing this well." George tried again in the March 21 meeting to get the participants' view of their needs on the table by sending out a survey. Pete first appeared to agree with this but then fluffed it off to suggest that sending out an article would work just as well to "get them thinking our way." In the last meeting before the retreat, the conflict over needs and purposes finally broke out fully and Pete directly used his power as vice president and organizational sponsor to tell George specifically what the retreat's purpose would be. Although George was able to sit at the table and tried to represent his own interests in participatory management as well as what he perceived to be the needs of the participants, the disparity of power effectively kept George from having much impact in defining the retreat's educational needs.

Because genuinely flat planning tables are much less common than most theorists presume and practitioners wish, it is difficult to negotiate the needs-assessment democratically without anticipating how power frames the process. But just being aware of power is like answering the telephone, saying hello, and then hanging up. Planners must also be able to anticipate others' use of power as well as effectively exercise it themselves. From the most mundane breakfast meeting to the irruption of racism, power matters because planners and stakeholders actively construct planning tables in terms of who gets there (or who does not) and what they are able to do (or not do). By framing participation and communication at the planning table, power relations directly affect whose interests the needs-assessment process represents and therefore the educational and political needs for a program.

Democratically Negotiate Needs

There has been a nearly ubiquitous charge in the literature for planners to involve adults in determining their own learning needs. Lindeman (1926) certainly thought that adults were quite capable of knowing their own learning needs. So did Bryson (1936), who described adults' felt needs as an important guide to developing adult education programs, although he cautioned planners to consult other sources as well. Tyler (1949) indicated that learners themselves could be a source of evidence in the needs-assessment process. Knowles (1950, 1970, 1980) enshrined the recommendation that planners and adult learners should jointly create a climate for needs-assessment. Boone, Safrit, and Jones (2002) provide a typical depiction of this long-standing injunction to include learners in assessing their own needs: "the adult educator as programmer, in collaboration with identified leaders of the target public(s) and their followers (potential learners), becomes intensely involved in a study of the situation to identify, assess, and analyze the immediate perceived needs of those publics. This process then becomes one of the organization's primary tasks in designing a program to meet those needs. The ultimate and desired outcome is . . . [to] identify and reach consensus on the expressed (felt) needs" (p. 140). Planning theorists routinely use words like "including," "collaborating," and "building consensus" to indicate the importance of learners assessing their own needs. Indeed, it is difficult to imagine how anyone could question including learners in needs-assessment. For a long time this invocation to involve learners in determining their own needs has been one of the ways adult educators have espoused their allegiance to a democratic heritage. As Brookfield (1986) notes, to "say one is meeting learner needs sounds humanistic, learner-centered, and admirably democratic" (p. 21).

Others have noted a tension in this claim to be democratic. Griffith (1978) argues, for example, that although many planners claim to be serving adult learners' felt needs, "there appears to be a pronounced reluctance on the part of many to report that they have designed programs to serve normative needs, as though such a confession were tantamount to rejecting democracy" (p. 392). Brookfield (1986) concurs: "To base education and training on a mix of felt and prescribed needs causes some educators to feel uncomfortable. It seems arrogant and authoritarian compared to the apparently democratic process of responding solely to the felt needs of learners" (p. 222). Monette (1977) reveals the practical dilemma: "The voluntary nature of adult participation and the democratic ethos of our society complicate the role of adult educators. They cannot ride roughshod over the values of adults even if they are judged ill-considered, and yet they must direct the traffic" (p. 123). This traffic-directing image is emblematic of how theorists and practitioners alike routinely acknowledge but disguise the political work of planning when making judgments about whose interests and needs matter. The image also reveals major limitations of equating the felt-needs approach with democratic needs-assessment. First, the traffic image reveals that learners are only one group of stakeholders whose needs should be assessed. But asking only learners about their educational needs falls far short of involving all stakeholders in these judgments. Second, asking learners to self-identify needs is not even necessarily democratic because it assumes that including learners eliminates power relations that influence needs making. It does not. Third, the image of directing traffic hints at but does not represent educators' political work because it assumes a flat planning table. Directing traffic requires more than neutral processing skills to manage the flow of power relations and interests. Directing traffic also requires the political skills of charting directions as well as exercising power in terms of who gets to the planning table. This is the essential dilemma: the apparent contradiction between assessing only learners' expressed educational needs—putatively the essence of democratic planning—and assessing the educational and political needs of *all* of the program's stakeholders.

So what are planners to do in order to democratically assess the educational and political needs of all stakeholders? The standard response (Boone, Safrit, & Jones, 2002; Caffarella, 2002; Houle, 1996; Knowles, 1980)—to develop needs "cooperatively"—falls short of informing practical action in the relations of power that frame the social and organizational contexts in which planners conduct needs-assessments. Saying that learners should be involved provides a good "first principle," but it fails to provide any workable recommendations for specific strategies. Planners typically work in asymmetrical relations of power that routinely thwart attempts to substantively involve learners—or most other stakeholders—in assessing needs. The key is for planners to make judgments about, first, which people should be involved, and second, how to best create conditions for their substantive participation at the planning table in the process of assessing the multiple educational and political needs of all stakeholders in a program. It is critical to understand that when needs are being assessed, stakeholders are always represented by someone at the planning table, regardless of whether the stakeholders themselves are actually present. Practically, then, the important questions are whether the representatives are legitimate, whether they are the best available given the situation, and whether they are able to exercise power in representing stakeholders' needs (Cervero & Wilson, 1994a).

Knowing which people should be at the table and creating the conditions for their substantive involvement in negotiating the needs-assessment can work only if planners carefully match their negotiation strategies to the structure of the situations that they face (Forester, 1989). Different contexts require different strategies for bringing people to the table to assess needs. Planners need a political analysis of the situation because "good intentions when blind to the context of action can lead directly to bad results" (Forester, 1990, p. 253). For example, as often happens when planners treat people equally under the guise of equal opportunity, they help to ensure that the needs of those who have the most power will be served (Forester, 1993). As planners assess how a situation is socially and politically constructed in order to negotiate needs democratically, they need to clearly see how their own place in the power dynamics allows for a "variety of modes of leverage, maneuvering, and strategic bargaining" (Isaac, 1987, p. 91). Knowing their own position in the web of political relationships allows planners to effectively use the consultative, bargaining, and dispute forms of negotiations described in Chapter Three.

Planners working planning tables in consultative conditions (Newman, 1994) have such common interests that even significant differences in power have relatively little impact on negotiating needs. For example, in the PI story Ron, as a project leader and full professor in the university, could exercise considerably more power than either Cassie or Dougie. Although Cassie and Dougie were experienced literacy practitioners, they were positioned as assistants on the project and as graduate students in the university. These power differentials were largely unimportant in the needs-assessment process because the interests among the three were so consensual about literacy practitioners' needs. Given Cassie's previous experience organizing and conducting practitioner inquiry programs, Dougie's previous experience as a literacy educator and previous participation in the first PI workshop, and Ron's eight-year leadership in the department's literacy staff development project, all three were led to promote their common view that literacy practitioners needed to research their own practice. Thus the needs-assessment was consultative, conducted largely through informal discussions among the three planners as they organized the workshops. Whenever possible, planners should take advantage of consultative circumstances to expand the representation of interests at the planning table. For example, the power differences between the PI planners and the learners were likewise consultative because the planners worked assiduously to ensure that the learners had different types of access to the planning table. Because both Cassie and Dougie were themselves literacy practitioners, they could identify with the experiences and practices of the participants. Furthermore, Dougie herself was a previous participant in the workshops, so she could draw upon that experience. Also, the planning for the third year of the project reflected the experiences of the planners and the previous participants during the first two years. In the third year the planners created a rotating advisory board of workshop participants to provide ongoing input to the planning. Even in the midst of the actual workshops, planners changed activities based on their consultative assessment of changing participant needs, as Cassie and Dougie did during the second session.

Although the theoretical literature presumes consultative conditions (without naming them as such), these are not nearly as common as the theories assume. Planners more often work with others who may share common interests but have conflicting ones as well. Planners will often describe the process of negotiating these common and conflicting interests as compromising, which represents bargaining situations (Newman, 1994). In seeking to find areas of common interests, planners should bargain to have all stakeholders represented in the assessment of educational and political needs for a program. At the major planning table at SVP where political needs for the program were assessed, there was virtually no opposition within the Professional Development Committee to changing the Society from a certifying to a teaching one, although there was residual resistance among members at large. Negotiating support for the new program at the board of governors, however, required considerable bargaining because some governors philosophically and financially opposed this organizational change. During the development of the *Fundamentals* program, learners were not at the table before the courses were offered. But the learners' interests were implicitly represented at the needs-assessment planning table through the course instructors, who had often been learners in other course systems. This implicit representation produced a rather uniform course format and teaching style in which instructors lectured and participants listened—and presumably learned. Because of Arthur's interest in promoting learner involvement, he bargained to involve learners more directly in expressing their needs by promoting experiential and interactive processes of learning in contrast to the dominant didactic ones. Experiential educational processes during the courses would place the learners at the instructional planning table, where they could express their practice needs directly to the instructors. But even though Arthur routinely promoted experiential learning processes in instructor training clinics,

Society instructors never actually used such experiential processes, because of the historical power of the dominant didactic approach. So he bargained with individual course instructors and designers by not challenging the lecture format in some courses and by encouraging and helping to design experiential practices in courses that would most benefit from them. He was only successful in such bargaining in three out of the five course sequences.

In dispute situations, winning is more important than reaching compromise (Newman, 1994). In disputes, one party often directly exercises its power in order to gain and keep control of the needs-assessment. The abrupt termination of the PI program is an exemplar of the consequences of power differences when assessing needs. Even if the planners had assessed the funding agency's political needs, they probably would not have had the power to change the final determination of whose needs mattered. The Phoenix story represents an educational program in which democratic practices were disputed. Pete believed he was the best representative of nearly all the stakeholders except for the president, and he carefully crafted the planning table to include only himself, Joan, and the president. When George joined the planning table he brought a specific democratic agenda, which Pete at first sidestepped, then bargained with, and finally quashed by exercising his power. At the final meeting a week before the retreat, as the planners were trying to make final decisions about the interactive exercises, George assured Pete the desert survival exercise would help them assess department managers' leadership needs and promote participatory decision making in the company. Because George's interests were in conflict with Pete's about improving the flow of information downward through the company, Pete directly told George "this retreat is not about participatory management. We can't use the retreat to criticize management." With this exercise of power, the dispute was over and Pete sustained his interests and power to define needs.

Summary

Planning theory has focused for decades on clarifying the concept of needs that "survives and thrives because of, rather than despite, its vagueness and multiplicity of meanings" (Griffith, 1978, p. 382). This confusion is more imagined than real, despite repeated calls for clarity. Needs are routinely defined as a gap between the present and the desired. The literature has focused mostly on measuring the first while ignoring the normative and political dimensions of the second. Even among those who have regularly noted the role of values and politics in assessing needs, the conversation essentially stops with this awareness. In this chapter we have moved beyond the awareness of how values and power shape needs-assessment to show how planners negotiate interests and power to construct needs in their historically evolving, communicative practices. To recognize that needs-assessments are the judgments that stakeholders make, as Houle (1972) so insightfully explained long ago, is one thing. It is quite another challenge to negotiate democratically the needs-assessments at the real tables that planners work. Knowing who to get to the planning table to assess needs is at best a risky, ambiguous endeavor because power always frames stakeholders' negotiation of interests in determining the program's educational and political needs. Depending on the power relations present in a situation and people's interests, planners should select from a variety of different negotiating strategies to democratically negotiate needs.

Chapter 5

Negotiating the Program's Educational, Management, and Political Objectives

Program objectives are a statement of the results people expect to achieve from an educational activity. Although many educators believe that explicitly stating them is a form of professional and regulatory busywork, program objectives are critically important because they are the "programmatic pivot" (Brookfield, 1986, p. 211) for the planning process. On one side of the pivot are stakeholders' various interests and needs; on the other side stand all of the judgments planners must make about the educational program, ranging from the instructional design to administrative tasks of budgeting and marketing. In addition, the formally stated objectives are used as benchmarks for evaluation because they "provide clear statements of the anticipated results to be achieved through an educational program. . . . At the heart of formulating program objectives is defining program outcomes" (Caffarella, 2002, p. 100).

We need to clarify two important misconceptions about objectives, which are commonly understood as statements formally expressed in writing that are determined before a program begins. In contrast, our conception is that people expect to achieve results from educational programs, whether or not these expectations are written down as objectives. As Houle (1996) explains, " . . . an objective is a purpose that guides a learner or educator, not the formal statement of that purpose" (p. 42) in written form. Second, people continually refine, or even change, the results that they expect from educational programs. Because "an objective may be known prior to the activity, emerge while it is occurring, or be perceived subsequently" (Houle, 1996, p. 260), the negotiation of program objectives is a process that usually begins before an educational program and continues throughout and after it ends.

Virtually all authors in the field agree with Sork and Caffarella (1989) that as the programmatic pivot, "program objectives should flow from the needs that have been identified and should be as explicit as possible" (p. 238). Indeed, assessing needs and negotiating program objectives are often bundled together as the "front end," or first step, in the planning process. This conceptual link was clearly made by Tyler (1949), whose first curriculum planning question, "What educational purposes should the school seek to attain?" (p. 1), incorporates both the collection of evidence central to needs-assessment and the prioritizing process necessary for negotiating objectives. Chapter Four discussed how our view builds upon a common observation of the relationship between needs-assessment and objectives: "Although needs assessment logically precedes setting program priorities, in practice purposes and objectives are often determined without a needs assessment having first been done" (Sork, 1998, p. 276). Our view is that whether or not planners collect evidence about people's needs, they always make judgments about stakeholders' needs in relation to the program. The people who have a stake in an educational program are likely to have many needs, only some of which will be addressed. Some of these needs may be widely shared; others can be in conflict. Of all the needs that could be met through a program, planners have to prioritize which ones should drive the instructional, administrative, and evaluation decisions they will make. Thus, priority setting is the key dynamic in how planners negotiate the program's educational, management, and political objectives. This chapter discusses four principles that should guide planners in this critical priority-setting activity.

Prioritize Educational, Management, and Political Objectives

Most planning approaches focus on educational objectives that are formally expressed in writing. However, experienced planners understand that people expect many outcomes from programs, only some of which are formally written as educational objectives (Beder, 1978; Cervero, 1984a). As discussed in Chapter Four, people have many educational and political needs that could be addressed through the program. In the critical activity of negotiating the program's objectives, planners have to prioritize the relative importance of many stakeholders' educational needs as well as their social and political needs. In negotiating these needs into the objectives that will guide program development, we recommend that planners: (1) prioritize educational, management, and political objectives and (2) use these three types of objectives to inform programmatic decisions.

Planning models consistently address the importance of developing educational objectives, which focus on what learners should know or be able to do as a result of participating in an educational program (Sork, 1998; Tyler, 1949). Many models, particularly those at the K–12 level, discuss only these types of objectives. However, there has been an increasing recognition in adult education (Boone, Safrit, & Jones, 2002; Houle, 1996; Knowles, 1980; Kowalski, 1988; Sork & Caffarella, 1989) that planners also need to identify a second type of objective directed at improving the quality of the program. Planning theorists have used different terms to describe this type, such as operational objectives (Knowles, 1980), management objectives (Boone, Safrit, & Jones, 2002), and facilitative objectives (Houle, 1996). Planners are urged to recognize these objectives because they are often essential to supporting the achievement of educational objectives. Houle (1996) explains that "in many teaching and learning situations, but particularly in those sponsored by institutions, objectives can be stated in terms not only of the outcomes of education but also of changes in the design components that will presumably make those outcomes better. These management objectives have to do with such matters as the acquisition of learning resources, the improved training of leaders, the establishment of more efficient counseling procedures, and the discovery of new sources of revenue" (p. 193). The development of an "instructor training clinic" in the SVP story is a good example of a critically important management objective. The Professional Development Committee members believed that instructor training was essential for the program's success and offered the clinic in March just prior to the five separate discipline courses in April.

Even as authors recognize the distinction between these educational and management objectives, they warn of a danger: "A threat to learning arises when facilitative objectives crowd out educational objectives" (Houle, 1996, p. 193). Although educational and management objectives are necessary, a balance in priority between both types must be maintained. Holding educational and management objectives in balance can be a problem, for example, when the educational objectives are compromised in order to increase the revenue stream needed to support the program. This is illustrated in the SVP story, in which no limit was set on the number of people who could enroll in the courses even though the educational objectives were more likely to be achieved with smaller numbers of participants.

Although educational objectives and management objectives are vitally important, they are only subsets of the results that people expect to achieve from a program. Planners need to recognize that people's political objectives are as much a part of the planning process as their educational and management objectives. These objectives are about the political relationships among people at the planning table and those not at the table—and the multiple political benefits that they seek to achieve there. People's political objectives are often defined as "hidden agendas," in contrast to the stated educational and management objectives. Thus, these types of objectives are seldom openly discussed, even though they influence educational and administrative judgments about a program. Our position is that although programs are not *only* about political outcomes, they are always about political outcomes. For example, Cassie and Ron had not only educational objectives for the teachers, but also the political objective of strengthening the reputation of the university so that the funding agency would support future programs. In this way students and faculty could be supported and the department could recruit students to the graduate program. Pete had not only four educational objectives for the management education program, but also the political objective of improving the standing of the human resources office, thus transforming his political relationship with the president and other vice presidents. The SVP president had not only educational objectives for the professional development courses, but also the political objective of using the educational program to respond to pending litigation pressures for licensure and reform.

These few examples illustrate the central point that people have educational, management, and political objectives that they hope to achieve through any program. Of the range of objectives that people have for a program, typically only the educational objectives are expressed in written form and shared publicly. For example, the planners for the PI program had three objectives for the first retreat: to create a learning community among the twenty-four teachers, orient the teachers to the practitioner inquiry approach, and help teachers find researchable problems for their projects. Not explicitly stated was the larger political objective of offering a form of staff development in which teachers were producers of knowledge instead of consumers of knowledge; this would be offered by expert presenters through the standard workshop format. Indeed, this objective was the motivating force for many of the educational and management judgments that the planners made about the PI program. This example illustrates an important principle: "However refined a statement of objectives may be, it can never be more than a notation in abstract terms of the goals that are actually sought. . . . Some writers on education have failed to make this distinction and have treated the statement of a goal as though it were the goal itself" (Houle, 1996, p. 191). This distinction has important practical implications as planners negotiate the program's objectives.

The practical implications occur in the divergence between program objectives that are expressed in written form and those that actually influence programmatic decisions. This divergence can occur for any of the three types of objectives, but is seen most clearly in relation to people's political objectives because they are rarely expressed in written form. For example, the planners of the PI program did not actually write an objective about their hope that the project would strengthen the university's relationship with the State Department of Education. Yet the importance of that objective was made visible as Cassie and Ron determined how many compromises could be made in order to keep the program funded without threatening the achievement of the central educational objectives. Such a disconnect also occurred in the PI story in relation to educational objectives, as there was not a written objective to "challenge racial power dynamics." However, the importance of that educational objective was brought into clear focus when Cassie was presented with the opportunity to address those dynamics arising from the wigger incident. At SVP, the chairperson of the Professional Development Committee had the explicit political objective of using the educational program to add new members to the Society, saying "one prime objective is to reach non-member appraisers through our education . . . programs and encourage them to participate in achieving professional certification." This objective was never formally expressed in writing, although it strongly influenced many educational and management judgments about the program.

There is a strong tradition for educational planners to make a distinction between the written objectives and the objectives that actually influence programmatic judgments. However, the examples from the three planning stories should make clear that this distinction simply confuses planners about what is going on. Houle (1996) suggests eliminating the need for this distinction, saying that planners " . . . must begin with the realization that they [objectives] are actual guides to action embodied in the learning program and express the hopes of those who take part in it. A first essential is to make written and orally expressed objectives conform as closely as possible to reality" (Houle, 1996, p. 191). This is particularly true for political objectives, which many people consider an inappropriate outcome of educational programs—even as they seek to achieve these objectives. In addition, people responsible for programs often consider these types of objectives too "politically sensitive" to acknowledge verbally, much less in written form. Nevertheless, because objectives are the results that people expect to achieve from an educational activity, planners must be aware of the full range of these expectations and realize that people will have these expectations regardless of whether they are formally expressed in writing.

Negotiate Objectives Before and During the Program

Most planning models (Knox, 1986; Kowalski, 1988; Queeney, 1995) agree with Knowles (1980) that "the starting point for developing program objectives is the pool of needs" (p. 122) that has been identified through a formal assessment process. The identification of needs creates the time boundary for the beginning of the process for negotiating objectives. The temporal end point of this process is typically taken to be the written expression of objectives, which are then used to design the educational program and set the criteria for evaluation. However, experienced planners know that this time frame for negotiating objectives is attenuated in both directions. For example, many educational programs derive from a previous offering and are deeply affected by that history. An increasing number of planning models recognize that objectives are continually developed, refined, or even changed during the educational program itself (Brookfield, 1986; Caffarella, 2002; Knox, 1986). Therefore, planners need to see their negotiation of objectives as a historically developing process that: (1) has a history predating the beginning of the formal planning cycle for a given program and (2) continues through the educational program and beyond. Whereas the previous section of this chapter addressed a wider scope of vision to include planners' political objectives, this section addresses a longer vision of the planners' temporal horizon for negotiating objectives.

In Chapter Four we discussed the importance of locating the program's needs-assessment in a specific time and place. Negotiating the program's objectives must have similar time and place horizons because setting priorities among the needs often occurs concurrently with needs-assessment. Even within the truncated time horizon of most planning models, there is a historically developing process from long-term strategic objectives to short-term educational objectives. As Blackburn (1994) advises Cooperative Extension planners, "Objectives can be tricky to formulate because of the potential for stating them at different levels. . . . Strategic and long-term objectives are at the institutional and overall program level; short-term objectives are [at] the specific project and teaching level. . . . As an Extension education programmer, you are interested in ultimately moving from the strategic, long-term overall objectives to stating the specific educational short-term learning objectives, to guide the specific learning or instruction required" (p. 95). A good example of this historical process from strategic program objectives to specific educational objectives is seen in the SVP story. That organization had a sporadic history of offering programs, mainly through its annual conferences and advanced discipline seminars. Unlike other professional valuation associations, SVP had never developed a formal system of training for appraisers because its mission was one of testing and certification. This changed when the Society decided to adopt a broad new strategic objective: to build an educational function that would provide systematic train-ing for the appraisal profession. The Professional Development Committee then developed the curriculum of five discipline courses for a candidate-to-senior education system. This was followed by the development of educational objectives by specific discipline course designers for each of the five courses.

In offering these five discipline courses for the first time, the SVP's system of training was started without a prior organizational history. This is much less common than the way in which the vast majority of programs are developed. The Phoenix Company story illustrates the more common situation, in which the historical process for planning a current program extends back in time to a previous program. As Pete negotiated program objectives for the 1992 retreat, he did so in the historical stream of retreat planning at the Phoenix Company. Although the program objectives for the 1992 retreat were different from the objectives of previous retreats, the priority-setting process was embedded in the ten-year history of annual retreats. Pete explained what happened as he planned the previous retreat in 1990: "Traditionally we had a spring retreat because it's the time when our budget information is put together and the administrators in the spring would get people together and kick off the year and say these are our major goals; this is what you need to think about in doing your budget. So we were anticipating the [1990] spring retreat and we wanted to do more of a communi-cation, interaction kind of thing and Mr. Jones was not ready to do it at all; he just thought too much was going on to do it." Even though the 1990 retreat did not incorporate the "focus on team building, communication with employees and communication among the department directors," Pete had this as a programming priority. This priority for team building and communication was reinforced when Joan was rehired in the fall of 1991. Joan said that "when I interviewed for this job, [the president] talked with me about the need to have better communication from department director level up and down." When Joan came back to the company, Pete said that "we really struggled with what does the job look like and . . . is she going to have enough to do?" In the review of Joan's job responsibilities, the retreat's educational objectives began to come into clearer focus; as Joan said, "we started talking about customer service and what some of the overall goals were, it just seemed logical that a retreat would be a good way to have accomplished some of the internal communication emphasis that we want to accomplish. So we started talking about 'it's time, we need to have one . . . first thing we have to do is talk to Mr. Jones and see what he would like to do.'"

The commonly accepted view of negotiating objectives would see this process beginning when Pete and Joan met with the president for the first time on January 3. However, it is clear that Pete was making his decisions about objectives for the retreat in the historically developing context of planning the previous retreat. For example, Pete was still reeling from the negative experience of planning the 1990 retreat when he and Joan began discussing ideas for the 1992 retreat and decided to approach the president on January 3. He said, "If I remember honestly, going into that [January 3] meeting, that meeting was more to cover me. To keep him [Mr. Jones] from coming up at the last minute and saying where's the retreat? I wanted to know if he had something in mind—we were ready but the purpose was not to have a spring retreat as much as it was to document that we talked to you so don't come back and say we didn't." Consequently, Pete's political objective of maintaining a positive relationship with the president was at least as important as the educational objective of solving a communication problem as he planned the 1992 retreat. The Phoenix story shows how the standard time horizon used to frame the negotiation of objectives is but a snapshot in an ongoing historical process. In contrast to this program, in which there was a significant change from the previous retreats, objectives for a new program often remain relatively unchanged from a prior effort. For example, the PI program was being offered for the third time but with the primary educational, management, and political objectives carried over from the previous two years. However, with the doubling of the group's size from twelve to twenty-four, one new objective was added: "To engage the knowledge and experience of teachers who were participating in the program for a second year without creating a hierarchy that privileged returning teachers." At the same time that the planners renewed their commitment to previously determined educational objectives, new objectives arose in response to the demands of the situation.

Planners' responsiveness to the ongoing historical situation also continues throughout the educational program itself. All objectives, especially educational objectives, are continually negotiated during the learning activity. This is an important point, because planners often do not have access ahead of time to the people who will participate in the program. The benefit of seeing that objectives are negotiated during the program is that learners' objectives can always be used to shape the program in real time. Others (Caffarella, 2002; Knox, 1986; Queeney, 1995) have stressed this point, agreeing with Brookfield (1986) "that the idea of continuous negotiation and renegotiation is stressed strongly as a feature of effective practice. Only if this renegotiation is possible can one abandon previously formulated goals as these become demonstrably irrelevant and begin to formulate ones that will allow learners to explore new directions" (p. 214). Although educational objectives can be developed before the program begins, they should "offer direction but leave some room for adaptation and interpretation" (Queeney, 1995, p. 212). The PI story demonstrates this common activity of negotiating the program's objectives in response to the conditions present during the educational program itself. Until the wigger incident occurred, the planners did not have an educational objective in the third retreat to address racism. However, when Cassie received Sonya's e-mail after the second retreat, she realized that "I probably needed to do something constructive about this issue with the whole group." Some of the participants also had this educational objective, with Sonya telling Cassie that she had talked with two other teachers who were in the group and that "they felt the same way—offended. Michael thinks the group needs to discuss it." With Cassie and at least some of the participants now wanting to achieve this educational objective, instructional activities would likely have been developed to address it in the third retreat. As it turned out, the continuing but ultimately failed negotiation of the overall management objective regarding the continuation of the PI program itself prevented the third retreat from happening.

The PI story illustrates that the importance of the ongoing negotiation of political objectives for an educational program cannot be overstated. This story presents an extreme example of how the fundamental political objective of maintaining the relationship with the funding agency should never be taken for granted, because it makes possible the achievement of educational and management objectives. In a similar fashion, maintaining positive relationships with the president and other vice presidents was central to Pete's planning strategy so that he could avoid a repeat of the circumstances of the 1990 retreat. In order to achieve this objective, Pete broke the normal chain of command at the company by meeting directly with Mr. Jones and bypassing the executive vice president. Pete's political objective was that "I was not going to include Brad at all. He was not part of the planning but I was going to make sure that Sam Jones was part of every step. And so, I intentionally excluded Brad because I did not want his input." He also involved other key vice presidents in order to achieve another of his political objectives: to secure their respect for the human resources department and for himself. As Pete said about the other vice presidents, "There are a couple of people in that group who just don't think I've got it together at all and I've got some critics." Throughout the planning process, before and during the retreat itself, Pete believed the political objective of earning this respect was achieved. This respect would be critically important as he planned management education programs in the future. After the retreat, he concluded that "I think we have taken a pretty big step. I think we have their confidence, and I think the VPs know that we have some skills and some background in this area that they probably don't have, and that's kind of a nice position to be in. . . . we have laid a foundation to build upon and that's what is exciting, because you gotta have that before you can move forward and I think at this point now, if we build on the momentum that we've got, then the sky's the limit." As Pete's strategy shows, negotiating the program's educational, management, and political objectives begins before the actual planning cycle for a program, continues during the program, and often extends after the program has ended.

Anticipate How Power Relations Frame the Negotiation of Objectives

People's educational and political needs have an effect on educational programs as they are negotiated at the planning table into actual program objectives. Houle (1996) highlights this move from the possibilities inherent in people's needs to the objectives that guide action: "Out of the complex array of complementary or conflicting possibilities present in the situation, dominant and guiding purposes emerge to give shape to the educational program" (p. 62). However, in negotiating objectives, planners move not only from the possible to the actual, but also from many possible needs to fewer actual objectives. As other authors have noted, planners are typically faced with the situation in which there are "many more potential objectives than your program can address" (Knox, 1986, p. 71). Therein lies the central dynamic at the planning table, because negotiating objectives is about making choices and giving priority to whose needs should shape programmatic decisions.

The role of power relationships in negotiating objectives is rarely mentioned in the literature, even though it is the central dynamic in practice (Rossing & Howard, 1994). Instead, this activity often focuses on "translating" needs into objectives (Boone, Safrit, & Jones,

2002), as if all needs are simply converted to objectives. As Queeney (1995) describes this process, "The first step in translating needs assessment findings into educational activities consists of converting those findings into learning objectives to guide development of educational activities that will address the discrepancies" (p. 211). The use of this translation metaphor may explain why a vast literature has been written on the needs-assessment process, yet "determining priorities is often neglected in the literature" (Sork, 1998, p. 276). Where planning models address the priority-setting dynamic, one of two strategies is recommended. The most common approach follows Tyler's (1949) model, suggesting the use of various "filters" that planners should use to determine the relative importance of needs (Caffarella, 2002; Knowles, 1980; Sork, 1998). For example, Knowles (1980) recommends translating management and educational needs through the three filters of institutional purpose and philosophy of education, feasibility, and interests of individuals. These filters would separate out the high-priority needs, which could then be translated into program objectives. Sork (1998) raises the point, however, that "no single set of criteria is suitable for all adult education settings . . . most priority decisions are based on a few criteria considered important by the decision makers" (p. 281). Sork's critique leads to the second strategy, which suggests the key to determining priorities is that decision makers will both decide on the criteria and use those criteria to set priorities (Boone, Safrit, & Jones, 2002; Knox, 1986). For example, Caffarella (2002) suggests that involving other people in determining priorities "is usually a good strategy, especially when large numbers of ideas have been generated from diverse sources. . . . People who are important players in these processes include learners, colleagues, education and training committee members, external parties, and/or other stakeholders" (p. 138). Houle (1996) adds some texture to using this strategy in practice with his metaphor of the "force field," in which potential conflict exists among the needs and the decision makers: "Any learning activity is, however, a force field in which many other purposes than the professed goals are in operation, some leading to harmony, others to conflict" (p. 180).

Our view is that although people do use criteria to set priorities, they do so in the context of socially organized relations of power that structure who is at the planning tables where these decisions are made. In the same way that we described in our discussion of needs-assessment in Chapter Four, negotiating objectives is fundamentally a political process framed at the macro level by who is at the planning table setting these priorities and at the micro level by the political dynamics that occur at the table. This is seen clearly in the ongoing meetings that Pete and Joan had with the Phoenix Company president. The organizationally defined relations of power structured the planning table, where the many possible needs that could have been addressed at the retreat were negotiated into four publicly stated educational objectives. When Pete and Joan had their initial meeting with Mr. Jones, he "helped clarify" their ideas for the retreat's focus. As Pete explained, "it was his idea that we focus on the department meeting and that specific aspect of communication in the facility." The people at the planning table remained intact as Pete and Joan came back to a second meeting, having written four educational objectives: (1) to improve department heads' and supervisors' perceptions of how they communicate and how they come across to their staff, (2) to give each individual an opportunity to lead a group and to receive feedback on her or his effectiveness, (3) to reinforce the value of good communication for managers, and (4) to provide an opportunity for team building within the management group. In identifying the sources of the four objectives, Pete made visible how power relationships structure the priority-setting dynamic. Pete explained that the objectives were determined in

> . . . our earlier discussion with him [Mr. Jones] because he feels it is really important that department heads and supervisors communicate well. . . . So we hit on the perception, how can we help people perceive what their strengths are in communication? I think that number 1 kind of came from Mr. Jones in our first discussion. We

really liked that idea. I think number 2 came from me more because I believe in actually forcing an individual to try it and practice it even in a dyad or triad and not necessarily to embarrass them but put a little pressure on them. I really think that's the way to change perceptions or to get information. Then I think 3 and 4 came more from Joan's point of view, from her program and from the needs we had identified in the fall to really reinforce this as a value because that's a big part of her role. This team building within the management group is something that Joan has really heard a lot about from this task force in the fall too. So they were kind of mutual but I feel like I kind of put number 2 in and Mr. Jones kind of put number 1 in and maybe [Joan] put 3 and 4 more together.

Using his location in organizationally defined relations of power, Pete constructed a planning table in which three people set the priorities for the management retreat objectives. Other stakeholders, such as the managers who would be the primary learners and the other 1,200 company employees, did not have a seat at the table where the retreat objectives were developed. Rather, they were represented by Pete, Joan, and Mr. Jones, who made the decisions based on what they perceived the other stakeholders needed.

Having a seat at the table, of course, does not necessarily ensure substantive involvement, because power relationships operate to structure the decision-making process. Having already decided on the retreat's educational objectives, Pete now had to sustain these objectives through three meetings with George, whom he hired to facilitate the two-day meeting. We see Pete exercising his power at the table especially as George attempted to renegotiate the retreat's overall purpose—from improving communication to a focus on participatory management. Early in the first meeting with George on March 7, Pete exercised his power by telling George that the company president had determined the retreat's purpose: "We feel like

we want to provide [a] skill-building opportunity on how to conduct a meeting and this comes directly from Mr. Jones and saying
that the information is not getting down to the lower levels of the
company." Later in the meeting, George attempted to renegotiate
this educational objective to a greater emphasis on participatory
management: "One of the questions that I have is the feeling on
the part of the company that this is participatory management
and this is something that has become part of our culture in our
department. . . . So that's another issue. But I don't know if that's
something [that you want to focus on]." Pete deflected this request
in the meeting and in the interview we conducted after the meeting explained why he had done so. He was concerned that the executives and managers "would be real threatened by opening the thing
up and really talking a lot about participation and participatory
decision making." Pete was able to exercise his power as the company vice president and the person who hired George to maintain
the four educational objectives that had been previously negotiated
with the president. Of course, George could have negotiated more
vigorously for a focus on participatory management, but he was constrained as he was also seeking to achieve his political objective of
maintaining positive relationships with Pete and other executives
at the Phoenix Company. In his role as director of a leadership
development institute at a nearby university, he was expecting that
additional business could be generated for his unit if this retreat
were a success as defined by company executives.

   Negotiating objectives is at the heart of any program development
process because these objectives will structure the instructional,
administrative, and evaluation decisions. Although people will use
filters to prioritize program objectives as suggested by other planning
models, power relations in the social and organizational context influence which people are present at (and absent from) the planning
table to use those filters. Further, the planning table where needs are
prioritized is not a neutral stage, because political dynamics will structure the negotiation of program objectives. In negotiating objectives,

planners need to anticipate how power relations frame the critical priority-setting dynamic at both of these levels.

Democratically Negotiate Objectives

Thus far in this chapter we have presented various lenses for seeing what happens in negotiating the program's educational, management, and political objectives. Planners must recognize stakeholders' multiple objectives and see negotiating objectives as a historically developing process that is structured by social and organizational power relations. But what should planners do to negotiate objectives democratically? We certainly agree with the sentiment expressed by Houle (1996) that "the understanding and acceptance of educational objectives will usually be advanced if they are developed coopera-tively. A person who has had a share in deciding what is to be done will understand it better and be more interested in doing it than she who must accept a goal developed by someone else" (p. 192). In this regard, there is universal advice to involve the learners (Knowles, 1980) as well as other stakeholders. As Caffarella (2002) explains, "Program planners should not develop program objectives in a vacuum. . . . Instead, other people, such as program participants, work supervisors, and external stakeholders, should be asked to help in developing or at least reviewing these objectives" (p. 159). Yet this advice falls short of informing practical action in politically organized social and organizational settings in which planners seek to have all stakeholders substantively represented at the planning table to decide the priorities for educational, management, and polit-ical objectives.

Although the strategic impulse is that all people affected by a program should be represented at the planning table to negotiate the objectives, determining which people should be involved and how to create the conditions for their substantive involvement is almost always an uncertain, ambiguous, and risk-taking activity. One of the main reasons is that planners must often work in situations marked

by asymmetrical power relations that thwart this vision. This is further complicated when people have multiple and sometimes conflicting objectives. Thus, no theory can unambiguously prescribe
whether the actual people selected to negotiate program objectives
are, in some transcendental sense, the right people. Rather, the planner must make a practical judgment in each and every situation
(Cervero & Wilson, 1994a; Reid, 1979). Our starting point in making these judgments is that people affected by a program are always
represented in some way at the planning table as program objectives
are being negotiated. Thus, the important practical questions
center on whether the person(s) representing the interests of the
people affected by the program: (1) is a legitimate representative,
(2) is the best representative in the given situation, and (3) can
substantively represent interests as decisions are made about program objectives (Cervero & Wilson, 1994a). For example, would
the objectives of the Phoenix Company's retreat have been different if representatives of the managers (the target audience) or the
nonsupervisory employees had been at the table in meetings with
the president or with George? Although they would have been legitimate representatives and possibly the best in the given situation, we
might ask if they had sufficient power to have their views on educational, management, and political objectives substantively represented. This third criterion is particularly important because it
illustrates a common situation in which people are at the table but,
even if they speak, have little "voice" in the decisions that are made
there. Thus, the planner needs to acknowledge that there are political costs of token representation before bringing people to the table
to negotiate the program's objectives.

Knowing who should be at the table and enabling conditions for
substantive involvement requires planners to match their negotiation strategies to the structure of the situations they face (Cervero &
Wilson, 1994a, 1994b; Forester, 1989). The situations most conducive
to the democratic development of objectives are those in which
people come together with common interests and seek to share

information and solve problems together. Most planning models assume these types of situations, in which everyone works together in a mutually supportive way and the negotiation of program objectives can be characterized as a consultation. Asymmetrical political relationships are not a barrier to people's being substantively involved in developing program objectives, as demonstrated in the PI story, in which common interests outweighed conflicting interests as the planners and the participants developed the educational objectives. The provisional statement of these objectives was derived from the planners' experience working with participants in the previous two retreat projects. The three original educational objectives were that participants would refine their research questions, learn about data collection strategies, and propose a design for their research projects. The participants had the opportunity to renegotiate these objectives through their evaluation of the first retreat meeting. In addition, phone interviews with the teacher advisory committee between the first and second meetings did not yield any revisions. Indeed, Cassie found that "several individuals said they trusted us completely to plan the sessions without their input." However, the PI story also illustrates the point that situations are not necessarily constant in any given planning process. As Cassie was negotiating the objectives for the third retreat meeting, she did so in a politically charged situation (because of the wigger incident) in which consultation was not the appropriate strategy. Cassie's difficulty in getting the two principal participants in the incident (Sonya and Jean) to discuss educational objectives for the next retreat changed the structure of the situation. Therefore, her negotiation strategy had to change from consultation to bargaining.

Negotiating objectives democratically becomes more complicated in situations in which people have both common and conflicting interests that affect the program. In these situations, bargaining is the appropriate strategy, and people negotiating objectives will seek to find areas of common interest (Newman, 1994). Cassie and the teachers used this strategy as they sought to determine the objectives for the third retreat. The specific activities in this strategy included phone calls, letters, e-mails, and ultimately a lunch two months after the incident. At that luncheon meeting, Sonya and Jean decided to raise the wigger incident at the third retreat because of the learning opportunity it would provide for all of the participants. Another example of a bargaining strategy is Arthur's initial restaurant meeting with the president of the SVP. In that meeting, Arthur sought to focus on the educational objectives, content, instructional methods, and teaching staff for the courses. He especially wanted to introduce experiential teaching methods into the courses. However, the president's focus was to ensure that Arthur accepted the political objective of the Society's new educational initiative, which was to help the Society survive, and that he understood who his allies and enemies would be in achieving this political objective. Arthur's position in that meeting is a good example of why the planner's place in the power dynamics affects their ability to negotiate objectives democratically. Cassie's place in the political relationships gave her a much wider range of bargaining strategies than were available to Arthur at his planning table. However, as Arthur gained more credibility in the organization, he achieved a greater power to bargain more effectively. For example, he was given responsibility to design the instructor training clinic in March, where his educational objectives were achieved. These bargaining situations are very common in educational planning and, while more complicated than consultations because of the trade-offs that need to be made, do not approach the difficulty of dispute situations.

Developing objectives democratically is most difficult in those situations in which people's conflicting interests outweigh any common ones. George encountered a dispute situation when he pushed Pete and Joan to involve the potential learners in negotiating the program objectives. Near the beginning of his first meeting with Pete and Joan on March 7, George asked, "Let me clarify again— the people who are there see the need and the value for these particular activities in terms of the objectives. Have they bought into the fact that we need some guidance and updating in how to conduct good meetings? We want to be provided opportunity to handle difficult questions." When Joan responded, "I don't know," she was simply confirming that the planners did not have an interest in developing objectives democratically. In this dispute, George could have used other strategies to expand representation at the planning table, such as asking to meet with a group of the managers who would attend the retreat or with the nonsupervisory personnel. Instead, he chose another strategy:

> . . . the reason I bring it up is, if they don't, that's OK as long as we let them know beforehand, this is what we are planning on doing. We don't want them coming to a meeting not clear on what the purposes and objectives are. And that they bought into the recognition, they recognize that there is a need and desire on our part to do this. Because if they don't see the need, then again it's somebody else's saying you need this. And Sam Jones has said this, you need this. But again, even though he thinks this is needed, they may not think it is needed.

Even as George recognized the importance of negotiating objectives democratically, he reframed the representation issue to one of informing the managers about what will happen at the retreat. George recognized the importance of learners' "buying in" to the educational objectives, but chose not to use a strategy appropriate to a dispute situation to ensure their substantive representation.

As is often true in negotiating objectives, there is a significant difference between "buying in" to an objective that has already been determined and substantively affecting the development of an objective. Having lost the dispute over substantive involvement, George seeks to achieve the lower standard of "buy-in" of the learners. He uses the strategy of sending a survey that frames the issue of "improving communication at the company" as simply improving meetings: "If we indicate through a communication prior to the retreat that one of the purposes is to see how we can have more effective meetings; and we can send out some type of survey form, which we ask them each to return to me; and then at the retreat, we say this is what you've said about your meetings." The strategy of using a mailed survey has the effect of appearing to involve the learners in negotiating objectives. George gives the rationale in explaining that the learners could "say we've had some input in the agenda for the retreat to the extent that this is now becoming our retreat and George's and the administrators are responding to something that we consider to be important." In reality, however, the objective had already been determined at the January meetings with the president.

The planner's location in the power dynamics matters most in dispute situations, as opposed to consultative or bargaining ones. George was not able to either renegotiate the overall objective from improving meetings to a focus on participatory management or win substantive learner involvement in negotiating the objectives. Pete, given his position as vice president in the company and the person who hired George, was able to maintain the overall objective and keep learners away from the planning table to negotiate objectives. On the latter point, he clearly did not see the survey affecting the objectives in any way. He enthusiastically agreed to send the survey, saying "this could plant the seed. We've had an announcement at our department directors meeting. We talked about it in a real positive, upbeat way. It's going to be fun, it's going to be interactive; we're going to get a lot done. But I think this would plant the seed of seriously thinking about what we're going to be talking about. And then if we could follow up between this survey and the retreat, we could send them a good article." Although Pete did not have the same ethical commitment as George to negotiating objectives democratically, he actually possessed the power to use strategies that would have nurtured a democratic vision.

Summary

Negotiating the program's educational, management, and political objectives is one of the most critical activities that planners undertake, because these objectives serve as the pivot between the many needs that could be met and the ultimate priorities that guide instructional, administrative, and evaluation decisions. As they negotiate objectives, planners need to widen their vision from the advice generally given in planning models. First, planners need to recognize that people who have a stake in the program have educational, management, and political objectives that they seek to achieve through the planning process. Second, planners need to enlarge their vision to see that negotiating objectives for a program has historical antecedents and that objectives will continue to be negotiated during the program and beyond. Third, planners need to anticipate how power relations affect both who is at the table to negotiate the development of objectives as well as the power dynamics that occur at the table. We urge planners to use these three dimensions of expanded vision and corresponding strategies in the service of the ethical commitment to negotiating program objectives democratically.

Chapter 6

Negotiating the Program's Instructional Design and Implementation

The instructional program is the most visible outcome of the planning process because "it involves designing the interaction between learners and instructors and/or learners and resource materials" (Caffarella, 2002, p. 167). Planners face a complex task as they consider a vast array of objectives and other criteria to make large numbers of interlocking judgments to design and implement the program. As Sork (2000) points out, "The instructional plan is the heart of the program; it's the place where philosophy, learning theory, understanding of group dynamics, availability of technology, understanding of motivation, and so on interact to influence how instruction is visualized" (p. 183). Planners often bring together a number of people—including instructional designers, subject-matter experts, instructors, learners, and those representing the sponsoring unit or organization—to make these interlocking judgments about the instructional program (Caffarella, 2002).

The three planning stories demonstrate the complexity planners face in negotiating the instructional design. The planners of the two-day retreat at the Phoenix Company had to make a bewildering number of decisions about content, format, scheduling, location, instructional materials, and instructional staff as they attempted to include, for the first time, many interactive learning activities. The SVP planners had no prior history of offering courses for entry-level professionals; they had to start from scratch to design

five new courses in a four-month period. Although the planners of
the PI project were conducting their program for the third time, the
size of the audience had doubled and now included teachers who
had participated in the previous program. The PI instructional
design was also quite complex because it included not only four two-
day retreats spread out over eight months, but also a listserv and site
visits to each participating teacher.

As explained in the previous chapter, educational objectives are
critically important in most planning models because they serve as
the programmatic pivot between needs-assessment and instructional
design. The stated program objectives are meant to serve as "concrete guidelines for program development" (Knowles, 1980, p. 121),
the "foundation for the instructional plan" (Caffarella, 2002,
p. 156), and the "reference point and focus for design of instruction
[and] the planning of course work" (Brookfield, 1986, p. 211).
Although educational objectives are an important consideration,
there is much more to consider at the planning tables when people
negotiate the instructional design and implementation. First,
people bring management and political objectives along with their
educational objectives to the planning table. Although political
objectives are usually not formally stated in written form, they are
brought to bear when people design the program's content, audience, format, and schedule. We might wish that these objectives
did not operate at the table, but they always do—as we illustrate
in the remainder of this chapter. Second, power relations at the
planning table also influence judgments about the instructional
design in a variety of ways. Of particular significance is how political relationships affect the involvement of learners in making these
judgments both before and during the program. Although planning
models in adult education have universally exalted involving "the
learner" in designing instruction, they fail to recognize that there
is no "generic" learner. Rather, adult learners have different locations in social and organizational power structures and thus have
more or less access to the planning tables where the instruction is

negotiated. These uneven planning tables must be acknowledged and addressed if all learners in a program are to have substantive involvement in this part of the planning process. As we show in the chapter's final section, power dynamics have broad implications for learner involvement, particularly in terms of democratically negotiating the instructional design and implementation.

A third major consideration raised by our planning theory is that, like needs-assessment and objective setting, negotiating the instructional design is a historically developing process. Planners typically make some judgments about the design shortly after they have an initial idea, even before they have negotiated a formal needs-assessment or the educational objectives. In some cases they know that the instruction must be offered in one of the classrooms in the organization's physical facility or on a time schedule that is preordained. This historically developing process is recognized by virtually all adult education planning models by the principle that participants should be allowed to renegotiate the instructional design during its implementation (Caffarella, 2002; Knox, 1986). As one of the steps in his planning model, Houle (1996) explains what should happen when the design is put into effect: "In this process, what was abstract is made concrete; education becomes in its fullest sense a cooperative art. Much of the direction and content of the activity may be determined only after it begins, particularly in learning that is centrally concerned with problem solving or human interaction. In other cases, constant adaptation is needed to adjust to problems or opportunities. Often it is wise to have a periodic reinspection of purpose and format to see whether they need to be adjusted to changing situations" (p. 69). Indeed, this need for flexibility and responsiveness is not simply accepted, it is highly valued as a central planning principle.

Although planning models recognize the continual renegotiation of the instructional design throughout the actual event, a distinction is generally made between design and implementation (Caffarella, 2002). In the context of Cooperative Extension, Forest and Baker (1994) explain that "The justification for maintaining the element of program implementation as part of the planning process is primarily that the intended actions seldom match exactly those activities which actually happen in the community" (p. 98). Thus, they offer the advice to: "'Plan your work and work your plan!' An old axiom but still true. Unless all your planning guides your work, the planning has no value. . . . You need to 'work' your plan: reflect, review, and redo as needed. The plan guides activity; it should not reduce our obligation to be open, flexible and responsive to specifics as they unfold" (p. 98). We believe the distinction between design and implementation is misleading and actually masks the continual negotiation that occurs among planners, teachers, and learners. We consider the negotiation of the instructional design to be part of the planning process whenever it occurs, whether before or during the program. As planners engage in needs-assessment activities and the development of objectives, they typically also negotiate the many elements of the instructional design. This negotiation continues throughout the actual program as teachers and learners together either enact the instructional design or revise it to better meet their needs.

Program development models in adult education have offered a variety of ways to outline the many judgments that planners make in negotiating the instructional design (Caffarella, 2002; Houle, 1996). Rather than comprehensively reviewing all of these design elements, this chapter uses our planning theory to illuminate the ways that people make the key instructional judgments about content, format and methods, and instructional leaders. In the following three sections, we illustrate how people negotiate the development of these parts of the instructional design. In the chapter's final section, we offer guidance on how to nurture substantively democratic planning for the instructional design and implementation. In order to nurture democratic planning, it is important to pay attention to the interlocking dynamics of power relations;

stakeholders' educational, management, and political objectives; and the historically developing nature of instructional design.

Manage the Politics of Selecting and Organizing Content

In contrast to the widespread attention that the program development literature devotes to instructional formats and techniques, there is much less focus on how to make content decisions. This is due in part to the persistent view of adult educators as responsible for the *process*, not the *content* of programs. Sork and Caffarella (1989) identify this as an issue about "how adult educators should design the actual instructional process. There seems to be a constant pull between the content of instruction and the process of instruction. Should we as adult educators primarily be facilitators of the learning process, with the emphasis on helping learners become more self-directed? Or should we be more content oriented?" (p. 240). Although the planner and teacher may be the same person, content is often selected and organized by someone other than the planner. In these situations the planner is not knowledgeable about the content and thus defers these decisions to the teacher herself.

The planning stories provide three common scenarios along a continuum that planners face in negotiating the instructional design. At one end of the continuum, Cassie and Dougie planned and led the retreats and were responsible for all content decisions. The SVP story represents the other end of the continuum, in that Arthur had no background in the valuation professions and therefore relied on the instructors to select and organize the content. His contribution to content selection was to lead the instructor training clinic, which offered a structured process for making these decisions. The Phoenix program represents a middle ground, as Pete was both a planner and one of the instructional leaders at the retreat.

However, George was another instructor who helped to select and organize some of the content for the retreat.

Most of the planning literature on how to select and organize content suggests that the educational objectives should be the starting point (Knox, 1986; Queeney, 1995). However, planners face a basic problem: "Selecting the content—that is, choosing what will be learned during a learning activity—is a challenge because instructors can rarely include all of the material they would like to teach" (Caffarella, 2002, p. 172). Thus, when planners are selecting content, in addition to the educational objectives they must use other criteria, including the amount of time allocated to the program, the backgrounds and experiences of the participants, and what the instructor knows. Theorists also recommend that there is no one way to organize the content, suggesting a variety of criteria that come into play (Buskey, 1987; Caffarella, 2002). Primarily, these criteria are learners' knowledge and learning styles, the nature of the content itself, and teacher preferences (Apps, 1991). The literature offers many possible ways to sequence the content, including chronologically, as a progressive development of concepts from simple to complex, as a development of broad principles from a series of specific illustrations, or showing the application of simple concepts or principles to more complex situations as the program unfolds (Buskey, 1987).

Beyond offering a set of criteria, theorists also give a clear sense of the historically developing negotiations for selecting content. The selection and organization of content does not end once a course outline or lesson plan has been written; rather, teachers and learners are constantly negotiating the content to be learned and how it is organized. Although in some programs learners find the original selection of content acceptable, Apps's (1991) description of his teaching experience is more common:

> In my experience . . . I find that I am constantly reorganizing content as the course or workshop moves along. Several factors cause this. Certain topics take longer

than I have planned—participants have more questions, there is greater interest in the topic, or several participants have difficulty understanding certain aspects of the topic. Thus I am constantly making decisions about topics. Some topics I move to succeeding sessions, some I combine with others. I add new topics and drop others. As participants become more familiar with the content and with their own reactions to it, they will often ask for a modification of what is taught. (p. 108)

Cassie and Pete, along with most teachers, would resonate with how Apps describes this continual negotiation about selecting and organizing content.

When we understand that people, rather than abstract criteria, make content decisions, we can more clearly see the role that their educational, management, political objectives, and power relationships play in this vital planning activity. The selection and organization of content in the Phoenix story offers several examples of how planners and teachers continually negotiate about what content to include. Pete and Joan exercised their power to select the Executive Adventure firm to conduct the Thursday segment of the program. Joan provided the rationale for selecting the content of the Executive Adventure to meeting the educational objective of improving communication: "I had participated a number of times in an Executive Adventure program . . . what that does is, it immediately breaks down so many barriers because a lot of our department directors and supervisors work together everyday but they don't really know each other. They've never socialized, they've never been together informally. And this program does that and if we had one day basically to do a retreat, we need to break down those barriers and build that quickly and this to me does it faster than anything else I've ever done." In other words, this exercise would temporarily allow the learners to cross the borders created by organizational power relationships in order to meet the educational objective of improving communication. Joan goes on to explain how she would work with the firm to ensure that the content addresses the educational objective: "They will work with us, they do the same basic things but they will pull their things that do the best job of facilitating communication, which is what our goal is, and they will be sure, with facilitation after the exercise, that [communication] is stressed." This was a consensual negotiation between Joan and Pete, as they both agreed on the organization of content: "Based on our conversations, we felt this [Executive Adventure] was real crucial to do first thing and do it and let's move on quickly."

Their selection of the desert survival exercise as one of the activities for Friday shows that political as well as educational objectives also affect the selection of content. At the March 21 meeting, George suggested using the content learned from this exercise to meet the objective of team building. However, Pete and Joan both had reservations about this focus on an "abstract" problem instead of real company problems as the content for the Friday sessions. As Pete explained after the program had ended, "I really would probably redo the desert survival thing and spend more time dealing with the real issues. I'm really finding in practice that if you can deal with a real issue in your environment that it's just so much more helpful than dealing with a simulation in a desert." In spite of this reservation, Joan explained that their negotiation with George about the content also included a political objective to maintain a positive relationship with him. She explained that "from my perspective I was trying to delegate some to George, I was trying to let him have some autonomy and not just be so directive." By giving George ownership over some decisions, Joan hoped to create a collaborative relationship so other instructional design tasks might be negotiated more smoothly.

The selection of content for the SVP courses occurred at the intersection of educational and political objectives for planners, course instructors, and the organizational leadership. One of the primary political objectives of leaders within the organization was to influence the discipline's development as a profession, which they accomplished by controlling the content of the courses. In addition to deciding to inaugurate the *Fundamentals of Valuation* at the second PDC meeting in December, the committee members also agreed that each of the five discipline committees would be responsible for designing its own individual three-day course for the first program. This decision created planning tables for each course that were led by discipline committee chairs and included only members of the discipline committee. Given that SVP had never undertaken this level of program development, the selection of content depended almost entirely on who was selected as the first course instructors, which meant that quite different versions of content would often appear as "official course content," depending on who was the instructor. For example, the Business Valuation instructor for the first-level course was the same person for the first few years of the program. His design of the first course presented in April had met with considerable acceptance among his discipline peers, such that his version of the course became the "official" version. In other cases, several different instructors taught the first-level introductory real property course during its inaugural year, each with their own version of the course. Because the Society had yet to procure its own real property textbook or successfully establish an agreed-upon course content outline, the strategy of rotating instructors resulted in conflict about what "official" knowledge the Society was endorsing and promoting. This led to an ongoing struggle about what constituted actual course content, because for the first few years this often depended on the specific expertise of the instructor. Thus, it became common practice for only discipline chairs or discipline committee members to teach courses, because they were then able to control the content.

The struggle over controlling the content, based on political objectives, also played out at the program level. For example, the Personal Property Committee was the impetus behind promoting general valuation theory as the foundation for all the discipline courses in the new program. As a result, it was not just coincidence that the professor chosen to provide the content of general valuation theory in plenary sessions was not only the professor chosen to write the Society's new textbook on theory but also the director of a graduate valuation sciences degree program. However, while the idea of cross-disciplinary, "general" valuation theory was typically supported, most discipline committees each had a different version of valuation theory, depending on the academic and professional origins of their appraisal work (for example, personal property in the arts, machinery and equipment in engineering, business valuation in accounting). But even though there was general consensus regarding the need for valuation theory, each of the disciplines addressed that need differently, producing conflict at the program level that played out through the process of negotiating individual discipline course content. The selection of content for individual discipline courses, the overall program, and the course instructors were also about meeting the political objective to establish the profession of valuation science. Developing course content also helped members to achieve their political objective of gaining more power over decisions in the organization. When Arthur attended his last board of governors' meeting after three years, he was given an "official standing ovation" for his contribution. When he looked around the room of governors, he realized that a majority had been or currently were instructors in the new education program.

Manage the Politics of Selecting Formats and Instructional Techniques

Since as early as the 1920s—when Lindeman (1926) argued that adult education is focused on situations, not subjects—the field has claimed its identity through formats and instructional techniques that are problem centered rather than subject centered. Indeed, people often refer to "principles of adult education," by which they mean designing instruction that builds on learners' experience. The centerpiece of these principles is a horizontal relationship between teachers and learners—the basis for educational approaches that involve significant interaction among learners and between learners and a teacher. This suggests that a teacher would have a different role because she is "no longer the oracle who speaks from the platform of authority, but rather the guide, the pointer-out" (Lindeman, 1926, p. 160). So cherished is this principle that some would claim that instead of content, "at times the method is the message" (Fellenz, 1998, p. 372). It should be expected, then, that rather than focusing on negotiating the selection of content, "the largest single body of literature in the field is concerned with processes; there are many methods and techniques available" (Buskey, 1987, p. 117). Every book on program development pays attention to selecting formats, and entire books are devoted to an explanation of formats and techniques, as well as the criteria to be used for selecting the best "adult learning methods" (Galbraith, 1990; Seaman & Fellenz, 1989).

There is consensus in the program development literature that as planners decide on format and instructional techniques, they organize the relationships among educators and learners in order to achieve program objectives. Building on Verner's (1964) typology, Fellenz (1998) makes the distinction between format and techniques in terms of the scope of instructional design: "It [format] has commonly come to refer to the way learners are organized by the instructional agency. As such it is an administrative task usually the responsibility of the programmer. Techniques are the ways in which the instructional agent arranges the interaction between the learners and the content or material to be learned. This lies within the province of the teacher" (p. 349). In the Phoenix story, the format was a two-day retreat and the instructional techniques used in the retreat included the outdoor adventure activity on Thursday and the desert survival exercise on Friday. In the SVP story, the instructional format refers to the three-day course, and the techniques included instructors' use of lectures and case studies.

The format for the PI program included four two-day retreats, the listserv, and site visits to the teachers' classrooms. Various techniques were used (see Exhibit 2.2), including a "concept mapping activity" and the "critical friends' discussions." There is also consensus in the literature that, as with needs, objectives, and content, a program's format and techniques are continually negotiated by the planner, teacher, and learners "in order to come to terms with changes brought about by the desires and abilities of other people or the specific instructional resources available. . . . The methods used are not exactly like those in the lesson plan" (Houle, 1996, p. 42).

With the wide array of formats and instructional techniques available, planners are always faced with having to make judgments about which ones to use. Given the principle that "there is no one best way of assisting people to learn" (Sork & Caffarella, 1989, p. 240), planners have been advised to consider a variety of factors as they negotiate about this important dimension of the instructional design (Apps, 1991; Caffarella, 2002; Galbraith, 1990; Knox, 1986). The consensus about these factors is summarized as follows: "The talents of the teacher(s), the level and objectives of the content, the situational factors, and the varied personal, social, and cultural systems in which learners are operating must be taken into account if the right format for learning is to be selected" (Fellenz, 1998, p. 353). However, as experienced planners know, these abstract criteria often lead to contradictory choices, which are further complicated by people's political objectives and the power relations in the context in which they make those choices.

Each of the planning stories offers a window into the real-time negotiation of instructional formats and techniques, which can be marked by either consensus or conflict. In both the SVP and PI programs, the course format and the retreat format, respectively, were agreed upon by the planners and institutional leaders. For example, the SVP planners chose this course format because it had been widely used in programs offered by its competitor associations, and thus all who were involved in selecting the format for this new effort were in agreement. In the PI story, the retreat format had been successful in the two previous projects, and the negotiation around selecting it for the third project was highly consensual among the planners. As shown in the three planning stories, techniques—rather than the program format—are more likely to be renegotiated. For example, although the retreat format did not change in the PI program, Cassie and Dougie were constantly making adjustments to the techniques. As Cassie explained in Chapter Two, they had planned to conduct a "concept mapping exercise" during the first retreat but negotiated right on the spot that the group would be better served with a less intense activity. Thus, Cassie and Dougie negotiated a shift from one large group discussion to two concurrent ones, each led by one of them.

In contrast to these consensual negotiations about the selection of instructional techniques, more conflict appeared in the Phoenix program negotiations among George, Pete, and Joan. The two-day retreat format had already been negotiated with the president when George proposed the desert survival exercise as a technique to be used for a block of time on Friday. He presented this to Joan and Pete to address their educational objective "of working together as a team, particularly supporting others, leading in a positive manner, working cooperatively. In order to survive we have to work cooperatively and support each other, have to listen to other people's ideas, and they may be incorrect, but we're going to analyze that later. Why did someone with an incorrect solution or idea, why did his or her idea prevail? Why did they listen to you when you said 'we should save this rather than what I want'?" But more was at stake than simply whether to use this common, highly interactive instructional technique. As the three planners were discussing how to construct the small groups of eight to ten people, Pete suggested that "we might want to pull out our vice presidents to let them observe. I want them to be as involved as they can, but I wonder if in this kind of exercise it might be good for them to be floaters." He was deeply concerned that the vice presidents would dominate the

discussion and then, in the debriefing that followed, this domination would be named and seen as a problem in the flow of communication at the company. If the vice presidents were embarrassed by
being perceived as a source of the communication problem in the
company, Pete's political objective of increased recognition for
the human resources department would be threatened. George
responded to this concern, in an attempt to directly meet the educational objective, by explaining that "if they do dominate, I am
going to process it in such a way [as to ask], who dominated? Well,
the president did. Well, let's analyze that. I would rather have them
participate because they're members of the team, otherwise we're
having a dichotomy."

As Pete tried to resolve this potential conflict between meeting
the program's educational objective and meeting his political objective, he recognized the importance of the social position of the person who would lead the discussion. Joan and Pete clearly understood
that they could not lead the discussion of "who dominated" in the
desert survival exercise because of their place in the company's
power relationships. In contrast, George could lead the discussion
because he was from outside the company and therefore was not
part of those same political relationships. Pete ultimately decided
to include the vice presidents and the president in the small groups,
with a political analysis of the situation that suggested the educational objective was most important: "I started thinking, well damn,
I'm going to let him stick his neck out because then maybe we'll get
somewhere. Maybe it will happen and maybe he will do it. . . . I
think it gets us closer to confronting the issue that top managers
don't really feel they have to participate and follow some of these
expectations that we're trying to get them to. I think it's a very difficult thing, but what we have to do is to convince top managers
that they need to examine their own values." They made this decision knowing that George could handle this discussion without
embarrassing the vice presidents; as Joan explained, "[George] is
diplomatic enough that I don't think any one of them would be

threatened by it." Even with this safeguard, Pete recognized the level
of risk to his political objective in using this instructional technique,
and he planned to meet with the vice presidents before the retreat to
"give them instructions and say, 'OK, you are a participant, you're to
try to act as much a team player and as an equal as you can and not
intimidate and not try to have all the answers before anyone else has
a chance.' I'll go over the agenda with them and I'll explain their role
as diplomatically as I can." By telling them to "act" as "equal as you
can," Pete is seeking to protect them—and ultimately himself—from
any negative fallout at or after the retreat. Thus many factors played
out in selecting the desert survival instructional technique, including the educational objectives, the instructional leader's capacities,
Pete's political objectives, and the power relations at the company.

Manage the Politics of Selecting and Preparing Instructional Leaders

Leadership is vital in every human endeavor, and educational programs are no exception. Along with instructional formats, techniques, and materials, instructional leaders are the primary means
by which content is conveyed and learned in educational programs.
Indeed, decisions about these dimensions of the instructional design
are so interdependent that they must be made in reference to each
other. When selecting leaders who can help learners best meet the
educational objectives, there is a good deal of consensus about
the criteria: content knowledge, competence in the process of
instruction, responsiveness to learners' experience and culture, credibility, and enthusiasm (Caffarella, 2002). These criteria were
among those the planners in our three stories used as they selected
leaders. In the SVP program, for example, content knowledge was
an important criterion for identifying instructional leaders for the
five new courses. Mastery of educational processes can also be a criterion, as was the case when the planners selected George for the
management retreat. In addition, instructional leaders can be

selected because some aspect of the situation confers credibility on them, as when the planners selected Mr. Jones for the concluding presentation at the retreat. Cassie's role in the PI story is a good example of another type of frequently occurring situation in which "the planner of a program intends to become its leader, as when a teacher organizes a class. In such a case, this element becomes the starting point in constructing the format, influencing from the beginning all other aspects of design, including the objectives" (Houle, 1996, p. 202). The PI story also highlights the importance of the leader's social and cultural positionality, as Cassie, a White woman, negotiated a resolution to the wigger incident.

Given the wide range of settings in which programs are planned, "the selection and use of leaders in an adult education program is usually not a task of filling well-defined slots in a table of organization with people already trained for their work" (Houle, 1996, p. 202). Without this stable body of teachers to draw upon—as might be provided in formal educational settings such as schools—negotiating the selection of instructional leaders is highly sensitive to the power relations in the social and organizational context, the program's educational objectives, and stakeholders' political objectives. One key selection criterion that is used in practice, but which does not receive sufficient attention in the program development literature, is the leader's positionality in the social and organizational power structure (Brookfield, 2001; Hart, 2001; Tisdell, 2001). Planners need to understand that there are no generic instructional leaders "because the power relationships that structure our social lives cannot be checked at the door to the workshop setting. There is no magical transformation that occurs as teachers and learners step across the threshold of the classroom" (Johnson-Bailey & Cervero, 1997, p. 42). In some instances, the instructional leader's position in an organization is a critical factor in being selected. For example, Mr. Jones was selected to give the retreat's closing speech precisely because of his position as president in the company's power structure. Although Pete explained how "we gave him an outline, we assigned his speech" at the end of the retreat to tie together the retreat's discussion of communication in the company, the same speech given by George, or even Pete, would have had a much different meaning to the retreat participants. In other instances, a leader's positionality in terms of power relations based on race, gender, or class matters. For instance, Cassie, Jean, and Sonya's cultural locations as Black and White women mattered as they negotiated who might lead the discussion of the wigger incident at the third retreat. As this example shows, an instructional leader's positionality can be especially critical to a program's success when the leader is a major player in the ongoing negotiation of the educational program.

The SVP and Phoenix stories both illustrate the complex dynamics that planners face when selecting leaders to address both educational and political objectives. The selection of the instructional leaders for the five SVP courses shows that planners often attempt to achieve both objectives simultaneously. The instructors selected for the first course offerings in April not only met the criteria of having appraisal expertise and previous teaching experience, but also supported the president in his effort to create the program for the Society. The SVP story showed that the organization tried to build in policy stability by creating a succession of presidents who had agreed on the creation of the new program. Likewise, in forming the Professional Development Committee, the president tried to further cement this new initiative by appointing new discipline committee chairs or reappointing current chairs who supported the program. Since instructors came from this pool of committee chairs and members, a critical selection criterion was support for the new program. The Phoenix story also shows that political objectives are as important as knowledge and skill criteria. Joan described the telephone call in which she interviewed George to make sure "he understood our values and our objectives and that he would be flexible and do what we feel needs to be done." His alignment with their political and educational objectives was as important as was his fit with a second criterion: "someone who could be a facilitator, could do different exercises and help the group to realize the importance of good communication based on some of the experiences."

In addition to technical process skills, George brought credibility "because he had some maturity and some recognition in the community so that the president and the vice presidents would buy into" the program.

A common issue that planners face is whether to select an instructor who is internal or external to the organization conducting the instruction. There are a number of reasons for seeking an external person, including a need for specific expertise, short-term expansion of staff, or cost-effectiveness (Caffarella, 2002; Flannery, 1998). Power relations also play out in this decision; for example, "an outsider may have greater stature or be more credible than an insider" (Flannery, 1998, p. 461). There can also be political liabilities with an external instructor if that person has a conflict with the values and goals of the organizational sponsor (Munson, 1992). All of these criteria came into play as Pete and Joan considered hiring George as an outside consultant for the retreat. As we already discussed, they believed that George supported their goals and values in reference to the retreat and had the process skills they needed. Nevertheless, his biggest asset was that he was from outside the Phoenix Company. Although Pete and Joan believed they "could have done the whole thing" themselves, Joan concluded that "it was very good to have George there. I think he brought some credibility as opposed to the administration" (Pete or Joan, for example) leading a discussion on communication problems. George's positionality as a cultural outsider not only contributed to the educational objectives of improving team building and communication, but also to Pete's political objective of improving his own credibility and that of the human resources department. Pete explained that George's presence helped his own "credibility with some of the skeptics, with some of the top managers. There are a couple of people in that group who just don't think I've got it together at all. I've got some critics and that's one reason I thought to have a neutral person who has a good reputation, who Sam Jones respects."

Once planners have selected someone to be an instructional leader, it is often essential to "reinforce the efforts of such people in any way necessary" (Houle, 1996, p. 202). These efforts at formal and informal staff development occur at planning tables subject to the same political dynamics as the educational program itself. The SVP story shows these dynamics playing out in the traditional format of the instructor training clinic in which Arthur wanted to introduce the ideas of learning from experience and interactive techniques into the courses. He used the clinics not only to promote this vision but also to develop his own professional power in the organization. He ran the organization-wide instructor training only once because he quickly realized that (1) the differences among disciplines were greater than the similarities, (2) he could exercise more control over smaller groups (six to ten) than over large ones (twenty-five to forty) to promote experiential learning, and (3) it gave him face time with discipline leaders to develop more productive working relationships. For example, his success with getting the machinery and equipment instructors to try an actual case study was largely dependent on having hit it off with them early on. Having developed those working relationships in instructor training contexts, they were willing to consider his advice as an educator and try out these unfamiliar strategies.

Preparing Mr. Jones for the final speech at the retreat is an example of a more informal, but no less effective, means of preparing instructors. As Joan explained, "He really tied in the whole communication [objective] and how employees want to be communicated to. He did a beautiful job with pulling all that together." Pete and Joan felt it was important to prepare "some points for him to make" because "he is not a real good speaker, and he tends to ramble." However, the key to preparing the president for this instructional role occurred much earlier, at the retreat planning tables "in January, [because] we built this whole retreat around issues that were near and dear to him . . . communication and not having good department meetings. Because they were his issues, he was able to process everything we did and built it into his own words and from his perspective was able to give this kind of talk." There are many intersecting planning tables at which planners negotiate the selection and preparation of instructional leaders. Planners should pay attention to historical dimensions of these negotiations, stakeholders' educational and political objectives, and the power relations that shape and operate at these planning tables.

Democratically Negotiate the Instructional Design

The leaders of adult education have so consistently stressed the voluntary character of adult education programs that the planning literature has taken this as a bedrock principle (Knowles, 1980; Lindeman, 1926). This is seen as the single most defining characteristic that separates the context of program planning for adults from curriculum development for children in schools. The planning vision to involve all stakeholders, especially adult learners, in decisions about the instructional design is compelling. Kowalski (1988) explains the standard wisdom about the connection between this vision and the expected outcomes: "Most adult educators accept the idea that program planning is enhanced significantly by involving the potential learners in planning activities. . . . It stems from the beliefs that involvement creates a sense of ownership, helps build motivation, results in more relevant educational experiences, provides a democratic procedure that is valued by most adults, and even influences achievement" (p. 103). These preferred strategies for learners' involvement are recommended as essential to ensure a successful educational program. Knowles (1980) suggests that "the ideal situation is when a group is small enough for all participants to be involved in every aspect of planning every phase of a learning activity" (p. 226). He recognizes, however, that in most situations the planning needs to be done "before the participants assemble" and a planning committee should be appointed "that is as representative of the participant population as possible" (Knowles, 1980, p. 226). Another commonly prescribed strategy to involve learners in the instructional design is to use methods during the needs-assessment process to collect "information on the target population's preferences regarding, for example, delivery mode or scheduling" (Queeney, 1995, p. 213).

The strategies for learner involvement in the instructional design also recognize the historically developing character of planning, which is seen as "an iterative process—objectives, organization contexts, and evaluation mechanisms will change both during the planning and implementation phases" (Caffarella, 2002, p. 174). Because learners are always at a planning table as participants, planners and teachers have many opportunities for renegotiating the program once a program begins. Although some decisions are very difficult to change, such as the instructional staff or the location, other decisions can remain provisional until the actual learners have been involved. In terms of organizing content, for example, Apps (1991) makes this suggestion to planners: "For most classes and workshops, particularly in those areas where learners have some experience and have questions and problems, include their ideas in your organizational scheme. If you teach a five-session class that meets weekly, you might tentatively organize topics before the first session, and wait to organize more specifically after that" (p. 107). In sum, planners have two different strategies for planning instruction because "in some situations it is possible to involve learners or their representatives in planning and thus foster a collaborative approach. In other situations, educators must act alone, drawing upon their experience and knowledge of people to design the program and then being alert to adjust it to meet the realities encountered when embarking upon it" (Houle, 1996, pp. 45–46).

Even though these strategies may accommodate learners' involvement, unless planners address people's political objectives and the network of power relations that frame the negotiation of instructional design, negotiating it democratically becomes a hit-and-miss activity. Democratic planning is a framework for organizing power relationships in the decision-making process and thus must always address the objectives of many stakeholders, not just learners, in developing the instructional design. There has been some recognition that nurturing substantively democratic planning for instruction is not as straightforward as simply "involving learners." Kowalski (1988) stresses the point that "curriculum planning in adult education appears to be more open-ended than in traditional schooling. But appearances can be deceiving. An examination of critical variables which impinge upon planning decisions suggests that the programming of adult education may be less structured, but not necessarily less restricted" (p. 141). These contextual restrictions include political considerations, such as "gaining the approval of powerful executives," and management objectives, such as increasing a revenue stream. But an even more difficult problem in democratic planning is how to handle conflict in values or objectives. When developing the instructional design, "a recurring concern throughout program planning is dissonance in values among the planner, the organization, and society. Where such discord exists, conflict is apt to be intense and pervasive. Determining the content and sequence of learning experiences is a process quite vulnerable to this problem. Whose values should dominate? Whose needs should dominate?" (Kowalski, 1988, p. 146). Unfortunately, the discussion often ends here, and planners are told, "A pragmatic approach synthesizing all values and biases is advisable" (p. 146). Without a way to anticipate how power relations and political objectives are likely to affect the process of developing the instructional design, planners are left with few options when reacting to situations.

There is much more explicit attention to the impact of power relations once the instructional design is being implemented. By illuminating the positionality of learners, instructional leaders, and other stakeholders in socially and organizationally structured power relations—including race, class, gender, and sexuality (Brown, Cervero, & Johnson-Bailey, 2000; Hart, 1990, 2001; Horton & Freire, 1990; Johnson-Bailey & Cervero, 1998; Manglitz, 2003; Shor, 1992, 1996; Tisdell, 2001)—democratic planning, though still precarious, becomes more likely. There is a clear recognition that strategies must be rooted in an analysis of power, which means that the "leader cannot be a laissez-faire facilitator, exercising a minimum of control. Taking this stance only serves to allow patterns of inequity in the wider society to reproduce themselves automatically in the classroom. Instead, the teacher must intervene to introduce a variety of practices . . . to ensure some sort of equity of participation" (Brookfield, 2001, p. 221). These interventions to nurture democratic planning are often complicated because there are inherent tensions, necessary trade-offs, and outright contradictions that must be negotiated between educational and political objectives in contexts of socially structured power relations before and during the planning. Planners need to understand their own social and cultural positionality and that of learners and other stakeholders as they undertake these negotiations in consultative, bargaining, and dispute situations.

Given that Cassie was working in a consultative situation in planning the instructional design, she was able to make use of three specific strategies in working toward democratic planning. The funding agency, institutional leadership, planners, and instructors had interests that supported the educational objectives of the program. Therefore, her main challenge was involving learners in instructional design decisions. The first strategy, which is common to programs that are repeated, is to have the participants in a program evaluate their experience, making suggestions for a subsequent program. Cassie did this by using her prior experience with learners in another state as a basis for the instructional design of the first project in Georgia. She then conducted a rigorous evaluation of the first two projects that she had led as a basis for designing the third project. This evaluation involved surveys and interviews with the learners as well as other stakeholders, such as the administrators of the literacy programs in which the participants taught. In this situation, then, the learners from previous programs sat at the planning table as representatives of the learners in the current program. The second strategy builds on this by having learners from the current program be members of an Advisory Committee and thus be sitting at the planning table where at least some of the instructional design decisions would be renegotiated during the program. The third strategy is to use formats and techniques that build on learners' experience, thus bringing to life the content that is to be learned. Indeed, the actual content that is taught is often highly dependent on what is said (and not said) by learners and instructors during these interactive learning activities.

The early stages of the SVP story illustrate a bargaining situation, as Arthur sought to represent learners at the planning table in negotiating the instructional design. As noted earlier in this chapter, the dominant understanding of education was as knowledge transmission: instructors were the acknowledged experts who decided on what content to include and how it would be organized. In this sense, the instructors represented the learners at the table in negotiating the design. Given that Arthur was not an appraisal expert, he had little leverage to bargain with the instructors to have learners at the table, as these decisions were made before the courses began. His best hope was to convince the instructors to move from lectures to more interactive instructional techniques, thereby bringing learners to the planning table during the programs themselves. He had relatively little success with this in some disciplines (real property and business valuation) and more so in others (personal property and machinery and equipment). For example, he helped the instructors design a case study for the third course in the machinery and equipment series. The entire three-day course was then devoted to the analysis of the case. The instructors would present parts of the case with specific appraisal tasks, and the course participants would work in appraisal teams (much as they would do in actual corporate contexts) on each task. Participants had to produce an actual appraisal report of the case by the third class, and they spent the last part of the course presenting and critiquing their various interpretations of value. As the SVP story aptly demonstrates, a planner's positionality matters in seeking to nurture democratic planning. Especially in situations like this one, in which the planner is working within a network of power relations that do not abide by a democratic vision, it is critical to view the implementation of the instructional design itself as a planning table so that more opportunities become available to democratically negotiate its features.

Pete's positionality, in contrast to Arthur's, offered a great deal more leverage to democratically negotiate the instructional design. Not only did Pete fail to take advantage of this situation, but he chose instead to represent this as a dispute situation in which the learners should not be present at the tables where the instruction would be negotiated. He certainly could have used focus groups, written surveys, or planning meetings with the learners at the management and executive level to decide on the content or instructional formats or techniques. In fact, Pete had the president's "permission to involve participants in planning for our yearly calendar" of programs. But he consciously did not involve participants because "this retreat has been a real sacred cow . . . [the president] planned it and it was an opportunity for each vice president to outline what we are doing next year." He chose to exercise his power to "intentionally exclude Brad because I did not want his input. But I had the power and support to get around him." Pete also knew, based on his presentation of the retreat plan at a department meeting, that some significant number of participants were "real resistant" to the outdoor adventure. So he was very positive about George's suggestion to send out a preretreat survey to the participants so that it would "help warm them up and get some buy-in. Allow them to participate but not to dictate what we're going to be doing." In this dispute situation, Pete drew up sides, saying, "I see myself as representing top management and then focusing it for my values." On the other side of the dispute were the vast majority of employees at the company, who would not have any substantive role in negotiating this program that was intended to have an impact on their working relationships. Of course, the power relations at the company supported this because "the way we do things here is we generally don't think a whole lot about how people feel about participating; it's an expectation and if we think it's important then they think it's important." Thus Pete's response to George's suggestion to negotiate the instructional design more democratically is that this vision is not applicable because "he's not coming from a business. He's coming from a leadership development institute and we're running a business." Because of Pete's defining it as a dispute situation, the planning of the retreat ended up being more about the long-term political objectives of strengthening the standing of the human resources unit than about the educational objective of improving communication at the company. Ironically, the way Pete and Joan negotiated the instructional design reproduced the very problem of communication the retreat was intended to address.

Summary

There is no more universal injunction in the planning literature than to involve learners in negotiating the instructional design. As we have shown in this chapter, enacting this vision at the planning table is as complicated as it is important. As planners seek to democratically negotiate the instructional design, they need to anticipate the opportunities as well as the dangers at the planning tables where people make multiple and interlocking judgments. To do so, they first need to see that people will bring political as well as educational and management objectives to the table in making judgments about content, formats and techniques, and instructional leaders. Second, learners and other stakeholders have different levels of access to the planning tables at which people make these judgments, due to their positionality in social and cultural power relationships. Thus, abandoning the idea of a generic stakeholder (for example, learners, teachers, and planners) is critical to constructing planning tables where people can have a substantive impact on the instructional design. Finally, these opportunities and dangers also exist at the planning tables as the instruction is enacted. This historically developing outlook is particularly important because many aspects of the instructional design continue to be negotiated as the program occurs in real time.

Chapter 7

Negotiating the Program's Administrative Organization and Operation

A variety of administrative tasks must be completed in order to bring educational programs into existence. For example, most programs need to be financed (and therefore they need a budget) and marketed (and therefore they need a promotional plan). Knowing how to budget resources or design marketing is just as important as knowing how to survey needs or write objectives. However, naming these tasks is not sufficient to effectively organizing and operating educational programs. Being told what the tasks are is akin to entering a theater for a play, being handed a script, and then being told there are no actors or stage. Embodying the actors and building the stage requires us to locate a program's administrative dimensions in a world of power and interests, as we have done with other major tasks such as needs-assessments, objectives, and instructional design. In this chapter we focus on budgeting, marketing, and program location to illustrate how the technical aspects of program administration also have political outcomes. We explain how being in a marginalized political position frames this task of program administration.

Donaldson and Edelson (2000) critique structural-functional theory as a straitjacket that reduces leadership "to a form of management focusing on regularity and control" (p. 194; see Capper [1993] for a similar critique of educational administration in general). In structural-functional analysis, difference and conflict are "nuisances to be avoided, controlled, or managed so that a high level of efficiency and productivity can be achieved" (2000, p. 193). They argue that by ignoring the role of power, this understanding of leadership has "replaced vision with technique and moral purposes with best practices" and ask, "if power and moral dimensions are overlooked . . . then what is leadership?" (p. 195). Transcending the trait, behavioral, contingency, transactional, and transformational schools of leadership thought, they answer that leadership is better understood as a relational social process. Beyond the surface template of form and function, organizations are really "'informal,' relational, processual social constructions, produced through human discourses in localized contexts where power plays a central role in how and by whom discourse is created and accepted as rationalized projections of reality" (p. 197). Power-engendered relationships produce and govern organizational activity and interaction. Consequently, people develop, maintain, or alter these organizational relationships as they work the planning table.

Because "the effective use of power is an essential ingredient in leadership" (Donaldson & Edelson, 2000, p. 200), educational leaders do more than develop and enact procedures designed to avoid conflict and produce efficiency. They also create and convey socially constructed understandings and use power to establish "patterns of social discourses that should contribute to democracy" (p. 199). Donaldson and Edelson's arguments for democratic leadership "join the issues of power, agency, and marginality because . . . they are connected in our practice, if not in our literature" (p. 199). Their perspective helps make sense of much organizational leadership practice in a way that organizational charts of functions and authority cannot. Administering programs is not simply about seeking consensus, working collaboratively, and providing support. Those terms disguise the sometimes chaotic, always power-engendered relational work that leaders engage in to create organizational understandings and messages ("discourses") about their programs. Creating support for educational

programs by crafting coalitions and communicating messages to stakeholders about the program's meaning and purposes is an outcome of
relational work at the planning table. As planners work the table to
develop organizational relationships, they also work to develop their
power to make such messages heard. Planners work their messages by
working the planning table.

Revisiting Clark's (1956, 1958) notion of marginality explains
why planners have to work their messages. The description of adult
education as "marginal" had been percolating in the literature for
some time (Burch, 1948; Essert, 1951; Knowles, 1950; McClusky,
1950) when Clark penned his trenchant analysis of the marginalized
Los Angeles public school adult education programs as distillates of
an enrollment economy and a "cafeteria" curriculum characterized
by goal diffusion, tenuous student ties, and institutional drift. Such
a detailed interpretation of marginality should not diminish, however, its broader delineation of adult education as being peripheral
to and dependent upon organizations with other primary goals. Most
adult educators have a visceral sense of such second- or third-class
organizational citizenship. As Donaldson argues (in a separate voice
in Donaldson & Edelson, 2000), however, "The field's understanding of marginality has been primarily informed by functionalist
thinking" (p. 202). By reinterpreting the traditional understanding
of marginality, Donaldson rhetorically reveals why planners have to
work their messages by asking, "How, then, through what processes,
and as a result of whose agency have our administrative units
remained marginal while the adult education function has become
increasingly central?" (Donaldson & Edelson, 2000, p. 202). This
paradox of expanding opportunities and demands for adult learning
leaving in its wake a diminished call for adult education (Edwards,
1997; Finger & Asun, 2001; Usher, Bryant, & Johnston, 1997) represents a new form that might be termed *turbo-marginality*.

Even though Clark (1956, 1958) had established the centrality
of marginality for the administration of educational programs,

Brookfield (1986) still worried that organizational marginality might well become accepted by adult educators and other organizational decision makers as "the defining characteristic of adult education" (p. 228). Donaldson (in his own voice in Donaldson & Edelson, 2000) substantiates that worry when he argues that the language of marginality has indeed created adult education's reality: "The language of marginality also defines membership—that is, who belongs [or does not belong] to the marginal group, unit, or function" (p. 202). Donaldson's poststructuralist analysis of organizational life as the relational construction and interpretation of "narratives" (that is, the stories we tell ourselves and others about who adult educators are and what we do) shows marginality to be "about power." In order to "explore the place of power in defining" marginality, Donaldson charges educators "to be critical of our narratives, both locally and as a field, in order to inquire about the extent to which our own language reproduces marginal status" (p. 202). He points out that it should be known "whose discourse, both locally and distally, frames decision-making conventions and membership in decision-making bodies that impact our organizational realities" (p. 202). Recognizing marginality as partially self-constructed and partially imposed "habits created through discourse" (p. 197) encourages planners to ask, "What new narratives do we need to invent to change the discourse and in so doing innovate by redefining meaning and membership, establishing new patterns of social engagement, and regaining authorship of ourselves?" (p. 202). This view of organizational life, in which power "flows" like a current through networks of relationships (Foucault, 1977), forces educators to see how they "are both empowered and constrained by structures of meaning (including our rules of practice and conventions) and membership (who legitimately can participate in the organization and in decision making) we and others have created and will create" (p. 201). Planners work messages at the planning table to sustain support for their programs. But working the message can also enable planners to alter the practices, conventions, and relationships that they participate in and coproduce. In working the table, planners can change their access to and effect upon decision making that matters.

Marginality is understood as a self-constructed identity that contributes to reproducing adult educators' peripheral location in organizations. An awareness of marginality is useful for understanding not only planners' marginalized self-perception but also their actual location as "low" on organizational hierarchies of responsibility and authority. This view also provides strategies to change that location, perception, and capacity. Ask adult educators about their role in their organizations and the answers routinely returned are "I really don't have much influence on things," "I just do what I'm told," or "I really don't make any decisions that matter." Whatever the words, they are really saying that they have no real power to act meaningfully in their organizations—a perspective often voiced by administrative theorists: "Most adult education administrators have relatively little formal power compared with administrators elsewhere in the organization" (White & Belt, 1980, p. 230; see also Goody & Kozoll, 1995; Knox, 1991). Given such a widespread practical and theoretical perception, only a few theorists in adult education have addressed systematically the question of power (Beals, Blount, Powers, & Johnson, 1966; Brookfield, 1986; Donaldson & Edelson, 2000; Ingham, 1968; Jiggins & Shute, 1994). Although many tip their hat with a sideways glance to the awareness that power matters—with references to the need for collaboration, the importance of consensus, the effort to avoid conflict, and the awareness that superiors and stakeholders determine the focus and outcomes of adult education programs— power remains a "hallway" word that once spoken will typically stop any theoretical discussion of administration. However, understanding power is essential for seeing the conditions in which planners act as well as for changing those conditions—something the actions of the planners in our three stories well illustrate.

Theorists have tended to describe program administration as a disembodied phenomenon defined by the delineation of tasks. In this view, planners have no faces, just tasks; no stage, no actors, just script. Along with Giddens (1979, 1984) we reject the notion that organizations somehow exist independently of the people who construct and embody them. Planners act in their social and organizational settings to produce educational outcomes and, simultaneously, to maintain or transform their political relations with others in those settings. Thus, planners exercise power to represent interests as they work their messages at the planning table to create support for their programs. We use this perspective to show that as the planners in each story went about the seemingly mundane and technical activities of administering programs, they deliberately sought to alter both the social and organizational power relations and the discourses about themselves as planners. There are many operational tasks and decisions we could focus on (Courtenay, 1990); we choose to discuss how the "routine" decisions and tasks of budgeting, marketing, and managing program location present obstacles as well as opportunities for planners to promote their organizational messages and to renegotiate power relations in their social and organizational contexts. We conclude the chapter by addressing the possibilities of creating substantively democratic participation in these administrative tasks.

Finance the Message

Caffarella reminds planners "to recognize that budget management and other behind-the-scenes tasks are integral components of the planning process and serve as the driving forces behind program development efforts" (2002, p. 305). She lists such "critical details of the budgeting process" as estimating costs, creating contingency plans, conducting cost-benefit analyses, and managing budgets. As with many administrative texts, she provides principles, worksheets, and rules of thumb to help planners complete these essential operational tasks. Knowles (1950) provides sample budgets and cost accounting records from his long tenure as continuing education director at a Chicago YMCA, to serve as guides to and illustrations of projecting program costs and accounting for expenditures. Most administrative manuals have suggestions for how to prepare, manage, and analyze budgets (Caffarella, 2002; Galbraith, Sisco, & Guglielmino, 1997; Nadler & Nadler, 1987; Simerly, 1990). Such technical skills are important because knowing what a program costs or how much revenue it produces matters.

In the Phoenix story Pete notes at one point that he is more critical of the Executive Adventure part of the program because he knows "how much this is costing us." Yet there is a "big woops" after the program because neither Pete nor Joan had ever calculated the cost of (1) having more than sixty staff out of the company for two days, (2) paying for their travel and lodging expenses, and (3) financing the outside facilitators of George and Executive Adventure. When they finally did itemize the costs, well, they were more than surprised—so much so that Pete sent Joan to the president with the cost report because he was worried that the success of the program would be sullied once top management learned how expensive the retreat would be. The potential for political disaster was considerable. On the organizational chart (see Figure 2.3) Pete would appear to have the same capacities and responsibilities as other vice presidents. Yet Pete's power had historically been marginal to the other units of the company. One of Pete's major interests was to use the retreat to change that marginality. This was evidenced by Pete's contentious relationship with the executive vice president, his belief that other vice presidents did not think "we have it together at all," and his actions prior to the previous retreat, when he implemented the directives of the executive vice president rather than work with the president to develop those directives. The previous retreat and the new one represented, more than anything else, Pete's reworking of his relationship with the president in order to both increase his personal power and that of human resources. Whether Pete's focus was on assessing needs, prioritizing objectives, or organizing instruction, it was also about reshaping his political relationships with other organizational leaders (the president, the other vice presidents) and outside leaders (George). Pete intended to change these relationships to enhance his organizational power and to develop and convey the organizational message that management training should be experiential rather than directive. The planning of the Phoenix retreat illustrates an organizational leader's recrafting of his unit's marginal location in the company by redefining his working relationships with other leaders and by constructing, communicating, and enacting a new understanding of organizational development.

So why is the budget important? Although never systematically tallied until just before the program, the retreat budget was crucial for supporting the resources such as Executive Adventure and George as well as all the usual behind-the-scenes costs such as travel, lodging, food, and entertainment. That would be the usual response. But there is a more significant answer. The fact that Pete and Joan never did any cost projections, contingency planning, cost-benefit analysis, or even preliminary accounting for a program that could easily be described as a significant cost overrun, yet no one in the company raised so much as an eyebrow, speaks volumes about how successful Pete had been in renegotiating his power and the importance of human resources. If the retreat had not been so positively experienced by the senior management team, if Pete and Joan had not effectively reshaped their working relationships with senior management and the president, and if they had not significantly altered the expectations for and practices of the training unit, then such a "woops" could have produced even worse consequences than the disastrous start of the previous retreat. A mismanaged budget can cost people their jobs. Yet the cost overrun in the Phoenix story did not elicit even a whimper of complaint because the message Pete and Joan created with the retreat made it seem "worth it."

Financing lay at the heart of the SVP story because creating an educational program that would produce a new revenue stream for the Society was a chief interest of the education coalition. Even before Arthur was hired—with no official budget line for his position—financing the expanding activities of the Professional Development Committee had quickly become a costly endeavor. Funding a two-day PDC meeting, which typically required covering the travel, lodging, and other expenses of twenty to twenty-five people to meet in an urban business hotel, could cost $20,000 or more. Within the first months of the PDC's existence, the Society expended more than $50,000 (two PDC meetings plus directing the executive director to find and fund an education director) on a program that was barely imagined, much less actually producing income to finance itself. This was a considerable amount of financial commitment to an organizational change that was still encountering resistance. So financing the start-up activities of the program was contentious right from the beginning. In effect, the organization had to borrow from itself to create the opportunity to change its message (to convert the mission and goals of the organization to those of a teaching society) to its members, its public, and its regulators.

The costs of the PDC and *Fundamentals* courses became a point of conflict at the interim board of governors' meeting three months after Arthur's hiring. Recall the creative accounting incident from the story. When challenged about how to finance the costs by members of the budget committee, the Society's president responded by creating a $150,000 "income" category from book royalties that the Society did not yet have rights to and program revenue that did not yet and might not ever exist. Amazingly, the strategy worked because the projected expenditures for program development now were "balanced" by an "income stream." But politically this was a crucial moment in the Society's new educational program, for if the negotiations at the budget level had failed, then the lack of allocated funding would have stopped the planning. Losing funds for planning would have seriously restricted not only the educational program but the message of signaling the Society's transformation. But with the imagined income stream in place to underwrite

planning and start-up costs, the planning team's financing continued, and resources could be drawn upon to conduct the first program in April that the PDC had directed Arthur to organize.

Such financial juggling probably seems rather normal in a
business context, and it is important to remember that this was a
Society run by and for businesspeople. Understanding this event
from the marginality perspective provides a richer view of how crucial this initial budget conflict was for enabling the Society to
reconstitute its identity. The importance of this budget incident
stemmed from the resources that became available for the Society
to change how it understood its purpose (its narrative) and how it
conducted business (its discourses). On one level this imagined
budget line was about continuing to pay for meetings, air travel,
lodging, conference rentals, overhead projectors, instructor salaries,
and rental cars. On another level it was about how the formal allocation of resources enabled a demarginalization of the Society's
new educational efforts—literally moving them from a peripheral
(actually nonexistent, budgetwise) location in the organization to
a visible place as a formal budget initiative (the board of governors
voted on and approved the budget). With its approval, not only did
the PDC's power increase in the organization, so did Arthur's power
as the educational organizing arm of the PDC. Furthermore, it provided official sanction not only to plan programs but also for the
message that the Society was changing from testing to teaching.
Prior to any formal sanctioning and endorsement of the new educational program itself by the board of governors, the educational
program became real because it had a budget line. Thus the
approval of this initial budget line was an important indicator
that the Society actually believed the message about its new identity and mission.

A lesson typically learned early and never forgotten is the political power of the budget. Perhaps the most obvious example was the
power of the budget to completely stop not just the PI program but
its message and purpose of explicitly altering power relationships in

adult literacy staff development. The PI story shows planners creating messages that they intend to use to maintain or alter power relations. Not only is adult literacy education a routinely marginalized endeavor organizationally, so too is practitioners' staff development. Within such an environment there can be little doubt that a program focused on professional self-inquiry would seriously strain organizational tolerances because of the limited availability of resources to support more traditional forms of staff development based on expert-driven models. But Ron, as a high-ranking professor with many years of leadership for the staff development project, used his power and his working relationship with Cassie, with her years of practical experience and success in promoting and implementing practitioner inquiry, to develop an innovative staff development project that deliberately challenged the traditional power arrangements between university experts and literacy teachers. Cassie and Ron developed the program to promote the message that practitioners' experience and reflection are an important source of staff development. The entire program was designed to communicate this message not only to the participating practitioners but also to the sponsoring organization itself. Even though the program's demise was ancillary damage from the cancellation of contracts for other staff development programs, it was still the budget, or its rescission, that did the damage. Budgeting matters—not just in getting the numbers right but in getting the politics right as well.

Market the Message

Adult educators have long known how important marketing programs can be. But there has always been a tension between what planners presume about adult learners and why planners need to market programs. Bryson (1936) names the tension clearly: "It is part of our theory of adult education that men and women take part in it because of their own felt needs," but he quickly cautions that "the administrator who is promoting a program cannot safely rest in the belief that the adult or his [sic] community will come to him of their own accord" (p. 119). The tension is between the idea of felt needs and the oft-repeated view "that people do not know what they are interested in," that "people are not always the best reporters of their own permanent interests" (pp. 122–123). Consequently, "promotion is necessary" (p. 119). Knowles is also clear that "no program will succeed that is not interesting to the people it is meant to help" but offers the same "caution . . . don't take their responses too seriously" (1950, p. 179). Both Bryson and Knowles are heeding Lindeman's (1926) injunction that adults can and should determine their own learning needs, but because of their practical experience Bryson and Knowles know that the principle of learner-centeredness alone does not fill seats. Educators often need to market their programs to ensure participation.

By 1958, however, Clark was becoming quite critical of what he calls an "orientation of a service agency . . . formed around and defined by unmediated responsiveness to clientele" (p. 6). Clark describes adult education as a "cafeteria" in which "the short-run need for clientele, set by the enrollment economy, strains against the long-run need for respectability as the basis for legitimacy. Agencies in the field are torn between a service character and a school orientation" (p. 10). And there the debate between felt needs and marketing more or less remains. The primary justification continues to be the standard marketing mantra that promotion is about "ensuring participation" because the most important marketing task is to "communicate a message that this program is useful and meaningful to potential participants" (Caffarella, 2002, p. 316). While occasionally repeating the cautions learned earlier, most discussion focuses on the mechanics of marketing borrowed from the business professions (Kotler & Fox, 1985). For example, the fact that some programs fail is sometimes laid at the feet of planners because they have not marketed effectively enough so that potential "clients" will know where they can satisfy their needs—a case Beder (1986) makes in promoting the "Four Ps" of marketing (product, promotion, place, and price). Caffarella (2002) presents a comprehensive overview of marketing purposes, techniques, and checklists (see Caffarella's references for other sources of marketing principles and techniques; see also Galbraith, Sisco, & Guglielmino, 1997; Knowles, 1980; Kotler & Fox, 1985; Nadler & Nadler, 1987; Simerly, 1990). We should point out that Caffarella adds, "It is crucial to communicate well to other publics, such as sponsoring organizations, funding agencies, and the general community the value and importance of the planned program" (2002, pp. 316–317; see also Kotler & Fox, 1985). Although theorists focus on marketing principles and techniques, marketing is just as much political as technical because it is also about crafting "narratives" and "discourses" that "sell" programs not just to clienteles but to other stakeholders as well. Thus marketing is also about power and marginality.

Marketing is often assumed to be more necessary in market-driven settings such as university continuing education or continuing professional education and less so in intraorganizational staff development contexts like that in the Phoenix story. Yet internal marketing was a significant dimension for creating a new organizational message about human resources and for altering political relationships framed by the marginalized status of the human resources unit. Recall George's repeated efforts to get the learners involved in making decisions about what the retreat would focus on, as well as his promotion of participatory management. When George tried to get Pete to survey what managers thought of communication practices in the company, Pete sidestepped him by suggesting that they send out an article about the retreat's objectives about communication in order to get the managers "thinking our way." Another example is Pete and Joan's series of informal talks with the president and the other vice presidents about the importance of participating in the retreat as team players so that the experiential learning techniques would work. So even in a situation with no need for a formal marketing plan because the audience was captive

("We're pretty directive here," Pete reminded us), it was still crucial to work the message of how the retreat should operate. As Pete said, they wanted "buy-in"; Caffarella (2002) notes that the key to obtaining buy-in is communicating a message of importance. To promote the retreat's objective of focusing on communication, Pete excluded George's interest in participatory management. A question of who would participate in determining objectives was changed into a problem of promoting the objectives that the president had already endorsed. By converting a question of objectives to a question of marketing, Pete exercised his power to say whose needs mattered as well as to communicate the retreat's message to the stakeholders. Communicating that message to the participants would make his interests more influential at the company—that is, he demarginalized his position through formal and informal marketing of the retreat objectives.

Arthur faced a different situation. The new *Fundamentals* courses would need to be successful in a highly competitive market in which other appraisal organizations already had recognized educational "products" for sale. To compete in this market, Arthur believed that SVP would need to create an educational program that developed a competitive reputation because it was a good *educational* program. Thinking educationally was not what this Society was used to doing, but they were good at thinking in marketing terms. So he used marketing strategies to plan the courses. At its December meeting, the PDC directed Arthur to organize the Society's first presentation of new courses for the following April. However, there were no courses designed, no textbooks selected, no course exams prepared, no instructors decided upon, no site selected, no fees established, and no instructor salaries agreed upon. These were all essential administrative tasks, yet Arthur and the PDC had all that to do and more. And, of course, there was no marketing plan.

Among these many operational demands, Arthur had to negotiate two major issues to get the first *Fundamentals* program organized and delivered. He had to get the instructional aspects of the new courses organized and he also had to get the appraisal public's attention about the availability of these new courses. Recall that at the December PDC meeting each discipline committee began developing courses by assigning committee members to specific course preparation tasks. Arthur sent out a memo after the meeting requesting each course designer to send him course objectives, course descriptions, instructors' names and qualifications, and a "what's-in-it-for-me hook" for publicity. Receiving no responses, he tried again at the governors' midterm meeting in January and again by memo after that, still to little avail. By then it became clear that he would only be able to develop the promotional materials by taking advantage of the already planned instructor training session held in March. Several members of the education coalition, including the PDC chair, the Education Committee chair, and several discipline committee chairs had decided that part of changing the Society's orientation meant doing more than offering courses. It also meant emulating other societies' educational activities, one of which was to require instructor training for SVP course instructors. But even though the Society did indeed need to "train its instructors," it needed more urgently to get courses designed and promoted. So Arthur used the March training clinic for those purposes.

It is not unusual to have major administrative functions overlap or "bleed into" each other as the course design, instructor training, and marketing did in the SVP story. Indeed, there are clear practical connections among those three, although they are theoretically treated as discrete tasks. Nonetheless, Houle (1972) long ago noted this simultaneity in planning programs, at which effective practitioners are skilled; Caffarella (2002) presented this as the key dynamic in her interactive model. In current vernacular, such multitasking is consistent with administering large educational endeavors.

So what did marketing, with its attendant issues of course design and instructor training, have to do with creating messages, demarginalizing education, and altering power relations in administering the SVP *Fundamentals* program? In terms of creating "new narratives . . . to change the discourse" (Donaldson & Edelson, 2000, p. 202), consider how the discourse of marketing—well understood and practiced by the Society members as businesspeople—enabled the course designers and instructors to develop courses. The discourse of marketing was used to create a discourse of education. By responding at the instructor training clinic to Arthur's request for course information to be used in promotion efforts, the course designers also began to determine what the objectives and content would be. All the discipline committees had agreed at the December PDC meeting to organize their curricula, but as of March very few had done so. Consider also that in an organization in which professional preparatory education was traditionally marginalized, Arthur was actually considered to be primarily a logistics manager and conference planner. By getting the course developers to think educationally by thinking about marketing, Arthur began altering his power to act as an educator in the organization. Arthur's attempts to change what the PDC and others thought of as managing program delivery to designing the program educationally was one of his first major efforts to change those power relations, those "habits of discourse." As with the budget at the interim governors' meeting, the complex interplay of marketing, course design, and instructor training helped to change the overall message of the new program to the organization itself, the appraisal education consumers, the regulatory agencies, and the general public: continuing and certifiable *education* (not just testing) was crucial to promoting a message of professional confidence and public trust. By using the discourse practices of business to promote educational discourse practices, Arthur altered his power in the organization by working educational tasks and issues, not just managing program logistics. Enabling Society members to develop their courses as educators helped to create the larger organizational message of shifting from testing to teaching.

In such a commercially competitive market, publicizing and promoting the valuation courses was a constant issue because the program's success depended in large part on producing an income stream regardless of whether it was educationally effective. As Arthur organized the marketing for each new phase of the overall valuation program, he would add or alter policies about many operational aspects, including enrollment, exam schedules, grade reporting, costs, and attendance requirements. After three programs had been presented by the end of the first year, Arthur designed a complete schedule of locations, costs, curricula, and instructors for the entire second year of the program. Produced for wide distribution, a year's schedule of programs was meant to signal SVP's expanding presence in the appraisal education market. Although a major promotional publication was necessary, it was risky because the organization was still unsettled about this change in identity. At the urging of a governor who was also a program instructor, the education chair proposed a resolution to the board of governors that this promotional brochure be sanctioned as the official definition of program curriculum and participation policies for the *Fundamentals of Valuation*. It was a bold move. The adoption of the resolution officially endorsing the brochure as a statement of the program and its educational policies accomplished three things. First, the governors' endorsement meant that education was now a legitimate mission of the organization; previously only the budget had been so endorsed, not the program itself. Second, this endorsement sent a message to the membership, the public, and regulatory agencies that the Society had officially reoriented its mission from just testing to include teaching. Third, again as with budgeting, marketing helped to move education to the center and away from the periphery of the organization. A marketing tool had become policy that changed relations of power and organizational identity.

Use Program Location to Work the Message

Planners know that arranging and managing the delivery and presentation of programs, often referred to as "logistics," is important. Because program logistical management can be quite overwhelming, there are many checklists for ensuring attention to every delivery and presentation aspect, from the minute to the major (Caffarella, 2002; Knowles, 1980; Nadler & Nadler, 1987; Simerly, 1990). Indeed, it seems that there may be no end to the nightmares of operational details that can disrupt a program. For example, in one SVP program, as Arthur hurriedly surveyed the classrooms on the first day, he noticed that the tables and chairs in one classroom were quite uncomfortably arranged, but he thought there wasn't enough time to rearrange them. An experienced instructor showed up just minutes before the class was to begin, quickly sounded the alarm, and got Arthur to rearrange things to be more conducive to adult learning. Planners have long known that technical details such as room arrangements are crucial to establishing what is often referred to as "climate" (Knowles, 1950, 1970, 1980). Logistics are about climate, and much more. Beyond getting the climate details right, there are also opportunities in managing logistics, because through them the impression, the message, the meaning, and therefore the identity of the program can be created (or lost).

In this section we focus on one logistical detail: program location. Seemingly only a technical detail and routinely delegated to support staff, the task of locating programs is really about creating program messages and establishing program identity. Pete and Joan met with the president and discussed at length where to locate the retreat—in town or out of town? Pete had already discussed this issue with certain vice presidents prior to negotiations with the president. Why were *they* talking with the *president* about where to locate the program? Because it mattered in constructing the message and identity of the retreat. Removing the retreat from the company site itself to a conference center was intended to alter the normal patterns of interactions in the company. Experiential learning would be more effective because of the more relaxed environment. In such a setting, the normal power relations of the company could be temporarily suspended in order to achieve the retreat goals without any real alteration of power back in the company itself.

In the PI story Cassie and Dougie believed it was important to shift the location of one workshop from the conference hotel on the first day to a rustic retreat on the second. Why did that matter? Because it presented to the participants a particular message about the purpose and identity of the program. The new location signaled a change in state of mind. As with the Phoenix story, by shifting the location the planners altered the identity and message of the program. In all three stories, program location signaled important messages to participants and other stakeholders. As these examples show, locating programs is just as political as any other planning task. We have discussed (Wilson, 2001; Wilson & Cervero, 2003) what is broadly termed the "politics of place" to argue that there is a "politics of identity" to locating programs. In this section we use the SVP story to illustrate the implications of politics of place and identity in program administration. The seemingly low-level logistical decision of selecting program sites actually produces important outcomes about identity, messages, power, and marginality.

In the SVP story, program location was intricately enmeshed with producing the reoriented mission and identity of the organization— but not without conflict. At the time of SVP's entry into the appraisal education market, there were several other organizations marketing well-recognized programs. Given that such appraisal education was largely conducted in a business context, there was a standard model of program delivery and location: typically, concentrated courses of approximately five days, almost always conducted at business hotels and resort conference centers in major urban centers or vacation destinations throughout the country. Among the many messages signaled by such locations was that such endeavors represented successful businesses or they would not be able to afford to locate programs in expensive places. Some SVP leaders felt that their educational program should follow this strategy in order to indicate their business stature as well; historically they had located their annual conferences in such locations. Others, however, believed the SVP courses should not be located in expensive business conference sites. These PDC members were also involved in establishing a graduate degree of valuation science, and the organization itself had had an interest in establishing advanced degrees for some time. As appraisal was an unlicensed profession, the only official endorsement of professional competence was voluntary membership in an appraisal organization or advanced degrees in ancillary professions such as engineering, business, economics, or art. This group believed that a more productive route to establishing higher valuation as a profession lay in the well-established practice of locating the study and training of professions in higher education (Larson, 1977; Schon, 1983). Therefore, they wished to locate their appraisal courses on college campuses and arrange for participants to earn credit (through continuing education units) that could be used in a graduate program they had established at a small liberal arts college.

By locating its programs on college campuses rather than in business conference centers, SVP was trying to link its educational endeavors to higher education. If that association was to be established, it would suggest an academic and professional legitimacy not just to SVP's courses but to the profession of valuation science itself. So the location directly represented a specific construction of identity that could deliver a message to appraisers, the public, and the regulatory agencies: a message that appraising was a legitimate profession—like accounting, law, architecture, engineering, medicine, or others located in higher education—and therefore entitled to regulate itself. The major professions have long established the power to regulate their work by locating themselves in higher education, by educating a select few, and by requiring testing and licensing in order to practice. SVP sought the same route and result because up to that point appraising had been more of a quasi-profession. Nearly anyone could practice appraising because experience, rather than training and certification, enabled people to value property. Thus, locating the program physically and symbolically on college campuses was an attempt to move from the professional margins to the mainstream. Some SVP leaders believed that if the training of professional valuators could be established as requiring advanced study in higher education and professional society certification through testing, then the profession would develop more power to conduct its work. So the location of SVP programs was a major issue from the very beginning because it was a key to establishing an identity of professional legitimacy. During Arthur's tenure the programs were routinely (although not always) located on college campuses or their continuing education conference centers and were academically associated with a valuation science degree program. After Arthur's departure and as the overall valuation program became more successful, it increasingly emulated successful business by locating programs in high-end resorts and business centers.

Democratically Administer Programs

When program administration is framed solely around technical tasks, there would appear to be no need to carry out those tasks through a substantively democratic process. However, an ethical commitment is always enacted because these tasks also have political outcomes. Because democratic participation has always been on the field's philosophical agenda (Bryson, 1936; Lindeman, 1926), it is not surprising that theorists in the 1950s and 1960s were particularly emphatic that adult education should be administered democratically (Beals, Blount, Powers, & Johnson, 1966; Brunner, Wilder, Kirchner, & Newberry, 1959; Essert, 1964; Hallenbeck, 1948; Knowles, 1950; Liveright, 1959; Mathews, 1959). Knowles eloquently and forcefully proclaims what he calls the "group process" planning of adult education as "a laboratory for democracy" in which "people may have the experience of learning to live co-operatively" (1950, p. 9). He argued that there is no better place to learn democracy than in group-centered leadership: "The foundation of good organization . . . is a democratic philosophy"—which "means that policies will be determined by a group that is representative of the participants. It means that there will be a maximum of participation by all members of the organization, that there will be co-operative sharing of responsibility" (p. 169). He follows with principles to define representative committees because committees are a major tool of democratic process in organizations. Essert (1964) claims that "the final approval over any phase of operation in adult education in public organizations should be placed by law as close to those affected as feasible" (p. 192). Brunner, Wilder, Kirchner, and Newberry (1959) proclaim that "there is practically unanimous agreement in all studies that the maximum involvement of potential and actual constituents in program building produces the best results" (p. 133). Although the rhetoric cooled in the 1980s and 1990s, the adherence to democratic philosophy remained intact (Brookfield, 1986; Donaldson & Edelson, 2000; Donaldson & Kozoll, 1999; Howard, Baker, & Forest, 1994; Jiggins & Shute, 1994; Knowles, 1970, 1980; Waldron, 1994). The central credo of this prolific discourse is to involve people in decision making about matters that affect them—a not-at-all-extraordinary directive and one centrally representative of American popular notions of democracy. Involving people in decision making comes with essentially one practice prescription: be collaborative. Knox, for example, defines the essence of administration as establishing procedures for collaboration and "gaining agreement on desirable goals and contributions to goals" (1991, p. 220; see also Donaldson & Kozoll, 1999; Knox, 1980).

But something has gone awry in these prescriptions of collaborative decision making: democratic practice has resulted in planners continuing to reproduce their own marginality. Brookfield captures the problem: "the chief element missing in my own professional preparation . . . was the awareness that adult education programs were created in political situations, were open to alteration as a result of political decisions, and were dependent on a favorable political climate for continuance" (1986, p. 228). Although Brookfield notes that this political dimension to adult education is "rarely acknowledged," there are frequent asides about the political dimensions of planning, as if theorists' practical experience were seeking to find voice but had no way to express that experience. For example, Essert argues that adult educators are better able to do their work "only if there is complete understanding of these objectives by the administrative heads" (1951, p. 175). Clark says the "acceptance" of adult education depends upon "principally those with power" (1956, p. 60). Brunner, Wilder, Kirchner, and Newberry (1959) warn that planners often "neglect essential differences among neighborhoods" because they too seldom realize the "fact that socio-economic factors have a very real influence on the effectiveness of programs" (p. 133). These whispers of insights continue (Goody & Kozoll, 1995; Robinson, 1970; Smith & Offerman, 1989; White & Belt, 1980), but never as more than practical asides—as if there is concern that, if spoken too loudly, they might sully the dominance of structural-functional administrative theory.

There have been a few attempts to think more systematically about power in adult education administration theory. Beals, Blount, Powers, and Johnson (1966) discuss the role of power in planned social action for community change. Ingham (1968) chides adult educators for failing to draw upon organizational theory and introduces a view of power in administration drawn from organizational sociology. Although noteworthy, such attempts are primarily functionalist interpretations with only limited insight for working real planning tables. Most theories are bereft of any mention of power, and the exceptions allude to power only as a force that influences planning or as a commodity that planners lack. It is rare for anyone to discuss power as Jiggins and Shute (1994) do with anything other than euphemistic allusions. As Donaldson and Edelson observe, "We believe a major part of the field's problem with power is its general absence in our literature" (2000, p. 200). Part of the reason for this sanitizing in adult education lies in the theoretical insistence upon rationalized scientific problem solving as the basis for administrative action (Wilson & Cervero, 1997; see also Chapter Nine)—hence the continuing invocation of "collaboration" as the central practical action of planning. The real problem with prescriptions for collaborative, rational decision making as the basis of democratic program administration is that such prescriptions embody democratic principles only in highly selective conditions. Collaborative prescriptions for participatory decision making are likely to be conducive to substantive democratic involvement primarily in situations where stakeholders share highly consensual interests. For example, when Pete, Joan, and Mr. Jones gathered around the planning table, their negotiations were quite collaborative because their interests were nearly consensual, despite the power imbalances. Nearly all prescriptions for collaborative strategies presume consultative situations.

Consultative strategies aren't effective for handling bargaining or dispute situations in which interest conflicts and power imbalances make a difference. Although George attempted to collaboratively negotiate the instructional strategies of the retreat with Pete, he was unsuccessful because their interests were different and their power relationships were asymmetrical. The real irony of the Phoenix story is the lesson of how power, when unchecked by an ethical framework of democratic principles, reproduces the interests of those with greater power. Because of the high confluence of interests, Pete, Joan, and the president easily agreed on the company problem: an ineffective flow of information. George, representing a democratic stance of promoting participatory decision making, attempted to question the problem definition but was ultimately neutralized by Pete. Nearly all of the action in the Phoenix story, from deciding on location to determining the audience to financing to instructional design, can be interpreted at one level as carrying out a series of administrative tasks. But the full range of actions at the planning tables is only visible through a political lens. That lens shows the conflicts and the effective use of power to maintain the dominant interests of the company's leadership.

Likewise, in the PI story, much of what Cassie, Dougie, and Ron planned and implemented can easily be interpreted in traditional administrative terms. Those terms leave unintelligible, however, the wigger incident, which participants at first ignored, only later reluctantly coming to understand that they had to address such "unpleasantness." Cassie struggled about what to do throughout this protracted planning incident. Because of her commitment to participatory practices and her power as a workshop organizer, Cassie negotiated the beginnings of a resolution between the protagonists. Managing this dispute would have been a major objective if the group were to have met again.

Collaborative decision making is not a universal planning strategy, for it is effective only in highly consensual circumstances. In the face of power, consultative decision making is wishful thinking and a self-marginalizing practice. Adult educators have prescribed this one response to power for so long (from Essert, 1951, and Knowles, 1950, to Donaldson & Kozoll, 1999) that they have been disempowered by this marginalizing discourse. Although collaboration is highly admirable for promoting democracy at flat planning tables, it is hardly helpful in addressing the power dynamics that most planners face at the uneven tables in their everyday practice.

Summary

Planners play many roles by working on organizational philosophy and vision and resource allocation. We address this in Chapter Nine, in which we develop the view of planner as strategic organizer in the struggle for knowledge and power. In this chapter our focus has been on specific administrative tasks necessary to organizing the noninstructional dimensions of educational programs. A colleague once described financing, marketing, and program location as rather black-and-white decisions, suggesting they typically are uncontroversial and routine. We have used this chapter to show how such seemingly technical tasks are always also about power.

Administrative tasks have political outcomes because they provide venues for planners to "work their messages" as they work the planning table. The need to communicate their message and to reshape political relationships is essential because the acquisition of resources to organize and operate educational programs is marginalized in many social and organizational contexts. Getting other stakeholders to understand and support that message is a major outcome when planners complete administrative tasks.

Chapter 8

Negotiating the Program's Formal and Informal Evaluation

There is virtually universal agreement that program evaluation is a political process (Brookfield, 1986; Knox, 1986). This political awareness is much more evident than for any other planning activity, perhaps because there are clearly evaluative judgments that people must make about the program. This awareness may also have developed because planners have paid attention to their experience in the real world, in which "every adult education program is a unique psychosocial drama. The cast of characters will never be exactly the same from one program to another, and the publicly stated reasons for conducting an evaluation may bear little relation to the private agendas possessed by the actors in the drama" (Brookfield, 1986, p. 266). This is why Chapter Five urged planners to pay attention not only to stakeholders' educational and management objectives, but to their political objectives as well. As a response to these conditions, many evaluation theorists (for example, Ryan & DeStefano, 2000; Weiss, 1986) suggest that "no evaluator would offer up an evaluation that did not at least pay lip service to the notion that stakeholders and their interests ought to be included in an evaluation" (Mathison, 2000, p. 85). Theorists have also highlighted the conflicted relationship that planners have about their obligation to conduct a formal evaluation. Program evaluation is seen both as a necessary activity essential to effective planning as well as an activity that produces more feelings of guilt, inadequacy, and frustration than any other planning activity (Knowles, 1980).

As an essential activity, planners have received a great deal of advice about conducting evaluations for program improvement and accountability (Boone, Safrit, & Jones, 2002; Caffarella, 2002; Knox, 2002). The scope of program evaluation has broadened considerably since Tyler's (1949) conception, which focused solely on the achievement of a curriculum's educational objectives. Most understandings of formal evaluation now focus on producing evidence about a wider set of issues that decision makers face, including, but not limited to, the educational outcomes. One widely used definition, for example, explains that formal program evaluation is "the systematic collection of information about the activities, characteristics, and outcomes of programs to make judgments about the program, improve program effectiveness, and/or inform decisions about future programming" (Patton, 1997, p. 23). There is so much emphasis on program evaluation that it has now taken on a life of its own outside of the planning process, with its own resources in adult education (Boulmetis & Dutwin, 2000; Fenwick & Parsons, 2000; Knox, 2002; Ottoson, 2000) and in education and social sciences more generally (Kellaghan & Stufflebeam, 2003; Patton, 1997).

In spite of this focus on evaluation as necessary for effective planning, there is plenty of hand-wringing by planners about the value, need, and feasibility of actually conducting formal program evaluations. A typical reaction from practitioners is: "'Program evaluation: Why bother with it? Why is it important?' Often times among action-oriented practical Extension professionals, these are the reactions and questions when the topic is raised" (Forest, Brack, & Moss, 1994, p. 177). These doubts about the value of formal evaluation contribute to a lack of systematically collected evidence for many programs, and when it is collected it is often in the form of "smile sheets" that simply ask learners about their reaction to the program (Caffarella, 2002). Many reasons are given for this, such as the perception that "evaluation is just plain hard to do" (Boone, Safrit, & Jones, 2002, p. 194). The explanations that planners offer for not conducting formal evaluations fall into four groups: (1) many important outcomes from educational programs are not measurable; (2) evaluation cannot actually demonstrate that the program "caused" the outcomes, so why bother with the effort; (3) evaluation costs too much in terms of time and money when compared with other planning tasks that "must" be done; and (4) decision makers often cannot or will not take action on the basis of the evaluation results (Caffarella, 2002). Recognizing the paralysis that planners often feel when faced with the expectation of conducting a formal evaluation, Houle (1996) counsels planners to do the best they can given the situation: "Whenever possible, data . . . should be collected from the beginning of the educational activity. . . . While it is useful to have many kinds of evidence to provide for the balanced appraisal, only as much measurement should be undertaken as the situation allows. Otherwise evaluation becomes an end in itself, which may be appropriate in research investigations but which distorts its proper purpose in most educational activities. Sometimes the concept of an exquisitely refined assessment of achievement is so daunting that it keeps educators from doing any evaluation at all" (p. 232). While this advice may be comforting to planners, it does not offer an analysis of the causes of—and, therefore, potential solutions to—the paralysis they experience.

If planners are to take practical action, they need to move beyond feelings of guilt, inadequacy, and frustration in their stance toward program evaluation. This chapter offers an approach to practical action that connects formal evaluation to the judgments that stakeholders make about programs regardless of, and often in spite of, such an evaluation. Our approach is built upon three enduring realities. The first was expressed in Chapter Five, in which we urged planners to articulate the program's political objectives as well as educational and management objectives. Second, we urged planners to recognize that people will continue to hold their own educational, management, and political objectives even if they are not on a publicly shared list. Finally, the fundamental point about program evaluation is that people will make judgments about whether these various objectives were achieved through the program, regardless of whether planners provide evidence as part of a formal evaluation. Indeed, there is universal agreement in the literature (Caffarella, 2002; Deshler, 1998; Forest, 1976; Forest, Brack, & Moss, 1994; Grotelueschen, 1980; Houle, 1996; Queeney, 1995) that "informal evaluation is going on all the time. Some kinds of judgments are being made continuously about the worth of the program. Participants are constantly making complaints or paying compliments. Teachers and leaders are never without feelings about how well or how poorly things are going. The directors of programs are sensitive both to these judgments and to their own feelings" (Knowles, 1980, p. 203). Of course, there are times when planners need to collect evidence as part of a formal evaluation. Even when planners conduct a formal evaluation to assess the objectives, however, they must recognize how this process intersects with the ongoing judgments that people make about the achievement of their educational, management, and political objectives. Although people sometimes use the results of the formal evaluation to make these judgments—particularly about the educational and management objectives—they generally use a wider range of evidence to judge the worth of the program, particularly in relation to their political objectives.

Everyone who writes about evaluation (Forest, Brack, & Moss, 1994; Houle, 1996; Tyler, 1949) is resolute that "evaluation is more than just a process for providing data. Rather, the essence of evaluation, as defined . . . in much of the literature, is making judgments about the value or worth of a program" (Sork & Caffarella, 1989, p. 241). This is precisely the point we made in Chapter Four about needs-assessment. At the heart of needs-assessment is making judgments, which may or may not be informed by evidence collected to make those judgments. As with needs-assessment, planners can conduct a formal evaluation by which they intentionally provide evidence to people who have a stake in the program. However, they should not lose sight of how these activities intersect with the informal evaluations that people are making at the same time (Forest, 1976). Therefore, the purpose of this chapter is to provide the conceptual tools to negotiate the development of a program evaluation, which includes an understanding of how these activities intersect with the full range of evaluative judgments that stakeholders make about an educational program. There are three interconnected elements at the heart of program evaluation: what is evaluated (objectives), how it is evaluated (using criteria and evidence), and who evaluates it (whose judgments matter). The first section addresses the importance of using people's educational, management, and political objectives as the focus of the program evaluation. The second section explores the politics of the evaluation process, specifically in relation to the collection of evidence and the criteria people use to make their evaluative judgments. Third, we discuss how power relations frame whose evaluative judgments about these objectives matter. Finally, we discuss the challenges and opportunities that planners face in nurturing a substantively democratic approach to negotiating the program evaluation.

Evaluate Programs Based on Educational, Management, and Political Objectives

The three planning stories offer commonplace examples of how formal evaluation as it is often conducted in practice makes a small, and relatively insignificant, contribution to people's judgments about a program's objectives. Although the planners in each story administered surveys as part of the formal evaluation, this evidence primarily addressed the learners' judgments about some of the stated educational objectives. Arthur administered a survey to learners, asking about their reactions to the course content and process.

He also surveyed the instructors, asking them to self-evaluate these same dimensions. Based on this evidence, he wrote a formal memo to each instructor and course designer that provided specific rec-ommendations and "elements to think about in the revision process." Pete and Joan asked the learners to complete an eight-item survey to gather their reactions to the achievement of the educa-tional objectives "related to communication and department meet-ings" and the retreat processes. Cassie spent the last forty minutes of each retreat session on evaluation, with participants completing a survey about their reactions to the two-day program and dis-cussing what could be changed for the next meeting. As valuable as these formal evaluations might have been to assess the achieve-ment of some educational objectives, they failed to provide evidence regarding other stakeholders' judgments about the educa-tional objectives or the management and political objectives. Although these planners no doubt recognized that stakeholders evaluated their multiple objectives using either a wider range of evidence than these surveys or no evidence at all, they probably conceived of the surveys as the sum total of the evaluation. This bifurcated mind-set is not only politically naïve but also program-matically ineffective. Given the twin realities that "all programs are being evaluated continually by many people related to them" and that "informal evaluations are used to make decisions" (Forest, 1976, p. 173), planners need to base the evaluation on the full range of stakeholders' objectives. Therefore, the evaluation should be framed around the programmatic pivot of the educational, management, and political objectives, regardless of whether they are formally stated. Although there are some common issues in addressing these different types of objectives, each also presents its own challenges.

There are several challenges in using educational objectives as the basis of the program evaluation, the first being which ones to use. In contrast with the typical situation for management and political objectives, planners often have some stated educational objectives that could serve as a basis for evaluation. For example, the PI program had objectives for each retreat, and the Phoenix management retreat had four educational objectives that served as the foundation for the formal evaluation. Thus, Cassie could judge the worth of the first retreat in reference to the objective "to help teachers find researchable problems for their projects" and Pete could assess the retreat's objective "to develop skills in handling difficult questions, conflict, and confrontation when conducting a meeting." However, challenges arise because there are many programs that have only "teaching objectives" as opposed to "learning objectives." A good example is the management retreat objective, "to provide skill building opportunities on 'How to Conduct a Meeting.'" An evaluation of this objective would simply determine that opportunities were provided, not that any learning or change occurred. To provide a better basis for evaluation of educational objectives, Pete could have reshaped the objectives to focus on knowledge, skill, or organizational change outcomes.

Another challenge is that programs often do not have formally stated educational objectives, as illustrated by the SVP planning story. This is a very common situation: although "the critical first step [for a formal evaluation] is specifying objectives for the program . . . getting these statements back from programmers is often a difficult task" (Forest, Brack, & Moss, 1994, p. 181). For example, Arthur asked the course designers at the January interim governors' meeting to provide him with objectives for the upcoming April courses. Receiving no response at the meeting, he followed up later in January with a memo asking for the information. Again receiving no response, he incorporated writing course objectives into the March instructor training clinic.

A third challenge is that educational objectives can change during the program, as illustrated in the PI story. As Caffarella (2002) points out, "Program processes and even outcomes may need to be negotiated throughout the program, which in turn makes the evaluation process both more complex, and yet also more realistic"

(p. 228). For example, the wigger incident presented Cassie and the participants with the opportunity to add the educational objective of challenging racially organized power dynamics in the third retreat.

Perhaps the most difficult challenge for planners is the fact that stakeholders have multiple educational objectives, only some of which are formally stated. In Chapter Four we showed that people have many needs in relation to a program, which are then reduced in the priority-setting process central to the negotiation of objectives. For example, the primary educational objective for the management retreat was "to increase the awareness of the importance to the Phoenix Company of communicating as a team member." We have already seen that George's educational and political objective was to promote participatory management at the company, which was much more ambitious than "communicating as a team member." Mr. Jones was clearly not interested in participatory management. Rather, he saw a need for the retreat based on the problem that hourly employees would regularly tell him, "we don't know what's going on; our supervisor doesn't answer our questions." The managers and supervisors, who made up the retreat's primary audience, were not aware of either of these objectives. Although they were informed of the planners' objective about team building, the participants had their own hopes about the retreat's educational outcomes, which never received any formal expression. This is fairly common, and indeed, "often the learners' objectives are different from those stated in the program, or those of the instructor" (Forest, Brack, & Moss, 1994, p. 181). Arthur offered one strategy for handling this situation when he evaluated the SVP courses in terms of learners' own personal objectives, asking, "How successful do you feel that you were in accomplishing your objectives in taking this course?"

Management objectives for a program are critical because they "identify the things that will be done to improve the quality of the institutional resources for meeting educational needs" (Knowles, 1980, p. 124). We gave many examples of these in Chapters Five and Seven, showing that program objectives often have to do with matters such as adequate physical facilities for the program, the revenue stream for the program, collaborative relationships with other institutions, selection and training of teachers, and the quality of materials and technology for the program. The single biggest challenge in evaluating management objectives is the fact that they are generally not stated and therefore not subject to formal evaluative processes. As Knowles (1980) points out, these objectives "tend to be more implicit than explicit. For example, I do not believe I have ever seen 'to achieve a balanced budget' in writing in a list of instructional objectives, but everyone understands that it exists. Perhaps one of the bonus benefits of formulating evaluative questions is that many of these implicit objectives are brought to the explicit level" (1980, p. 205). Of course, stakeholders continually evaluate the achievement of a program's management objectives even when they are not formally stated. For example, planners and institutional leaders often evaluate a program based on its revenue or profit, either because that funding source is needed to support the program or because the "profit" from the program fees is used to support other institutional functions and services.

As shown in the SVP story, the Society leaders clearly judged the worth of the five new courses based on how much profit was made to support other Society functions and how many new members were recruited to the Society. Consequently, no limit was set on the number of people who could enroll in the SVP courses. Another example of evaluating management objectives is that the Professional Development Committee members, believing that instructor training was essential for the program's success, offered the clinic in March just prior to the five separate discipline courses in April. Although only a cursory formal evaluation was conducted, using a learner satisfaction survey, Arthur and the PDC members used other informal forms of evidence to continually evaluate the success of these clinics in preparing new course instructors.

The PI story provides a dramatic example of the importance of evaluating the management objective of "achieving financial support for the PI program." The evidence used to assess the achievement of this objective was continually collected in the form of receipt of grant funds. As is often the case, Ron and Cassie paid attention to this management objective only when new evidence, in the form of the nonrenewal letter, threatened the program's very existence. Often program evaluations are made at the intersection of educational and management objectives, as shown in the Phoenix story. Pete did not simply evaluate participants' learning in Thursday's Executive Adventure activities, but rather assessed the learning in relation to the cost. Because of this, Pete was "more critical" because "I was painfully aware of the cost. . . . I kept saying: Is this worth the money, are they doing a better job, and what's happening here, is the group getting the benefit of this?"

While some evaluation models stress the importance of evaluating management objectives, there is significantly less focus on the need to evaluate stakeholders' political objectives. This is unfortunate because, as we have shown throughout this book, people seek to achieve many political objectives through the educational program. Therefore, the primary challenge here is recognizing these as worthwhile objectives to address as part of the formal evaluation process. These objectives are suggested in some of the more expansive approaches to program evaluation, such as when Grotelueschen (1980) advises evaluators "to consider the totality of program variables including general program description, explicitly stated program goals, program states, and the central concerns for and about the program" (p. 77). Knowles (1980) also suggests that attention be paid in the evaluation to the "organizational climate and structure" where it is important, for example, "to assure participation of all relevant parties in policymaking and management of the adult education operation" (p. 206). Although Knowles identifies an important objective in this example, it is fairly bloodless in comparison with many other stakeholders' political objectives. What makes these objectives difficult to evaluate is that they are often considered agendas that people wish to keep hidden. Given the recognition that stakeholders will always evaluate the program based on their political objectives, the primary decision for planners is whether it is possible or desirable to include these in the formal evaluation.

Political objectives were vitally important in all three stories and were evaluated by multiple stakeholders, although none were part of the formal evaluations. In the SVP story, political objectives for organizational change initiated and drove the *Fundamentals of Valuation* program. The Society was clearly expecting these courses to change the organization from a testing to a teaching society. Another political objective was to position the Society favorably if the federal government used continuing education as a basis for mandatory licensing. None of these objectives was part of the formal evaluation, although the Society leadership did informally monitor their achievement.

Cassie and Ron informally evaluated the achievement of their political objective: "to maintain the long-term relationship with the State Department of Education." Although they did not write down this objective or include it as part of the formal evaluation, it turned out to be central to their evaluation of a program outcome when the relationship was threatened. When the possibility of the program's cancellation arose, not only were the educational objectives put at risk but more important, the long-term relationship that would support future programs was also in jeopardy. In contrast to the PI program, at Phoenix Pete was much more explicit about the retreat's political objectives, although they also were neither written down nor formally evaluated. Pete spoke openly about his political objective to improve the standing of the human resources unit, thus transforming his political relationship with the president and other vice presidents. Consequently, Pete's political objective of maintaining a positive relationship with the president was at least as important as the educational objective of solving a communication problem when planning the 1992 retreat. As explained in Chapter Five, this objective was very much on his mind as he evaluated its achievement after the retreat, saying that "I think we have taken a pretty big step. I think we have their confidence, and I think the VPs know that we have some skills and some background in this area that they probably don't have, and that's kind of a nice position to be in. . . . We have laid a foundation to build upon, and that's what is exciting, because you gotta have that before you can move forward, and I think at this point now, if we build on the momentum that we've got, then the sky's the limit." Because the informal evaluation of political objectives is important, we recommend that planners put an explicit focus on these alongside the educational and management objectives in the formal evaluation process.

Manage the Politics of Evidence and Criteria

Once planners have identified the three types of objectives against which programs are evaluated, their next task is to negotiate the evidence and criteria that people use to make their judgments. Caffarella (2002) explains how the interlocking relationships among objectives, evidence, and criteria are central to people's judgments about the worth of an educational program: "Judgments about programs . . . are reached by comparing results of the data analysis with the criteria that were set (or emerged) for each evaluation question or objective" (p. 256). Political and technical considerations regularly intersect as planners negotiate the program evaluation around two key factors: (1) the criteria people use to judge the achievement of an objective and (2) the evidence people use in making those judgments. In making judgments, stakeholders use many forms of evidence as well as criteria that often are not explicit, particularly in their informal evaluation. One reason that judgment criteria can be implicit is that planners often fail to distinguish between objectives and criteria. Houle (1996) discusses the necessity of making this distinction: "Criteria of evaluation are suggested by the objectives; some people would argue that the two are interchangeable. But 'to learn the basic principles of economics' is related to but different from 'to learn the content of a specified textbook on economics.' The second establishes a criterion for the decision as to how well the first has been accomplished" (p. 217). Planners also need to be aware that the evidence upon which people base their judgments is much broader in the real world than in research textbooks. Even in relation to the formal evaluation, "the type of data you collect will be determined by . . . stakeholders' motives and purposes. Some will demand rigorous evaluation and others will be more satisfied with anecdotal data and description" (Forest, Brack, & Moss, 1994, p. 184). This variation in acceptable evidence is also influenced by stakeholders' values because evaluation "is more than mere data gathering, [as] values are reflected by the indicators used—standardized test scores, verbal testimony of program participants, or the criticism of a program observer" (Grotelueschen, 1980, p. 77). Other political considerations can influence decisions about evidence, as Brookfield (1986) explains: "Stakeholders are those individuals who have a stake (an investment) in securing a favorable evaluation for a certain program. They will attempt to provide the evaluator with information that shows the program is successful and is accomplishing the goals for which it was established" (p. 265).

There are many sources of advice about producing evidence for formal evaluations, particularly for educational objectives. Sork and Caffarella (1989) offer the standard set of procedures: "The next steps in the evaluation process include determining the evaluation design, planning the collection of data, specifying the data analysis procedures, and establishing evaluation criteria. The most widely used means of collecting evaluation evidence are written questionnaires, tests, interviews, observations, product reviews, and examinations of organizational records" (p. 242). Other authors offer practical strategies for the overall evaluation design and data collection (Boulmetis & Dutwin, 2000; Caffarella, 2002; Knox, 2002), evaluation for program improvement (Deshler, 1998), evaluation of program failures (Sork, 1991), evaluation of learning outcomes (Fenwick & Parsons, 2000), and theory-driven evaluation (Rogers, Petrosino, Huebner, & Hacsi, 2000; Russ-Eft & Preskill, 2001). Program evaluations are also informed by Kirkpatrick's (1994) framework for four levels of evidence (see also Caffarella, 2002; Cervero, 1988) that "represents a sequence of ways to evaluate programs" (p. 21). The levels are focused on participants' reactions to the program, their learning, their behavior change, and results that occur because of their behavior change.

As helpful as these strategies can be, there is a relative lack of advice on managing the issues that arise at the intersection of technical and political considerations that planners face in producing evidence. In conducting a formal evaluation of educational objectives, there is some recognition that political issues such as resource constraints "often force program planners to choose a less than ideal design and methodology" (Sork & Caffarella, 1989, p. 242). Of course, what is ideal is dependent on political considerations. For example, because the cost and difficulty of measurement increases in moving from reaction to results, planners are advised "to check with stakeholders on whether this extra preciseness is required" (Forest, Brack, & Moss, 1994, p. 180). However, managing the politics of what counts as evidence in the informal evaluation process, particularly for management and political objectives, usually is planners' greatest challenge. As Forest (1976) points out, "informal, grapevine feedback and pressures from other people influence [stakeholder] decisions at least as much as the data we can present. Let's not fight the natural inclinations of people; let us instead be part of the reality and encourage more of it" (p. 174). This advice that stakeholders will use many forms of evidence to make judgments shows that political considerations often overshadow the technical quality of the data collection processes, so that "any information on program merit contributes to the evaluation process, aiding an administrator deliberating between alternatives" (Grotelueschen, 1980, p. 80).

The Phoenix story illustrates this point, as Pete and Joan managed the politics of evidence in evaluating the retreat's educational objectives. On the one hand, they took care in the technical design of the eight-item survey to formally evaluate the educational objectives. The evidence produced by the survey was at Kirkpatrick's (1994) first level, as the items asked participants about their reactions to whether the objectives were achieved. On the other hand, there was much more evidence being produced outside of the bounds of the technical survey design. They intentionally produced some of this evidence when Joan asked her staff to "get some feedback for us. So they have been talking to supervisors, and they sincerely appreciated the opportunity to be there and have a chance to meet and interact with people that they talk with over the phone but they never really had a chance to work with." Stakeholders often make judgments using evidence that planners cannot manage. Pete's lack of control over evidence in stakeholders' informal evaluation did not have negative consequences because participants' reactions to the retreat were very positive. Pete said that "all the vice presidents that I've heard from felt that we really accomplished the objectives." In fact, the executive vice president called Pete "just to say how well it went and how he enjoyed it, and how he had been around the company today and people came up to him and started a conversation, that he had never said anything but hello to before the retreat. He thinks it has really let down some of the barriers and opened up new communication, which he thinks is very valuable. Mr. Jones said it was excellent—that 'we did an excellent job' I think were his words." In contrast to this positive outcome, Pete's lack of control over evidence might have had negative consequences if Mr. Jones was using behavior change as the criterion of success. Mr. Jones saw a need for the retreat because employees expressed their frustration that supervisors were not communicating important information. The planners translated this need into the educational objective of improving communication at the company. It is likely that the evidence Mr. Jones could have used to judge the retreat's success is that since the retreat, hourly employees no longer complain about this problem in their monthly meetings.

When it comes to managing the evidence about a program's political objectives, the stakes are as high as the evidence is anecdotal. A central problem is that those objectives are rarely publicly stated and thus only informal evaluations can be done. Joan used anecdotal evidence from comments she received from the managers to judge whether the retreat accomplished the political objective of strengthening the role of the human resources department. She believed that now "we've got a united, focused group. And I don't think we had that before. So what we're hoping is that we're going to use this kind of as a stepping stone toward just a whole more supportive, united management training program." As explained earlier in the chapter, Pete used anecdotal evidence of comments from the vice presidents to conclude that the retreat had a positive impact on his own political standing in the company.

At SVP, the political objective for the new educational programs was to transform the Society's mission from being a testing society to being a teaching society. Although this major political objective was not formally evaluated, the Society's leadership was constantly judging the worth of the program in relation to this objective. The evidence that stakeholders used to make these judgments consisted of membership increases and increased applications from those wishing to be teachers for the program. Perhaps the most telling evidence people could have used to judge the success of this objective is that after three years the majority of the Society's elected leadership had gained organizational visibility through teaching in the program.

Managing the politics of the criteria that people use to judge an objective is an extraordinarily delicate task, because those criteria are inescapably based on stakeholders' values about what counts as having achieved an objective. There is no empirically based way, for example, to determine what counts as a passing score on a test of participants' learning. Rather, this determination "involves identifying and clarifying the bases for judging the data. These criteria are explicit statements of our values and expectations, and imply that all outcomes of the evaluation process are underlined by the values of those involved in the evaluation regardless of the accuracy or objectivity of the measurement" (Forest, Brack, & Moss, 1994, p. 177). When conducting a formal evaluation, there is an opportunity to publicly negotiate the criteria so that the ones "chosen indicate the level of learning or change that is considered acceptable" to all stakeholders (Caffarella, 2002, p. 233). In some situations "where the criteria cannot be predetermined, a process for how criteria will eventually emerge [should be] outlined" (Caffarella, 2002, p. 233). In these cases, planners can start with individuals' criteria that can be made public and then negotiated to ones that are agreed upon by all stakeholders. A final issue that adds to the complexity of managing the politics of criteria is that "as an activity proceeds, original criteria may change, some being altered or abandoned and others added" (Houle, 1996, p. 218).

Planners often do not have the opportunity to use these strategies for setting criteria in formal evaluations because stakeholders use privately held criteria to judge the educational, management, and political objectives. This was the case in all three planning stories. One form of evidence that Pete used in judging the first objective, "to increase the awareness of communicating as a team member," was that departments would request follow-up workshops on team building in their own units. Although he may have had a criterion for the number of departments requesting a workshop that would have allowed him to judge the retreat a success, he never made this public. Two key management objectives of the SVP courses were that Society membership would grow and that the courses would generate a profit to use in supporting other Society activities. However, there were no publicly stated criteria for how many new members or how much profit would be required to judge the courses as successful in meeting these objectives. Pete and Joan expected the Phoenix retreat to achieve the important political objective of increasing support for the human resources function at the company. In saying "we're not where we need to be," Joan implied that they had not quite reached the criterion of success. As mentioned in the section on evaluating programs based on educational, management, and political objectives, Pete identified the less rigorous criterion of simply laying a foundation to build upon. It is likely that the planners used this lower criterion, because they certainly judged the retreat a success in terms of the political objective.

Anticipate How Power Relations Frame Program Evaluation

While managing the politics of the evaluation process, planners must remember that evidence and criteria do not evaluate programs—people do. As Forest (1976) reminds planners and evaluators, "extensive data do not represent the value or worth of a program. We need to take our cues from the existing, pervasive, informal evaluations. These most prevalent, and thus more powerful, evaluations do not seem to need tables of data and computer printouts for making judgments. These informal evaluations by participants, funders, politicians, and other decision-makers are causing much frustration among data collectors and researchers" (p. 173). This focus on people making judgments explains why program evaluation is fundamentally a political process framed at the macro level by who is at the planning table making evaluative judgments and at the micro level by the political dynamics that occur at the table. By influencing which stakeholders are at the table, power relations play a central role in determining whose evaluative judgments matter about an educational program. This insight has resulted in the advice that planners need to know their audience for a formal evaluation (Caffarella, 2002; Grotelueschen, 1980). Although this is an important strategy, it is incomplete unless tied to the wider vision of whose judgments really matter about a program. In this section, we discuss the specific strategy of stakeholder-based evaluation as framed by the power relations in social and organizational settings.

The universal advice (Caffarella, 2002; Mathison, 2000) for planners conducting a formal evaluation is that if results are to be used in decision making, then they need to consider "who are the main audiences for the evaluation report, and what issues concern them that your evaluation could address" (Knox, 1986, p. 165). This is known as "stakeholder-based evaluation" (Weiss, 1986), suggesting that anyone who has a stake in the program is a potential audience for the evaluation. In this approach, "The key to evaluation payoff is to identify stakeholders, know their values and expectations, and design evaluations according to their agenda, values, purposes, criteria, and intended eventual use of the evaluation" (Forest, Brack, & Moss, 1994, p. 179). The central strategy, then, is to be able to identify the people who are making evaluative judgments about the program and to learn what matters to them. Just as when negotiating the needs and the objectives for the program, it is necessary to identify the groups of people who have a stake, such as participants, learners, teachers, financers, planners, institutional leaders, legislators, and the public (Cervero, 1984b; Forest, Brack, & Moss, 1994).

Although there are always multiple stakeholders for formal evaluations, most efforts typically "focus on only one audience while attempting to accommodate others as much as possible" (Grotelueschen, 1980, p. 96). This practice of targeting primary audiences was evident in all three stories as the planners designed the formal evaluation for some, but not all, of the major stakeholders for their respective programs. The teachers and learners were the primary audiences for the PI evaluation, which focused on how to improve the educational processes for the retreats. The planners and teachers were the primary audiences for the SVP evaluation, which also focused on improving the delivery of instruction for the courses. The planners themselves were the primary audience for the Phoenix evaluation, which focused on participants' reactions to the retreat processes and outcomes. Pete and Joan expected to use the responses to work with departments in the company requesting follow-up activities that could foster improved communication in their units. The planners in all three programs did not explicitly consider stakeholders with the greatest amount of power—such as the institutional leadership and funding sources—as the primary audiences for the formal evaluation. As we have discussed throughout this chapter, however, there is often a serious disconnect between the formal and informal evaluation activities as stakeholders judge the worth of a program.

Although all three programs were formally evaluated, the planners had a much broader view of who was at the table where evaluative judgments were made about the program. Their informal evaluation activities were consistent with the advice of Hood (2000), who speaks to the importance of the relationship between power and evaluation: "The contention that evaluation cannot be separated from institutional and social structure should not be whispered but rather shouted in the evaluation community" (p. 80). The planners recognized that the organizational power relations at SVP and at the Phoenix Company positioned the people in the leadership structure as the ones whose evaluative judgments mattered. As discussed in the previous section, Pete was especially attentive to the president's and vice presidents' judgments about the worth of the retreat, much more so than any other single participant. Likewise, Arthur was more concerned with the evaluative judgments made by the Society's president and the chair of the Professional Development Committee than those made by any particular learner. Viewed from the perspective of the overall evaluation effort, not simply the formal part, the primary audiences were composed of those stakeholders in social and organizational positions of power.

Political relationships play out at the table as stakeholders deliberate about the purposes of the formal program evaluation. Politically astute planners recognize that formal evaluations are used for many purposes other than to enhance program quality or judge program impact. Indeed, evaluation textbooks offer the clear recognition that "some purposes of evaluation could be viewed as manipulating the decision-making process. It could be used to justify a decision already made. It might be used as a technique for postponing decisions. It might be used as window dressing with no intent of the results ever being used" (Forest, Brack, & Moss, 1994, p. 179). The planners in all three programs did intend to use the evaluation results, so their formal evaluation activities could not be characterized as window dressing. Cassie used the evaluations at the end of each retreat session to adjust and improve future sessions, Arthur used the evidence from learners and teachers to improve future courses, and Pete used evidence from the managers to determine follow-up programs. However, planners and other stakeholders often conduct formal evaluations either with no intention of using the results for decision making or without a plan for how they will be used to inform decision making about the program. When a formal evaluation is being done for window-dressing purposes only, the stakeholders at the table still make their judgments about the program, and do so through informal evaluation activities.

Whereas calling an evaluation "window dressing" suggests it simply won't be used, stakeholders have other purposes for evaluations that are less benign. Stakeholders also use their power to negotiate at the planning table for evaluations that will support a particular outcome. Knowing this, "some people who plan programs may not want to make judgments about their programs or have others make those judgments. This stance is especially true in environments where no matter what the data show, evaluations of any kind are seen as punitive or are used primarily to advance political or personal agendas" (Caffarella, 2002, p. 227). These agendas can include supporting the continuation of the program, expanding important dimensions of the program, or eliminating or significantly altering a program. The formal evaluations for the programs in our three stories were not used in these ways, because the planners were seeking to improve their understanding to strengthen future programs. However, when a formal evaluation "is done to justify decisions (even if not admittedly), its motive is usually political. Evidence is gathered to support a political decision already made but not necessarily revealed. The evaluation outcomes are not only dictated a priori but the processes are also directly influenced. . . . an evaluator might be selected who was biased against the program" (Grotelueschen, 1980, p. 122). There are numerous ways that people can use their power during negotiations at the planning table to influence the evaluation outcomes, including the selection of an external evaluator to direct the formal evaluation activities. As evaluators come to the planning table, they become political actors in the program. As Brookfield (1986) explains, "It is important that external evaluators who enter a program setting to conduct a review of its accomplishments be aware of the political dimensions of such activity. . . . The external evaluator therefore needs to spend considerable time (if possible before accepting a contract) investigating the interpersonal conflicts, hidden institutional agendas, and covert purposes that may have surrounded the decision to call for an evaluation" (p. 265). Once engaged, however, evaluators become stakeholders in the program and must carry out their work in the matrix of power relations that structure the social and organizational context.

Democratically Evaluate Program Objectives

There is widespread intellectual and practical support for the proposition that planners should use democratic principles in negotiating formal program evaluations. This support is framed both in theoretical terms (House & Howe, 2000; Mathison, 2000; Ryan & DeStefano, 2000) and as an ideal based on practical experience (Grotelueschen, 1980; Kowalski, 1988). For example, Knowles (1980) recommends that every person who is in a position to make any kind of judgment about a program should be brought into the evaluation process in some way. He suggests that members of various groups are usually involved, depending on the type of program: participants, leaders or instructors, program director and staff, the advisory committee, outside experts, supervisory and management personnel, and community representatives. As a practical matter, this impulse arises from the real-world experience that those who have a stake in a program are constantly judging its value and worth. Therefore, it makes sense to involve them in the formal evaluation because they often are in a position to make decisions about the program: "Many program directors have learned the hard way that it is a mistake to perceive these populations merely as sources of data for the use of others in making an evaluative judgment. It is crucial to their ego-involvement and to the validity of the results that they be included also in the process of analyzing data and interpreting and applying the findings" (Knowles, 1980, p. 205).

Many program evaluation theories frame the enactment of this ideal to include all relevant stakeholders within the social and organizational setting. This orientation aligns closely with our theory, arguing that the major challenges to substantively democratic evaluation result from the asymmetrical political relationships in which the evaluation is designed and carried out. For example, House and Howe (2000) frame stakeholders as acting within the social and organizational political relationships that enable and constrain substantively democratic evaluation: "Genuine democratic deliberation would require that the interests of all stakeholder groups be central and the interests of all relevant parties be represented. . . . Some of the biggest threats to democratic decisions are power imbalances. . . . There must be some rough balance and equality of power for proper deliberation to occur. Evaluators must design evaluations so that relevant interests are represented . . . which often means representing the interests of those who might be excluded from the discussion. Determining and weighing interests is extremely complex and uncertain, and often controversial" (p. 5). Defining evaluation as a political process is just the starting point, however, because "there remains, of course, contention about who counts as a stakeholder, just what inclusion means, and the consequences for evaluation when stake-holders are included in novel ways" (Mathison, 2000, p. 85). As just one example, Hood (2000) argues that the educational interests of people of color often do not receive equal protection in deliberations because they are underrepresented at the planning table. Even in the theories that recognize the impact of power, few practical strategies are offered to carry out democratic approaches to evaluation (Mathison, 2000).

In order to take practical action, we need to go beyond an understanding that there are multiple stakeholders with divergent priorities and interests. A practical approach to democratically negotiating the formal evaluation must be seamlessly connected to the overall approach to planning offered in the previous chapters. Chapters Four and Five explain how planners can negotiate democratically both the assessment of needs and the resulting educational, management, and political objectives. Planners are likely to face similar challenges and opportunities in representing the interests of these stakeholders at the table to negotiate the formal evaluation. It is important that planners see the fundamental intersection of the planning tables for negotiating needs, objectives, and evaluation. In this sense, negotiations at evaluation planning tables occur throughout the planning process: "The inevitable role of values and criteria in interpreting and judging data again underscore the absolute importance of involving the appropriate stakeholders from the beginning of the evaluation process. Their values, expectations, and criteria are then known to us as we plan the evaluation, implement it, and ultimately interpret and use the results in the program" (Forest, Brack, & Moss, 1994, p. 187). In addition to negotiating the program objectives as part of the formal evaluation, democratic evaluation should also occur at the planning tables for criteria, data collection and analysis, and determination of worth and value. There are many diverse challenges to negotiating these parts of the formal evaluation, depending on whether planners are facing consultative, bargaining, or dispute situations.

Although learners must be at the table when negotiating the educational objectives (Deshler, 1998; Fenwick & Parsons, 2000), planners often do not consider other stakeholders in their vision of who matters. Kowalski (1988) explains that this "tunnel vision" pertains to both the data collection as well as the evaluative judgments that stakeholders make:

> Adult education literature contains many urgings that the learners should be highly involved in program evaluation activities (for example, Knowles, 1980). Although this recommendation is well founded, it often creates a sense of tunnel vision for the programmer; that is, the programmer concentrates on learner involvement and ignores the other potential participants. Involvement here pertains to the planning and appraisal as well as data collection. In addition to the programmer and the learners, other potential contributors may be persons not actively involved in the program but affected by its outcomes (such as supervisors), adult educators from other organizations, organization employees not involved with the program, members of a program advisory council, former students in the program, and consultants. (p. 155)

This tunnel vision may not have serious consequences in consultative situations in which all stakeholders are on the same page. For example, the evaluation results based on learners' reactions in the SVP programs were shared with instructors to improve future programs. It did not matter that other stakeholders did not assess the educational objectives nor were the results shared with them. The SVP leadership would continue to offer these courses based on learner attendance rather than on whether the objectives of any individual course were being achieved.

In bargaining and dispute situations, however, this tunnel vision of focusing only on learners in the formal evaluation can either produce negative outcomes or limit the opportunities to strengthen the program. The PI program clearly was located in a dispute situation, as its very existence was threatened. What would have happened, for example, if an effort had been made to follow Kowalski's (1988) suggestion to include all stakeholders, including a representative from the funding agency and the teachers' program directors, on an advisory committee to evaluate the program? Because only the learners were asked to evaluate the program, other stakeholders were not at the table to either provide evidence of program impact or make evaluative judgments based on that evidence. Although we do not know if this would have prevented the program cancellation, it is also possible that such an evaluation effort would have strengthened these decision makers' investment in the program's educational objectives. In the formal evaluation of the Phoenix management retreat, there was a similar lack of involvement of stakeholders other than the learners. In this bargaining situation, it would have been critical to know what evidence and criteria the president used to determine whether the program had achieved its educational objective of improving communication at the company. Would the evidence from the formal learner evaluation have been sufficient, or did he expect that employees would now stop complaining to him about communication problems in their monthly meetings? Pete and Joan could have put their program at risk because the president was not at the table when negotiating the formal program evaluation.

In contrast to the usual case with educational objectives, learners are rarely involved in formal evaluation of a program's management objectives. As pointed out earlier in the chapter, this happens because management objectives are typically not stated as such and therefore not formally evaluated by any stakeholders. The primary challenge, then, is to make management objectives public so that all stakeholders can be included in formally evaluating them. There is much to be gained if the primary stakeholders are at the table providing evidence and making judgments about such objectives as the physical facilities, program costs, teacher selection and training, and materials and technology supporting the program. A common strategy in consultative situations is to appoint a program advisory committee composed of the primary stakeholders for a program. These advisory committees become even more important in bargaining and dispute situations because they provide a public forum for adjudicating competing interests in judging the worth of a program. For example, Cassie and Ron could have appointed an advisory committee to evaluate the program's management objectives as well as the educational objectives. Such a committee could have collectively judged the adequacy and effectiveness of the infrastructure supporting the program. Since it was funded entirely by a single-source grant, one management objective could have been to develop multiple sources for financially supporting the program. With the primary stakeholders at the table—including learners, funders, program directors, and university planners—the end of the program might have been averted.

Planners' capacity to carry out a democratic evaluation of a program's political objectives is often hampered because, as is true for management objectives, they are often not stated. In consultative situations this problem can be overcome because the stakeholders' interests are not in direct conflict. For example, the PI program had enjoyed a great deal of support from all stakeholders, based on a successful track record of two previous projects. Cassie and Ron could have appointed a management committee to address the political objective of having all relevant parties continually involved in decision making and planning for the program. The additional complicating factor for political objectives, however, is that stakeholders often do not wish to make these objectives public, which clearly presents a problem in bargaining and dispute situations. This would have been the case with Pete's political objective to strengthen the credibility of the human resources unit at the Phoenix Company. It is possible that Pete could have put this objective on the table for other stakeholders to evaluate, with one form of evidence being other departments requesting similar follow-up retreats for their staff. Had Pete formally evaluated this political objective, his primary challenge would not have been to negotiate the criteria and evidence, but rather whether all stakeholders would accept the validity of this political objective.

Without agreement about the validity of a political objective, then, planners are faced with using informal evaluation processes to judge whether it has been achieved. Planners' key strategy in conducting a democratic formal evaluation for a program's political objectives is to seek common ground on those objectives that are acceptable for the collection of evidence and public deliberation.

Summary

In Part Two we have used Sork and Caffarella's (1989) conception to organize the five significant tasks that planners undertake to develop an educational program. They negotiate the needs-assessment, program objectives, instructional design and implementation, administration, and program evaluation. Although the planning tables at which these five tasks are negotiated may be separate in theory, they are interdependent in the practical judgments that people make in practice. This is particularly important to understand when negotiating the program evaluation because this task is often left to be negotiated late in the program development process, sometimes after a program has occurred. An important message of this chapter is that negotiating the program evaluation occurs at the same planning tables where the needs and objectives are negotiated. Thus, as stakeholders negotiate the program's educational, management, and political objectives, they are deciding on key dimensions of the formal evaluation. The power relations that structured the planning tables for needs and objectives similarly structure the decisions about whose evaluative judgments matter in judging a program's value or worth. Finally, these same power relationships offer opportunities and constraints as planners seek to democratically negotiate the program evaluation.

Chapter 9

Working the Planning Table in the Struggle for Knowledge and Power

As the planners in our three stories exercised power to negotiate interests, they illustrated the seamless integration of the technical demands and political dimensions of planning educational programs. Despite important advancements in understanding the politics of curriculum theory and practice in education generally (Apple, 1996; Petrina, 2004; Pinar, 1974; Pinar & Bowers, 1992; Pinar, Reynolds, Slattery, & Taubman, 1995; Schubert, 1986), most adult education planning theory remains based on the Tyler Rationale. But these Tylerian interpretations are unable to account for the political work of planning educational programs. Technical planning principles and procedures are necessary, but not sufficient, because it is not possible to talk about good planning without also talking about politics. In this chapter we propose an image of educational planners as strategic organizers of education in the struggle for knowledge and power. To that end, we review three traditions in adult education planning and administration theory to examine the long-standing theory-practice gap between what theorists prescribe and what practitioners experience. We argue that the gap will continue until theorists provide a working account of practical action in the everyday socially structured settings that routinely privilege the interests of some while disadvantaging the interests of others.

As a personal coda to our work, we conclude with a discussion about why we have used planning stories as a central feature of this book, why learning from planning experience is so crucial to becoming good planners, and how we teach planning.

Traditions in Adult Education Planning Theory

There are many traditions in educational curriculum planning (Pinar, Reynolds, Slattery, & Taubman, 1995). In our 1994 book (Cervero & Wilson, 1994a) we drew upon Schubert's (1986) historical typology of curriculum traditions to describe the classical, naturalistic, and critical traditions in adult education planning literature in order to situate our theory. As Schubert's recounting demonstrates and others confirm (Petrina, 2004; Pinar, Reynolds, Slattery, & Taubman, 1995), those broad curriculum and planning traditions have been evident for much of the last century and continue today. Indeed, these curriculum and planning traditions can be understood as representative and derivative of Habermas's (1971) theory of instrumental, practical, and emancipatory forms of knowledge and action. Our point is not to repeat that discussion, for it is available elsewhere (Cervero & Wilson, 1994a; Newman, 2000; Petrina, 2004; Pinar & Bowers, 1992; Schubert, 1986; Sork, 2000; Sork & Newman, 2004; Wilson, 2005; Wilson & Cervero, 1997). With a slight renaming, we briefly analyze these three planning traditions to argue that nearly all adult education planning theories provide guides to practical action predicated on rational problem solving. In a perfect world devoid of inequitable power relations and conflicting interests, such models of action might produce good planning. However, by not accounting for power and interests, rational problem solving fails to provide a workable guide for practical planning action. That failure has persistently reproduced the classic theory-practice gap that theorists tend to discuss (or ignore) and practitioners tend to (rightfully) bemoan.

Conventional Planning Theory

Conventional planning theory (Sork & Newman, 2004; Wilson, 2005) represents a rational problem-solving process replicating Tyler's (1949, p. 3) argument that "educational objectives become the criteria by which materials are selected, content is outlined, instructional procedures are developed and tests and examinations prepared." The planning process is routinely described as follows: first assess learning needs, then develop learning objectives from assessed needs, next design learning content and instructional formats to meet the learning objectives, and finally evaluate learning outcomes in terms of whether the objectives were achieved. Although the Tyler Rationale is routinely challenged by practitioners and debated by theorists, it remains the underlying theoretical starting point for much curriculum and planning theory. Moving beyond a K–12 school setting that is focused on classroom curriculum, planners of adult education programs also need to address the demands of different organizational contexts and the tasks associated with program administration. These planning and administration tasks, along with their sequential execution (often called "planning steps" and so enumerated), represent the principles and procedures to follow when planning educational programs for adults.

Conventional theory's structure of principles is what we have used to organize this book. The origins of conventional theory are routinely attributed to Tyler's enormously influential course syllabus from 1949, *Basic Principles of Curriculum and Instruction* (Boone, Safrit, & Jones, 2002; Sork, 2000; Sork & Caffarella, 1989; Sork & Newman, 2004), although the principles clearly emerged much earlier in the century (Petrina, 2004; Schubert, 1986). Despite his claim to the contrary, Knowles's *Informal Adult Education* (1950) represents an equally mature statement of planning theory for adult education, predicated directly on Tyler's curriculum theory but also incorporating his practical planning and administrative experience as a program director. As the history of conventional planning theory indicates (Sork & Buskey, 1986; Wilson & Cervero, 1997), the planning literature in the United States began to proliferate in the 1950s, and its production has continued apace since.

Yet amid an apparently bewildering diversity of planning theories exists a uniform depiction of program planning, which has elaborated upon—but has not changed or challenged—Tyler's and Knowles's principles. Because of this underlying uniformity, Sork and Buskey were able to synthesize a "generic planning model composed of nine specific steps" (1986, p. 89). Those nine specific steps directly mirror the sequencing of steps presented as the conventional definition of planning: analyze context, assess needs, derive objectives, design instruction, administer programs, and evaluate outcomes. Sork and Caffarella (1989, p. 234) subsequently refined this "generic model" as "a six-step basic model" representing "the most common logic found in the literature." This common structure of problem-solving principle and logic, which began emerging in the 1920s, promotes a specific interest in adult educators' use of "scientific"—that is, rational—problem solving as the professional approach for producing adult education programs (Wilson, 1993; Wilson & Cervero, 1997). It is this insistence on rationalism, in any and all situations and at any and all costs, to conduct practical human action in social and organizational settings that creates and sustains the theory-practice gap. Rationalism itself is an ideal prescription that is unable to enable action in the structural flows of power. Indeed, it has long been supposed that rational problem solving eliminates the "political noise" of working in organizational contexts (Forester, 1989; Freidmann, 1987). Despite promising movements in the general curriculum literature (Apple, 1996; Petrina, 2004; Pinar, 1974; Pinar & Bowers, 1992; Pinar, Reynolds, Slattery, & Taubman, 1995; Schubert, 1986), the logic and principles of the conventional tradition continue to frame and dominate the adult education planning literature

(Boone, Safrit, & Jones, 2002; Sloane-Seal, 2001; Sork, 2000; Sork & Newman, 2004).

The Deliberative Tradition

Practitioners often point out that the rational problem-solving principles upon which conventional planning steps are predicated rarely work in actual planning circumstances (Brookfield, 1986). In response to this observation, some theorists have described planning as a complex decision-making process of human interaction. This approach has been referred to as the deliberative or practical tradition in curriculum theory (Reid, 1979; Schwab, 1969; Walker, 1971). Represented most fully in Houle's (1972) theory of planning and implicated in nearly all adult education planning theory since that time (for example, Caffarella, 2002), it urges planners to analyze their contexts and then make judgments about what to do given the constraints and opportunities in those contexts. In addition to defining planning as making practical judgments, another major insight of this tradition is the recognition that when planning a program, planners may not need to complete all of the generic planning model steps in the traditionally prescribed order (Houle, 1972, 1996; Walker, 1971, 2003). This second insight seriously challenges the preferred sequential logic of the conventional view because it questions the underlying logical necessity of connecting needs-assessment to objectives to design to evaluation. Whether or not the steps have to be followed sequentially represents the only substantive theoretical debate in the adult education planning literature (Wilson & Cervero, 1997). The iterative, deliberative view of nonsequential tasks as a way to make conventional theory more "practical" dominates the planning literature today (see Caffarella, 2002, & Sork, 2000, as examples). Planning theory has moved from a steady avowal of a linear sequence of planning principles to a more practical understanding of planning work as humans making judgments (Houle, 1972, 1996) in order to address the theory-practice gap. While challenging the sequential logic of conventional theory, the deliberative tradition still rests solidly, however, on rational problem solving as the key understanding of practical action in socially structured settings. This tradition's invocation of "deliberation" as the defining practical activity (Reid, 1979; Schwab, 1969; Walker, 1971, 1990, 2003) actually is similar to what the conventional view holds as rational problem solving. Thus, while providing a more accurate accounting of actual practice by bringing people and context into the picture, the underlying rationalist prescription remains largely the same because deliberation essentially represents the decision-making aspects of implementing rationalist problem-solving steps. Thus the theory-practice gap continues because the deliberative tradition is a variant of the conventional tradition that foregrounds a rationalist approach to making decisions. As with the conventional tradition, the deliberative tradition hopes to use rationalism to minimize the political noise of working in organizations. But that noise does not go away just because planners fail to account for power and interests.

The Critical Tradition

Critical planning theory represents another significant planning tradition. Paulo Freire's *Pedagogy of the Oppressed* (1970) is an exemplar. Some theorists have seen implications for planning theory in Freire's *Pedagogy* (Sork, 2000); others have described it explicitly as a planning model (Boone, Safrit, & Jones, 2002; Wilson & Cervero, 1997). Freire's theory is both, because it contains planning theory and procedures that derive from his critical questioning of who gets (or does not get) what kinds of education. His theory shows that adult education is a political act in challenging repressive power structures that requires an ethical commitment to social justice. Freire's work represents a long tradition of planning adult education to redress social and political inequity—a tradition that continues today (Wilson & Cervero, 1997). This history of critical adult education planning theory has antecedents in nineteenth- and twentieth-century adult education that took place in, for example, labor movements; workers education; settlement organizations; civil rights and antiwar movements; churches, mosques, and synagogues—wherever people sought to change repressive social and political regimes (Foley, 1999; Neufeldt & McGee, 1990; Newman, 1994; Schied, 1993; E. Thompson, 1963; J. Thompson, 1997; Welton, 1987). Because adult education represents a struggle for knowledge and power (Cervero & Wilson, 2001), the various efforts for social justice today—to contest global capitalism, develop a more sustainable world, revivify democracy in the West, address the continuing epidemic of AIDS, and confront numerous other conditions of inequity—all provide fertile ground for improving the political practice of planning adult education. If the deliberative tradition introduced the importance of context and planner judgments, the critical tradition describes context in specific political terms of sociostructural oppression and urges adult educators to address questions of social injustice. Although there is still a tension between theory and practice in the critical tradition, this tradition moves us toward a more workable understanding of practical action in socially structured settings. It does so by recognizing the structural relations of power in which planners exercise agency to address social and political inequity. In the critical tradition, planners have to understand the consequences of how structurally organized settings benefit some people and disadvantage others, so that they can identify and address oppression with specific educational programs for adults.

Problems in Planning Theory

Action, Context, and Rationality

Although there has been an abundance of conventional theories offered in the literature, there has been considerably little critical inquiry providing alternative ways of understanding practice. The primary problem left to solve in the planning literature is thought to be the theory-practice gap. Initially, adult education theorists thought that the gap existed because of deficient or unprofessional practice. For example, Bryson's (1936) adult education textbook was an attempt to theorize the "unscientific" planning practice of adult educators. Knowles clearly noted that gap in 1950, saying it was time to get beyond "trial and error" and develop "scientific" theory about planning education programs for adults. In one of the few studies of actual planning practice, Pennington and Green (1976) concluded that planning theory did not account for planning practice, although they concluded this was a practitioner problem rather than a theoretical one. Later theorists began to suspect that theory was causing the gap problem. Sork and Buskey (1986) concluded that program planning theory was unsophisticated, that there was little cumulative analysis or integration, that differences among planning theories were more a matter of contexts than actual differences in planning (hence their "generic model"), and that theory had little to offer in describing what planners do. Then the suspicion grew that the gap may be inevitable. Sork and Caffarella (1989, p. 243) argued that because the planning literature was largely normative, the "gap that has always existed to some degree between theory and practice has widened" in recent years. They attributed that growing gap to practitioners' tendency to take shortcuts, the influence of context on planning, and the increasing irrelevancy of planning theory to planning practice. Newman (2000) and Sork and Newman (2004) point out the gender and North American bias in those who develop planning theory. By excluding other ways of thinking, this bias produces planning theory that continues to promote technical rationality and instrumental problem solving—synonyms for "professional activity . . . made rigorous by the application of scientific theory and technique" (Schon, 1983, p. 21). Technical rationality and instrumental problem solving remain the epistemological focus and practical stance, respectively, of most adult education planning theories.

Why does the theory-practice gap persist? Why the continued insistence on technical rationality at the expense of understanding practice? Although some would argue that technical rationality is a misrepresentation of the Tyler Rationale (Hlebowitsh, 1995), the continued existence of the gap is amazing given the advancements in understanding human action across the social disciplines (Bernstein, 1983; Giddens, 1979, 1984). Thus the gap persists because the perennial insistence on promoting instrumental problem solving produces a corollary problem: the inability to develop a theory of context for practical action. And the use of a rationalist ideology of instrumental problem solving has led directly to an inability to develop an account of human action in planning practice (Cervero & Wilson, 1994b, 2001; Wilson, 1993, 2005; Wilson & Cervero, 1997, 2002). The persistent promotion of instrumental problem solving as practical action produces and sustains the gap (Donaldson & Edelson, 2000; Newman, 2000; Sork & Newman, 2004). This is the problem: instrumental problem solving as a theory of action becomes dysfunctional in the messy human interactions, framed by power relations and interests, that characterize action in the real world. Technical rationality fails at the practical level because it does not enable people to see, much less provide strategies to negotiate, relationships of power. As we have illustrated in this book, power always trumps rationality.

Further, the inability to see and negotiate power is a function of the context problem. Most planning theories do not articulate the conditions of actual practice beyond the term *context*. Nearly all adult education planning theory since the 1960s has acknowledged the importance of context—but this acknowledgment has been outweighed by the theory's failure to describe what context is or how planners act in relation to that context (Cervero & Wilson, 1994b; Wilson & Cervero, 1997). To be sure, some theories name organizational structure, the role of resources, the importance of stakeholders, and other such features as significant dimensions of context (Boone, Sarif, & Jones, 2002; Caffarella, 2002; Clark, 1956; Houle, 1972; Knowles, 1980; Knox, 1980). But these theories typically do not provide any account of human action in context other than to prescribe rational problem solving. A practical understanding of context has not been addressed because technical rational planning theory assumes that contextual conditions do not matter as long as everyone acts rationally.

To be effective, planners need a repertoire of well-developed techniques and strategies. Yet conventional theory, with its focus on principles and procedures as its definition of practical action, only partially helps planners in their actual work. In the conventional perspective planners are technically skilled to conduct a series of steps; practical action is thought to consist of the action needed to execute the steps. In the deliberative tradition, educators are people who make judgments about what to do; practical action is thought to consist of the deliberation needed to make decisions. Both certainly represent dimensions of the practical action necessary to plan programs: tasks need to be implemented, decisions need to be made. Neither, however, provides a working theory of practical action in the lived world of educational planning, for the theory of practical action upon which both models depend is one of rational problem solving. But rational problem solving is not practical or effective in many planning situations that are defined by inequitable relations of power and conflicting interests. It is only the critical tradition that recognizes idealized prescriptions for rationality as unworkable for the political practice of adult education.

Administration and Leadership Theory in Adult Education

The Gap Persists

Where can we look for answers to the questions of context and practical action? Arguably, we would expect theorists of educational leadership and administration to explain the practical action necessary to organize and lead educational programs. And indeed they do. When Jack London rhetorically asked, in 1959, "What does the administrator do?" (p. 222), his reply surprised no one, because theorists already thought they knew what adult and continuing education program administrators and leaders did. As with conventional adult education planning theory, the standard answer in adult education administration theory has been to describe an array of administrative tasks for which leaders are responsible. Although there is variability in the terms used, the enumeration of leadership and administrative functions, often described as "the similarities of administrative processes in all systems" (Essert, 1964, p. 178; see also Courtenay, 1990), has remained remarkably stable through several decades (Boyle & Jahns, 1970; Bryson, 1936; Courtenay, 1990; Galbraith, Sisco, & Guglielmino, 1997; Knowles, 1950, 1970, 1980; Knox, 1991; Kowalski, 1988; London, 1959; Prosser & Bass, 1930; Smith & Offerman, 1989). Yet the leadership and administration theories, with close analogs in conventional planning theory, also promote overreliance on technical rationality and instrumental problem solving at the risk of misunderstanding context and practical action. We make four observations about these attempts to understand the context and action of administration and leadership, to show why this literature continues to reproduce the theory-practice gap and is only selectively helpful in understanding the action of real planners.

First, the adult education leadership and administrative literatures overwhelmingly derive from structural-functional organizational analysis, often unconsciously so. This approach to understanding organizations and leadership, which grew out of late nineteenth-century sociological analysis, tries to understand how organizations and other social phenomenon are structured and how their parts function in relation to structure. Structural-functionalism was employed by generations of organizational theorists to promote scientific rationalism in administrative decision making (Capper, 1993; Friedmann, 1987); until the late twentieth century it was the primary system of thought used to study organizations. Organizational study in business and in educational administration constitute two major areas of disciplined inquiry and professional practice that depend significantly upon structural-functionalist analysis. The literature of adult education administration and planning derives from educational administration theory, and its reliance upon the same school of thought is similarly pervasive. As Donaldson and Edelson note, "many in the field (ourselves included) have for too long been far too comfortable" (2000, p. 192) with structural-functionalist understandings of administration and leadership. Ingham (1968) suggested a similar observation when he illustrated how minimally adult education administrative literature drew upon the larger discussions of educational and organizational leadership and administration (see Capper, 1993, for similar observations about educational administration). With some notable exceptions (see Donaldson & Edelson, 2000; Jiggins & Shute, 1994; Robinson, 1970; White & Belt, 1980), this tendency toward theoretical monotheism has continued as adult education administrative theorists have tried to emulate structural-functionalist analysis in K–12 and other forms of educational administration.

Such dominance troubles us for several reasons. This nearly uniform structural-functionalist theoretical stance has produced a decidedly technical and procedural emphasis in the study and practice of adult education leadership and administration (Courtenay, 1990; Donaldson & Edelson, 2000). As a consequence, structural-functionalist accounts have reduced leadership "to a form of management focusing on regularity and control" by replacing "vision with technique" (Donaldson & Edelson, 2000, pp. 194–195). Such a l imited focus on control has limited consideration of other, more contemporary administrative analysis that incorporates feminist, poststructuralist, postmodernist, or other critical social analyses (Capper, 1993; Donaldson & Edelson, 2000). Reducing leadership to control and technique limits how we could understand practice—and therefore how we might change it (Wilson & Hayes, 2000). Finally, Giddens' long-standing criticism of structural-functionalism's fixation on the "anatomy" of organizations as "an arrangement of dry bones that are only made to rattle at all by the conjoining of structure and function" (1979, p. 23) really captures the problem: dwelling on the relationship of part to whole does little to help us understand or change how humans act in organizations—there literally is no life in such analyses. Although adult education administrative theory is quite helpful in enumerating many necessary administrative tasks and procedures (such as those for producing marketing plans or balancing budgets), it has remained distanced from the grime and heat of actual planning-table action—such as how to get to the table or what to say and do once there—by insisting on structural-functionalism's idealism of technical decision making. In this regard our complaint is the same for both adult education planning and leadership theory: such a limited theoretical view sustains the theory-practice gap.

Second, a quiet but important debate has simmered in the administration and planning literatures about the question of context. From the earliest writings in the literature of adult education administration, there has been a tension between trying to define precisely those leadership functions that are "necessary in all organizations" and trying to define how the specific organizational settings and circumstances affect administrative practice. Bryson (1936) reveals this tension when he argues that adult educators need to develop the kinds of administrative skill that educators of children already have: "For the person who directs the night [that is, adult education] activities of the public-school system, principles of administration are not readily distinguishable from those which govern the work of a day-school [that is, children's education] executive" (pp. 117–118). Yet, he goes on to say, "the [adult education] administrator is constantly making an adjustment between his [sic] present program and the marginal activities which he thinks might be welcomed by his clientele" (1936, p. 123), by which Bryson recognizes that the generic administrative function of assessing needs depends upon the context in which the program exists. This tension between the view that principles work in all contexts and the view that contexts determine the principles has teetered back and forth throughout the literature. Those arguing for educational administration as applied science or scientific management (manifestations of structural-functionalist analysis) have tended to promote administrative leadership as a set of generic principles that work in all contexts. For example, Courtenay (1990) derived generic administrative functions (just as Sork & Buskey, 1986, and Sork & Caffarella, 1989, had for the planning literature) from his review of administrative theory in adult education. Such "context-free" principles represent a long-established tradition in the adult education administration theory (Boyle & Jahns, 1970; Galbraith, Sisco, & Guglielmino, 1997; Hallenbeck, 1948; Knox, 1980; London, 1959; Smith & Offerman, 1989).

Others have emphasized the role and effect of context: "leadership is adaptive . . . in that purposes usually cannot be achieved unless the organization comes to terms with its environment. A major responsibility of leadership is the working out of satisfactory adjustments between organizations and environmental pressures" (Clark, 1956, p. 44). Ingham (1968, p. 61) claimed that his analysis provided "evidence to support the hypothesis that administrative principles may be valid for one type of organization but not for another." Brookfield (1986) has depicted each act of programming as a unique psychosocial drama in which characters and conditions constantly change. Clark's (1956, 1958) famous depiction of the administrative marginality of adult education programs has been redeveloped to include "conflicts resulting from different interests and power balances" (Donaldson & Kozoll, 1999, p. 45). In most cases those who acknowledge context do so, however, within a structural-functionalist framework in which analyzing context becomes just another technical decision-making step in conventional and deliberative planning models (Boone, Safrit, & Jones, 2002; Caffarella, 2002; Houle, 1996; Sork & Caffarella, 1989). But, as Giddens (1979) would say, such structural-functionalist analyses lack an understanding of the acting subject within a structuring social matrix. As with adult education planning theory, most administrative and leadership theory lacks an actionable account of people working in the real world of organizing and leading adult education programs, regardless of whether it recognizes or ignores context. As we have argued throughout, there is no question that context really matters, because there is no planning table that does not represent a complex interplay of organizational actors with specific interests working in and through relations of power. But it is not enough to say that context matters. We have to provide understandings of how context is constituted and what that means for human action in structuring, and structurable, relations of power, which the planners who live in this book have amply personified.

Third, what experienced practitioners know—but what too few theorists in either the planning or administration literatures have addressed—is that the leadership and administration of adult education programs are always political. As we have argued throughout this book, working in organizations means working with people in relations of power, and this is especially characteristic of those with administrative and leadership responsibilities. Even though the broader organization and administration literatures empirically and theoretically have long recognized the political work of administrative leadership (Benveniste, 1989; Bolman & Deal, 1997; Friedmann, 1987; Isaac, 1987; Lax & Sebenius, 1986; Morgan, 1986), the dominant structural-functionalist interpretations in adult education have tended theoretically to ignore or deny that political work (for exceptions, see Donaldson & Edelson, 2000; Ingham, 1968; Jiggins & Shute, 1994). Nonetheless, despite this dearth of theoretical insight, there are practical insights that have long lingered unarticulated in the administration literature—insights that adult education planners as organizational leaders have the responsibility to negotiate the conflicting and consensual interests of stakeholders, to anticipate the threats and opportunities in the settings in which they plan and lead programs, and to develop the kinds of political relationships that support their programs

(Beals, Blount, Powers, & Johnson, 1966; Brookfield, 1986; Clark, 1956; Goody & Kozoll, 1995; Jiggins & Shute, 1994; Knox, 1980). For example, Clark (1956) is very clear about how little power adult education leaders have in public school systems and how important it is to manage organizational stakeholders to be supportive of adult education programs. Such insights struggle to be heard, though, because theorists have lacked the language to make sense of and convey what they have learned from their experience. In contrast to Clark's analysis, Essert illustrates the theoretical inability of much of the administrative and leadership literature to get past wishful thinking to name and address the real demands and conflicts of actual practice: "leaders are best able to enrich and improve . . . and provide balanced programs . . . only if there is complete understanding of these objectives by the administrative heads of the respective institutions" (1951, p. 175). Such complete understanding is possible only in a world devoid of institutional and personal conflict, competition for scarce resources, and the intense influence of sometimes conflicting, sometimes consensual stakeholders. So there is a palatable tension between the rationalistic insistence of structural-functional analysis and the practical voice of experience as planners allude to the political dimensions of their work—still without a language in which to speak it, except with whispers in hallways.

Fourth, planning and administration theories continue to promote a "rationalist agency" view of planning and leadership practice. Because of the structural-functionalist origins of adult education planning and leadership theory, both theories have promoted a generic view of practical action as following a logical order of planning and administration steps that are to be used in all circumstances— following and executing the steps and tasks is believed to be the *action* of planning. In this view, practical action is the rational problem solving of an *individual* sometimes, but not always, working rationally with other individuals. Although this is certainly a significant component of practical action, such a view nonetheless overly empowers the individual, to the extent that the context of planning—as defined by power and interests—is thought to have no effect. Or put another way, rationalism is believed to exclude, or at least minimize, the "nastiness" and "noise" of organizational politics. Although some may rhetorically deplore this noise, others who are more politically astute work this noise to their advantage. In either case, organizational politics are considered to be "personal" (Cervero & Wilson, 2001) and therefore to be addressed only on an individual ad hoc basis. Such a stance woefully underestimates the socially organized reality of power relations that structure organizational life. Because theorists have long sensed this tension but have been unable to voice it, they have, by default or conviction, continued to promote the idealism of rational thought and action as a response to the vicissitudes of daily practice. Such an individual rationalist view has persisted in the literature for at least two reasons. First, theorists have been content to prescribe ideal principles for planners because they believe such principled practices will either order or negate the unruliness of actual practice. Second, they continue to prescribe such principles by not asking what people actually do when they plan programs. Like Knowles (1950) long ago, these theorists see practice as unprofessional and unregulated "trial and error" and thus seek the relatively high ground of conventional and deliberative theory, which attempts to impose orderly process on unruly practice. Conventional planning and leadership theory, by weighing us down with idealistic rationalism as the only form of thought and action, has left us with no way to see the actual terrain of planning and leadership or how to act to navigate it—and so the gap persists.

Working the Planning Table for Real Possibilities of Action

Sork (2000, p. 179) is "skeptical about the prospects of developing a theory or model" that helps explain what is really going on in planning and helps people be better planners—the classic theory-practice problem. His comment is not surprising, because, like so many other areas of social inquiry and practical action, adult education has tried to emulate the natural and physical sciences and in doing so has produced the theory-practice gap. The gap continues because theories have primarily analyzed administration in terms of the functionalist tasks leaders must manage and accomplish. Of course, carrying out tasks is important—organizations would have little use for leaders who cannot hire good teachers, balance budgets, and market programs. Yet those functionalist interpretations define too little of what counts in doing the work of administering educational programs. Identifying the tasks to perform does not tell us how to get them done in the midst of organizational relations of power that promote some interests while blocking others. Rationalist prescriptions developed from structural-functionalist accounts of line and staff communication and authority patterns just do not get us close to actual human practice in organizational settings. As Forester (1989) reminds us, knowing the organizational chart (structure and function) does not help us much with learning and using the organizational ropes (relations of power and human interests). Context and politics—and how we choose to interpret them—do matter, and perhaps never more so than in the leadership and administration of adult education programs. The conventional administration tasks are routinely presented as primarily technical in nature. Our theory presents a more complete view by showing how such technical tasks are always also political because people with interests use power to provide leadership in constructing educational programs.

So what good are planning and leadership theories if they cannot tell us what effective educational leadership is or how to do it? To be fair, the ideological justification and theoretical origins for technical rational planning and administration have roots in eighteenth-century Europe (Friedmann, 1987). Planning emerged then as disciplined inquiry by experts in scientific methods who produced facts for decision makers: "These specialists, expert in mediating knowledge and action, I shall call planners, although the

specific designation did not appear until the 1920s, when it was usually modified to mean a particular kind of planning. . . . In their
most general signification, however, planners-as-experts have always
argued the selection of means is primarily a technical question, to
be decided on grounds of efficiency" (Friedmann, 1987, p. 4). The
splitting of values from "facts" (see Chapter Four for how needs-
assessment has traditionally personified this logic) in eighteenth-
century Europe resulted from the conviction "that politicians . . .
should concern themselves primarily with general goals of policy
('values'), leaving the choice of the appropriate means ('facts') to
specially trained experts" (ibid.). In the tenor of the times, scientific investigation produced facts and laws that "would ensure the
steady forward march of social progress" (Friedmann, 1987, p. 5).
The simplicity and power of this worldview remains profound more
than two centuries later. That ideological consensus of scientific
method as the definition and practice of the professions is the target of Schon's (1983) critique of technical rationality, which has
itself been critiqued as not particularly critical (Usher, Bryant, &
Johnston, 1997). Thus the leadership and planning literature has
emanated from a deeply ideological and historically situated way of
understanding the relationship between context and action. Likewise, adult education leadership and planning theories have drawn
on such theory to define planners and leaders as technical experts
in means, not ends. Even with such a robust historical footing,
the splitting of means from ends relies on an unsustainable understanding of theory-practice relationships. This stance that professional practice is a technical exercise in locating means and does
not require value judgments is why theories predicated on this logic
are unable to provide an account that helps us understand and guide
planning in the real world.

This book has depended on a different approach to theory-
practice relationships, context, and action. In juxtaposition to
traditional "scientific" theory and practice, with its premises of
observing, predicting, and controlling human behavior, we have

used a different understanding of the relationship between theory and practice (Cervero & Wilson, 1994a, 1994b). Actionable theory has to be (1) plausible—that is, able to account for actual practice; (2) politically strategic—that is, able to analyze and act within and upon power relationships; and (3) ethically illuminating—that is, able to reveal and sustain ethical standards for judging practice (Bernstein, 1983; Cervero & Wilson, 1994a, 1994b; Forester, 1989). The point of such an understanding of theory-practice relationships is to understand and enable practical action (Foley, 1999). This requires breaking free from the "scientism" that has had a stranglehold on attempts to make sense of and improve educational practice. Until we sever those entanglements and move forward to embrace the enormous variability of human interaction in educational practice, theoretical work will continue to reproduce the theory-practice gap, and understandings of practice will remain impoverished.

Part of breaking free of our epistemological and ontological past is facing squarely the limitations of our traditional understandings of context and action. Many planning and leadership theories remain ensconced in a worldview in which the only solution to the messiness of actual practice was a prescription for idealized rational problem solving. Our work has sought to question and transcend that prescription by asking not only what planners do but also what they *should* do. We believe that planners who ignore the power relations and interests that constitute social and organizational settings limit their potential effectiveness. Planners cannot wish away or bemoan in hallway whispers the reality that power matters in terms of whose interests get to the planning table to shape their educational programs. Nor should planners be surprised that people have interests and will work assiduously to have those interests matter in planning programs. These are the conditions of social and organizational life that inspire us to use the metaphor of "working the planning table" to analyze the negotiations that occur there. Working the planning table offers a way to anticipate and negotiate the interests of stakeholders and the power they exercise to promote their interests. In the "old world," theorists could not "see" these phenomena (although many clearly sensed their presence and effect) and therefore had no way to deal with them. In our analysis, planners cannot only see power and interests, they can anticipate doing something with and about them. We have tried to move the theoretical conversation from seeing context as a step to account for in planning to seeing context as socially organized power and interests that frame all planning actions. We do not think this response is *the* answer to the question of what do planners do, for we intend our analysis to raise more questions. We are hopeful about the prospects of our theory's providing opportunities for understanding and enabling practical action in education.

John Forester, whose work (1989, 1999) has been both inspiration and departure point for us, has argued that planners selectively shape attention to possibilities of action. In drawing on the traditions Forester represents, we have argued that planning is better understood as a social process of negotiating interests in relationships of power (Cervero & Wilson, 1994a, 1994b). In developing that position we have emphasized that planning has technical, political, and ethical dimensions. Planners engage fundamentally in "people work" (Cervero & Wilson, 1996) and are "knowledge-power brokers" (Cervero & Wilson, 2001). People work planning tables to negotiate interests, and they do so by selectively organizing attention to real possibilities of action. As Friedmann (1987) argues, planning is about action and has consequences. Such consequences in education have to do with how planners strategically organize real possibilities of action in the struggle for knowledge and power. The intertwined ethical principles guiding such planning focus on enhancing participation at the table and taking a stance on who should benefit from the resulting educational programs. Our work addresses the criteria for understanding and enabling practical action because it provides plausible accounts of practice, provides politically strategic actions, and promotes an ethical standard of substantively planning. Further, our work addresses the theory-practice problem by introducing a theory of practical action within socially structured settings. Our theoretical stance continues to rely on Giddens' (1979, 1984) structuration theory as the model of action and context. A key message of this book is that educational planning produces educational and political outcomes that either reproduce or challenge social and political relationships. As people plan educational programs, they act in relations of power to negotiate interests while simultaneously acting on those relations of power to alter or maintain them. We recognize that our theoretical stance may be perceived as overly focused on what individual planners can do, as opposed to the structural dimensions they face. Yet we hope that this stance offers a vision for people to imagine and enact real possibilities of action in the struggle for knowledge and power.

Coda

Teaching and Learning About Planning

Readers may query, Why use planning stories to think about planning? We would answer that stories provide a very powerful pedagogy for learning and teaching about planning. We began to really learn about planning when we started listening to our own and others' stories about planning practice and began questioning what planning theory was telling us planning should be. Indeed, we developed the theory by observing real planning stories for our 1994 book (Cervero & Wilson, 1994a) and listening to what those stories taught us. In this last section we provide a brief justification for a "storied" approach to learning about planning practice, and we offer a short version of how we learned to learn from planning stories and how we use planning stories to teach planning.

Why Planning Stories Matter

We lack the space to engage in an extended discussion of the promising movement of "narrative inquiry" (Clandinin & Connelly, 2000) in qualitative research. But we want to indicate how we have taken advantage of this broad-ranging and discipline-crossing investigative approach. Narrative inquiry (which goes by many names, depending on whether its disciplinary base is anthropology, literary criticism, history, or education; see Mcquillan, 2000) seeks to understand the lived experience of people by revealing that lived experience rather than allowing the life of human phenomenon to be leached out as more traditional investigative techniques so often do. Storytelling as a way of learning about and making sense of adult education practice has become increasingly popular in recent years. Brookfield (1995), for example, has used vignettes of his and others' experiences to make his theoretical and practical points both lucid and accessible. Vella (1994) has popularized storytelling as a way of getting to deeper meaning of our educational work. In education more generally, Clandinin and Connelly (2000) have popularized theories and practices of narrative inquiry. Narrative inquiry for them is "a way of understanding experience . . . for experience is the stories people live. People live stories" (p. xxvi)—and through their stories they educate themselves and others about the meaning of their experience. Foley adds that using stories for such sense-making enables us to become "more deeply interested in the politics and ethics of our work" (2001, p. 164).

It is, of course, ancient wisdom that stories are good ways to learn and teach. But why are stories so good at making sense of experience? Cronon (1992) argues that stories translate the almost uncountable events of our lives into "causal sequences—stories—that order and simplify those events to give them new meanings" (p. 1349). Drawing on Aristotle, Cronon describes the distinctive rhetorical features of stories as having a beginning, a middle, and an end. Because of this rhetorical structure, stories can tell us "consequences that become meaningful because of their placement within the narrative" (p. 1367). Without such organizing of events chronicled in our lives—which we have come to term *plot*— "everything becomes much harder—even impossible—to understand" (p. 1351). Like Clandinin and Connelly, Cronon argues that stories help us find meaning in our lived experience by selectively ordering the events of our lives, but he adds a crucial dimension to such sense-making: "Completed action gives a story its unity and allows us to evaluate and judge an act by its result" (p. 1367). Because stories tell the results of actions that may be told and valued in different ways, there is no neutral position from which to tell or hear a story. Thus, Cronon argues that narrators—that is, storytellers—"are moral agents and political actors. As storytellers we commit ourselves to the task of judging the consequences of human actions, trying to understand the choices . . . so as to capture the full tumult of their world. In the dilemmas they faced we discover our own, and at the intersection of the two we locate the moral of the story" (p. 1370). Because the crafting of stories enables us to make meaning of our actions, stories are vehicles for learning about "the challenges of deliberative planning" (Forester, 1999, p. 13) by being "windows onto the world of planning possibilities" (p. 244). Forester's "practitioner profiles" (first-person accounts or stories of planning practice) "provide a complexity and specificity that teach judgment, enrich perception, and heighten sensitivity" (1999, p. 247). These are abilities that any astute planner must develop in order to imagine and organize new possibilities of action. So stories are a way of making sense of the overwhelming details of our lives and a way of organizing our experience so we can evaluate and learn from it. We have used the planning stories in this book to illustrate our framing and interpretive perspective in order to "see" in ways that structural functionalism and conventional planning theory cannot.

How We Use Planning Stories to Teach

Our own story of how we came to use stories in learning and teaching about planning may serve to illustrate the points just sketched. Ron had been teaching a graduate course on adult education program planning for several years when I (Arthur) entered the doctoral program in adult education at the University of Georgia. When I took the planning course from Ron, he was drawing significantly on the K–12 educational curriculum literature and specifically using Tyler's (1949) curriculum theory and Schubert's (1986) survey of curriculum theory. Schubert (1986) overviews the major curriculum traditions, and Ron was using them to organize the specific adult education planning literature. Because it was a doctoral course, the teaching was the usual theory-before-practice hierarchy, although not without gnawing concerns that the theory barely accounted for actual practice and thus was not particularly insightful for improving practice. Ron subsequently invited me to join him in a research project investigating program planning practice. That work, which culminated in our 1994 book, took the theory-practice gap head-on. In collecting data for the book, we first began to learn about the power of stories in making sense of human experience. Both of us have had extensive experience working in continuing professional education. Schon's (1983) analysis of the reflective practitioner—in particular, his use of first-person accounts (stories) of professional practice—had a huge effect on how we began to think about what planners do and how we could learn about planning. So we figured that to understand how people planned programs we needed to watch planners do their work, to listen to their stories—and the Phoenix Company dropped into our laps.

After we collected and had begun analyzing the data from the Phoenix Company, Ron had the insight to use the documents and transcripts of planning meetings and our postmeeting debriefings as teaching material to help create what Schon (1987) has termed a reflective practicum in the planning course we were teaching. Initially the basic pedagogy had course participants taking on the parts of the actual planners and using their actual words to act out segments of the case during class sessions. Because planning stories order and present consequences of action, they engage students in a way of thinking and learning about planning that presenting only theory and procedures could not do. With real action before them, which we could stop and interrogate at any moment, our students produced different interpretations of what was going on.

In provoking and managing such interrogations, we typically ask who was a good planner and what was good planning—and why. Students, at least initially, often instinctively bemoan such questions because they sense but are reluctant to confront their value-ladenness. Yet when we push the questions, students take sides on who was a good planner and who was not. For example, Pete is routinely judged by some students as a "bad" planner because he is viewed as overly self-interested, a manipulator, and too political. Students will make assessments of Pete's actions, such as "Pete is too political to be a good educator." Once the assessment is out on the table, we can then dig deeper into how people understand planning and why they make the choices they do. This is where Cronon (1992) gets the power of stories so right. When people hear the Phoenix story, they make judgments about the consequences of actions, and in those judgments they lay out both their perceptual schemes—their "theories" of how they understand and act in the world—and their values for judging planning actions. The normally unarticulated and taken-for-granted perspectives that people rely on to assess their own and others' planning actions are opened up for critical inspection by examining planning stories. And in that critical inspection of practice, in which we debate about what constitutes good practice and why, learning about planning can really begin. Whereas many educators typically regard theory as distanced and unimportant in "real life," when examining planning action they quite willingly (well, most do, eventually) risk opinions about who is and who is not a good planner and why. This juncture is where planners create their own "moral of the story." It is here that they engage in learning about the political tasks that confront them and decide the ethical ground upon which they will stand. With an ethically illuminated analysis of the political work of planning, planners are much more able to utilize their technical skills to plan good programs with and for adults, because they know whose side to be on. This is a different kind of learning than our more traditional theory-before-practice, knowledge-before-action pedagogies allow. As Forester notes, planning stories are not about learning the right things to do regardless of the situation but about "how to inquire, how to learn . . . [how to] call our attention through the details to the kinds of considerations we need to take into account in our own novel circumstances" (1999, p. 247).

Over the years we have continued to develop our pedagogy of using stories to understand and improve planning practice. As we continued our analysis of the Phoenix story (see Cervero & Wilson, 1998; our story of that story changes), we used more and more of the story. In addition, we asked course participants to craft and analyze their own planning stories because the stories effectively get people to see and analyze the political and ethical dimensions not visible within a conventional theory perspective. To say that planners have to be politically aware is one thing; to get them to live, analyze, and judge their experience is quite another. So we hope the stories in this book can be models for students to write and learn from their own planning stories. No matter what the medium of presentation, however, it is the many stories of the Phoenix Company retreat, as well as the stories produced by our students, that still provoke judgment and enable us to see what we value and how power shapes the choices we make in our planning practices. Without these stories, learning about what really matters in educational planning is not possible. This is why the Phoenix, SVP, and PI stories are at the center of this book.

A Concluding Note

Although we have empirically and theoretically documented the place of power and interests in planning, we are wary of ending with don't-cross-the-line claims because there is still much to learn. So instead we close with questions illustrative of further possible inquiry: What do planners do when planning in substantively democratic ways? What are the constraints on and opportunities for such democratic efforts in planning? What does practice look like when planners abandon the traditional guise of neutral facilitation to stand purposively for some interests against others?

Negotiation is a powerful descriptor of practical action but not an exclusive one. Like power, negotiation is not just one thing (as both are often taken to be); negotiation and power suggest many meanings and practices. What can we learn about the rich negotiation practices planners use to work their tables? In what other ways are planners anticipating and negotiating power and interests? We have used our image of working the planning table as a trope for seeing the terrain and action of planning in ways that allow us to ask such questions. We know why planning matters and we know the political and ethical risks planners face. We know that planners exercise power to negotiate people's interests at planning tables. This book is alive with illustrations that personify our interpretations. However, we are just beginning to learn about the myriad discrete negotiation tactics that people use at the planning table (Cervero & Wilson, 1996; Hendricks, 2001; Mabry & Wilson, 2001; Yang & Cervero, 2001; Yang, Cervero, Valentine, & Benson, 1998). This matters because, if adult educators are to contribute to creating a better world, then we need to better understand how planners work their tables in order to better that work.

References

Apple, M. W. (1979). *Ideology and curriculum*. New York: Routledge.

Apple, M. W. (1990). *Ideology and curriculum* (2nd ed.). New York: Routledge.

Apple, M. W. (1992). The text and cultural politics. *Educational Researcher, 21*(7), 4–11, 19.

Apple, M. W. (1996). Power, meaning, and identity: Critical sociology of education in the United States. *British Journal of Sociology of Education, 17*(2), 125–144.

Apps, J. (1985). *Improving practice in continuing education*. San Francisco: Jossey-Bass.

Apps, J. (1991). *Mastering the teaching of adults*. Malabar, FL: Krieger.

Archie-Booker, D. E., Cervero, R. M., & Langone, C. A. (1999). The politics of planning culturally relevant AIDS prevention education for African-American women. *Adult Education Quarterly, 49*(4), 163–175.

Baptiste, I. (2000). Beyond reason and personal integrity: Toward a pedagogy of coercive restraint. *Canadian Journal for the Study of Adult Education, 41*(1), 27–50.

Beals, G., Blount, R., Powers, R., & Johnson, W. (1966). *Social action and interaction in program planning*. Ames: Iowa State University Press.

Beder, H. W. (1978). An environmental interaction model for agency development in adult education. *Adult Education, 28*, 176–190.

Beder, H. (Ed.). (1986). *Marketing continuing education*. San Francisco: Jossey-Bass.

Benveniste, G. (1989). *Mastering the politics of planning*. San Francisco: Jossey-Bass.

Bernstein, R. (1983). *Beyond objectivism and relativism: Science, hermeneutics, and praxis*. Philadelphia: University of Pennsylvania Press.

Blackburn, D. J. (Ed.). (1994). *Extension handbook: Processes and practices.* Toronto: Thompson Educational Publishing.

Bolman, L., & Deal, T. (1997). *Reframing organizations: Artistry, choice, and leadership* (2nd ed.). San Francisco: Jossey-Bass.

Boone, E. J. (1992). *Developing programs in adult education.* Prospect Heights, IL: Waveland.

Boone, E. J., Safrit, R. D., & Jones, J. (2002). *Developing programs in adult education: A conceptual programming model* (2nd ed.). Prospect Heights, IL: Waveland.

Boulmetis, J., & Dutwin, P. (2000). *The ABCs of evaluation: Timeless techniques for program and project managers.* San Francisco: Jossey-Bass.

Boyle, P. G. (1981). *Planning better programs.* New York: McGraw-Hill.

Boyle, P., & Jahns, I. (1970). Program development and evaluation. In R. Smith, G. Aker, & J. Kidd (Eds.), *Handbook of adult education* (pp. 59–74). New York: Macmillan.

Brackhaus, B. (1984). Needs assessment in adult education: Its problems and prospects. *Adult Education Quarterly, 34,* 233–239.

Brookfield, S. (1986). *Understanding and facilitating adult learning.* San Francisco: Jossey-Bass.

Brookfield, S. (1995). *Becoming a critically reflective teacher.* San Francisco: Jossey-Bass.

Brookfield, S. (2001). A political analysis of discussion groups: Can the circle be unbroken? In R. M. Cervero, A. L. Wilson, & Associates, *Power in practice: Adult education and the struggle for knowledge and power in society* (pp. 206–225). San Francisco: Jossey-Bass.

Brown, A. H., Cervero, R. M., & Johnson-Bailey, J. (2000). Making the invisible visible: Race, gender, and teaching in adult education. *Adult Education Quarterly, 50,* 273–288.

Brunner, E., Wilder, S., Kirchner, C., & Newberry, J. (1959). *An overview of adult education research.* Chicago: AEA/USA.

Bryson, L. (1936). *Adult education.* New York: American Book Company.

Burch, G. (1948). Community organization for adult education. In M. Ely (Ed.), *Handbook of adult education in the United States* (pp. 281–288). New York: Institute of Adult Education, Teachers College, Columbia University.

Burns, R., & Cervero, R. M. (2004). Issues framing the politics of pastoral ministry practice. *Review of Religious Research, 45*(3), 235–253.

Buskey, J. (1987). Utilizing a systematic program planning process. In Q. H. Gessner (Ed.), *Handbook on continuing higher education* (pp. 103–124). London: Macmillan.

Caffarella, R. S. (1988). *Program development and evaluation resource book for trainers.* New York: Wiley.

Caffarella, R. S. (1994). *Planning programs for adult learners: A practical guide for educators, trainers, and staff developers*. San Francisco: Jossey-Bass.

Caffarella, R. S. (2002). *Planning programs for adult learners: A practical guide for educators, trainers, and staff developers* (2nd ed.). San Francisco: Jossey-Bass.

Capper, C. (Ed.). (1993). *Educational administration in a pluralistic society*. Albany: State University of New York Press.

Carlson, D., & Apple, M. W. (1998). *Power, knowledge, pedagogy: The meaning of democratic education in unsettling times*. Boulder, CO: Westview Press.

Carter, T. M. (1996). How people's interests affect empowerment planning in a health promotion coalition. In R. M. Cervero & A. L. Wilson (Eds.), *What really matters in adult education program planning: Lessons in negotiating power and interests* (pp. 27–35). New Directions for Adult and Continuing Education, No. 69. San Francisco: Jossey-Bass.

Cervero, R. M. (1984a). Collaboration in university continuing professional education. In H. W. Beder (Ed.), *Realizing the potential of interorganizational cooperation* (pp. 23–38). New Directions for Adult and Continuing Education, No. 23. San Francisco: Jossey-Bass.

Cervero, R. M. (1984b). Evaluating workshop implementation and outcomes. In T. J. Sork (Ed.), *Designing and implementing effective workshops* (pp. 55–67). New Directions for Adult and Continuing Education, No. 22. San Francisco: Jossey-Bass.

Cervero, R. M. (1988). *Effective continuing education for professionals*. San Francisco: Jossey-Bass.

Cervero, R., & Azzaretto, J. (Eds.). (1990). *Visions for the future of continuing professional education*. Athens, GA: University of Georgia.

Cervero, R. M., & Scanlan, C. L. (1985). *Problems and prospects in continuing professional education*. San Francisco: Jossey-Bass.

Cervero, R. M., & Wilson, A. L. (1994a). *Planning responsibly for adult education: A guide to negotiating power and interests*. San Francisco: Jossey-Bass.

Cervero, R. M., & Wilson, A. L. (1994b). The politics of responsibility: A theory of program planning practice for adult education. *Adult Education Quarterly, 45*, 249–268.

Cervero, R. M., & Wilson, A. L. (1995). Responsible planning for continuing education in the health professions. *The Journal of Continuing Education in the Health Professions, 15*(4), 196–202.

Cervero, R. M., & Wilson, A. L. (Eds.). (1996). *What really matters in adult education program planning: Lessons in negotiating power and interests*. New Directions for Adult and Continuing Education, No. 69. San Francisco: Jossey-Bass.

Cervero, R. M., & Wilson, A. L. (1998). Working the planning table: The political practice of adult education. *Studies in Continuing Education, 20*(1), 5–21.

Cervero, R. M., & Wilson, A. L. (1999). Beyond learner-centered practice: Adult education, power, and society. *Canadian Journal for the Study of Adult Education, 13*(2), 27–38.

Cervero, R. M., & Wilson, A. L. (2001). At the heart of practice: The struggle for knowledge and power. In R. M. Cervero, A. L. Wilson, & Associates, *Power in practice: Adult education and the struggle for knowledge and power in society* (pp. 1–20). San Francisco: Jossey-Bass.

Cervero, R. M., Wilson, A. L., & Associates. (2001). *Power in practice: Adult education and the struggle for knowledge and power in society.* San Francisco: Jossey-Bass.

Clandinin, J., & Connelly, M. (2000). *Narrative inquiry: Experience and story in qualitative research.* San Francisco: Jossey-Bass.

Clark, B. R. (1956). *Adult education in transition: A study of institutional insecurity.* Berkeley: University of California Press.

Clark, B. R. (1958). *The marginality of adult education.* Chicago: Center for the Study of Liberal Education for Adults.

Collins, M. (1991). *Adult education as vocation: A critical role for the adult educator.* London: Routledge.

Counts, G. S. (1932). *Dare the school build a new social order?* New York: John Day.

Courtenay, B. C. (1990). An analysis of adult education administration literature, 1936–1989. *Adult Education Quarterly, 40*, 63–77.

Cronon, W. (1992). A place for stories: Nature, history, and narrative. *Journal of American History, 78*(4), 1347–1376.

Davidson, H. (1995). Making needs: Toward a historical sociology of needs in adult and continuing education. *Adult Education Quarterly, 45*, 183–196.

Deshler, D. (1998). Measurement and appraisal of program success. In P. S. Cookson (Ed.), *Program planning for the training and continuing education of adults: North American perspectives* (pp. 301–328). Malabar, FL: Krieger.

Donaldson, J. F., & Edelson, P. (2000). From functionalism to postmodernism in adult education leadership. In A. Wilson & E. Hayes (Eds.), *Handbook of adult and continuing education: New edition* (pp. 191–207). San Francisco: Jossey-Bass.

Donaldson, J. F., & Kozoll, C. E. (1999). *Collaborative program planning: Principles, practices, and strategies.* Malabar, FL: Krieger.

Drennon, C. E., & Cervero, R. M. (2002). The politics of facilitation in practitioner inquiry groups. *Adult Education Quarterly, 52*, 193–209.

Edwards, R. (1997). *Changing places? Flexibility, lifelong learning, and a learning society*. London: Routledge.

Essert, P. (1951). *Creative leadership of adult education*. New York: Prentice-Hall.

Essert, P. (1964). Concepts of the organization and administration of the adult education enterprise. In G. Jensen, A. Liveright, & W. Hallenbeck (Eds.), *Adult education: Outlines of an emerging field of university study* (pp. 177–200). Chicago: Adult Education Association of the USA.

Fellenz, R. A. (1998). Selecting formats for learning. In P. S. Cookson (Ed.), *Program planning for the training and continuing education of adults: North American perspectives* (pp. 347–374). Malabar, FL: Krieger.

Fenwick, T., & Parsons, J. (2000). *The art of evaluation: A handbook for educators and trainers*. Toronto: Thompson Educational Publishing.

Finger, M., & Asun, J. (2001). *Adult education at the crossroads: Learning our way out*. London: Zed Books.

Flannery, D. D. (1998). Staffing. In P. S. Cookson (Ed.), *Program planning for the training and continuing education of adults: North American perspectives* (pp. 455–480). Malabar, FL: Krieger.

Flax, J. (1992). The end of innocence. In J. Butler & J. W. Scott (Eds.), *Feminists theorize the political* (pp. 445–463). New York: Routledge.

Foley, G. (1999). *Learning in social action: A contribution to understanding informal education*. London: Zed Books.

Foley, G. (2001). *Strategic learning: Understanding and facilitating organizational change*. Sydney: Centre for Popular Education.

Forest, L. B. (1976). Program evaluation: For reality. *Adult Education, 26*, 167–177.

Forest, L. B., & Baker, H. R. (1994). The program planning process. In D. J. Blackburn (Ed.), *Extension handbook: Processes and practices* (pp. 86–99). Toronto: Thompson Educational Publishing.

Forest, L. B., Brack, R. E., & Moss, G. M. (1994). In D. J. Blackburn (Ed.), *Extension handbook: Processes and practices* (2nd ed.) (pp. 177–189). Toronto: Thompson Educational Publishing.

Forester, J. (1989). *Planning in the face of power*. Berkeley: University of California Press.

Forester, J. (1990). Evaluation, ethics, and traps. In N. Krumholz & J. Forester (Eds.), *Making equity planning work: Leadership in the public sector* (pp. 241–260). Philadelphia: Temple University Press.

Forester, J. (1993). *Critical theory, public policy, and planning practice*. Albany: State University of New York Press.

Forester, J. (1999). *The deliberative practitioner: Encouraging participatory planning processes*. Cambridge, MA: MIT Press.

Foucault, M. (1977). *Discipline and punish: The birth of the prison* (A. Sheridan, Trans.). New York: Vintage.

Frankel, C. (1977). John Dewey's social philosophy. In S. M. Cahn (Ed.), *New studies in the philosophy of John Dewey* (pp. 3–44). Hanover, NH: University Press of New England.

Freire, P. (1970). *Pedagogy of the oppressed* (M. Ramos, Trans.). New York: Continuum.

Friedmann, J. (1987). *Planning in the public domain.* Princeton, NJ: Princeton University Press.

Galbraith, M. W. (Ed.). (1990). *Adult learning methods: A guide for effective instruction.* Malabar, FL: Krieger.

Galbraith, M., Sisco, B., & Guglielmino, L. (1997). *Administering successful programs for adults: Promoting excellence in adult, community, and continuing education.* Malabar, FL: Krieger.

Giddens, A. (1979). *Central problems in social theory: Action, structure, and contradiction in social analysis.* Berkeley: University of California Press.

Giddens, A. (1984). *The constitution of society: Outline of the theory of structuration.* Cambridge, MA: Polity Press.

Goody, A., & Kozoll, C. (1995). *Program development in continuing education.* Malabar, FL: Krieger.

Griffin, C. (1983). *Curriculum theory in adult and lifelong education.* London: Croom Helm.

Griffith, W. (1978). Educational needs: Definition, assessment, and utilization. *School Review, 86*(3), 382–394.

Grotelueschen, A. D. (1980). Program evaluation. In A. B. Knox & Associates, *Developing, administering, and evaluating adult education* (pp. 75–123). San Francisco: Jossey-Bass.

Guthrie, D. C., & Cervero, R. M. (2001). The politics of moving continuing education to the center of the institutional mission. In R. E. Reber & D. B. Roberts (Eds.), *A lifelong call to learn: Approaches to continuing education for church leaders* (pp. 179–190). New York: Abingdon Press.

Habermas, J. (1971). *Knowledge and human interests* (J. Shapiro, Trans.). Boston: Beacon Press.

Hall, B. L. (2001). The politics of globalization: Transformative practice in adult education graduate programs. In R. M. Cervero, A. L. Wilson, & Associates, *Power in practice: Adult education and the struggle for knowledge and power in society* (pp. 107–125). San Francisco: Jossey-Bass.

Hallenbeck, W. (1948). Training adult educators. In M. Ely (Ed.), *Handbook of adult education in the United States* (pp. 243–252). New York: Institute of Adult Education, Teachers College, Columbia University.

Hansman, C. A., & Mott, V. W. (2001). Philosophy, dynamics, and context: Program planning in practice. *Adult Learning, 11*(2), 14–16.

Hart, M. (1990). Critical theory and beyond: Further perspectives on emancipatory education. *Adult Education Quarterly, 40*, 125–138.

Hart, M. (1992). *Adult education and the future of work.* New York: Routledge.

Hart, M. (2001). Transforming boundaries of power in the classroom: Learning from *La Mestiza.* In R. M. Cervero, A. L. Wilson, & Associates, *Power in practice: Adult education and the struggle for knowledge and power in society* (pp. 164–183). San Francisco: Jossey-Bass.

Harvey, D. (1996). *Justice, nature, and the geography of difference.* Oxford, UK: Blackwell.

Heaney, T. (1996). *Adult education for social change: From center stage to the wings and back again.* Information Series, No. 365. Columbus, OH: ERIC Clearinghouse on Adult, Career, and Vocational Education.

Hendricks, S. M. (1996). Renegotiating institutional power relationships to better serve nursing students. In R. M. Cervero & A. L. Wilson (Eds.), *What really matters in adult education program planning: Lessons in negotiating power and interests* (pp. 37–46). New Directions for Adult and Continuing Education, No. 69. San Francisco: Jossey-Bass.

Hendricks, S. (2001). Contextual and individual factors and the use of influencing tactics in adult education program planning. *Adult Education Quarterly, 51*, 219–235.

Hlebowitsh, P. S. (1995). Interpretations of the Tyler Rationale: A reply to Kliebard. *Journal of Curriculum Studies, 27*, 81–88.

Hood, S. (2000). Commentary on deliberative democratic evaluation. In K. E. Ryan & L. DeStefano (Eds.), *Evaluation as a democratic process: Promoting inclusion, dialogue, and deliberation* (pp. 77–83). New Directions for Evaluation, No. 85. San Francisco: Jossey-Bass.

Hooper, B. (1992). "Split at the roots": A critique of the philosophical and political sources of modern planning. *Frontiers, 13*(1), 45–80.

Horton, M., & Freire, P. (1990). *We make the road by walking: Conversations on education and social change.* Philadelphia: Temple University Press.

Houle, C. O. (1972). *The design of education.* San Francisco: Jossey-Bass.

Houle, C. O. (1996). *The design of education* (2nd ed.). San Francisco: Jossey-Bass.

House, E. R., & Howe, K. R. (2000). Deliberative democratic evaluation. In K. E. Ryan & L. DeStefano (Eds.), *Evaluation as a democratic process: Promoting inclusion, dialogue, and deliberation* (pp. 3–12). New Directions for Evaluation, No. 85. San Francisco: Jossey-Bass.

Howard, T., Baker, H., & Forest, L. (1994). Constructive public involvement. In D. J. Blackburn (Ed.), *Extension handbook: Processes and practices* (2nd ed.) (pp. 100–114). Toronto: Thompson Educational Publishing.

Ingham, R. (1968). A comparative study of administrative principles and practices in adult education units. *Adult Education, 29,* 52–68.

Isaac, J. C. (1987). *Power and Marxist theory: A realist view.* Ithaca, NY: Cornell University Press.

Jiggins, J., & Shute, J. (1994). Participation and community action. In D. J. Blackburn (Ed.), *Extension handbook: Processes and practices* (2nd ed.) (pp. 115–123). Toronto: Thompson Educational Publishing.

Johnson-Bailey, J., & Cervero, R. M. (1997). Negotiating power dynamics in workshops. In J. A. Fleming (Ed.), *New perspectives on designing and implementing effective workshops* (pp. 41–50). New Directions for Adult and Continuing Education, No. 76. San Francisco: Jossey-Bass.

Johnson-Bailey, J., & Cervero, R. M. (1998). Power dynamics in teaching and learning practices: An examination of two adult education classrooms. *International Journal of Lifelong Education, 17,* 389–399.

Kellaghan, T., & Stufflebeam, D. L. (Eds.). (2003). *International handbook of educational evaluation. Part two: Practice.* Dordrecht, The Netherlands: Kluwer.

Kirkpatrick, D. L. (1994). *Evaluating training programs: The four levels.* San Francisco: Berrett-Koehler.

Kleiber, P. B. (1996). Leveling the playing field for planning university-based distance education. In R. M. Cervero & A. L. Wilson (Eds.), *What really matters in adult education program planning: Lessons in negotiating power and interests* (pp. 59–68). New Directions for Adult and Continuing Education, No. 69. San Francisco: Jossey-Bass.

Knowles, M. (1950). *Informal adult education.* New York: AAAE.

Knowles, M. (1970). *The modern practice of adult education: Andragogy vs. pedagogy.* New York: Association Press.

Knowles, M. (1980). *The modern practice of adult education: From pedagogy to andragogy* (Rev. ed.). Chicago: Association Press/Follett.

Knox, A. (1980). Approach. In A. Knox & Associates, *Developing, administering, and evaluating adult education* (pp. 1–12). San Francisco: Jossey-Bass.

Knox, A. (1986). *Helping adults learn.* San Francisco: Jossey-Bass.

Knox, A. (1991). Educational leadership and program administration. In J. Peters, P. Jarvis, & Associates, *Adult education: Evolution and achievements in a developing field of study* (pp. 217–258). San Francisco: Jossey-Bass.

Knox, A. (2002). *Evaluation for continuing education.* San Francisco: Jossey-Bass.

Kotler, P., & Fox, K. (1985). *Strategic marketing for educational institutions.* Englewood Cliffs, NJ: Prentice-Hall.

Kowalski, T. J. (1988). *The organization and planning of adult education.* Albany: State University of New York Press.

Larson, M. S. (1977). *The rise of professionalism: A sociological analysis.* Berkeley: University of California Press.

Lax, D. A., & Sebenius, J. K. (1986). *Manager as negotiator: Bargaining for cooperative and competitive gain.* New York: Free Press.

Lindeman, E. (1926). *The meaning of adult education.* New York: New Republic.

Liveright, A. (1959). *Strategies of leadership.* New York: Harper & Brothers.

Livingstone, D. (1983). *Class ideologies and educational futures.* London: Falmer.

London, J. (1959). Problems of the adult administrator. *Adult Education, 9*(4), 222–231.

London, J. (1960). Program development in adult education. In M. Knowles (Ed.), *Handbook of adult education in the United States* (pp. 65–81). Chicago: Adult Education Association.

Mabry, C. K., & Wilson, A. L. (2001). Managing power: The practical work of negotiating interests. In R. O. Smith, J. M. Dirkx, P. L. Eddy, P. L. Farrell, & M. Polzin (Eds.), *Proceedings of the 42nd Annual Adult Education Research Conference* (pp. 263–268). East Lansing: Michigan State University.

Maclean, R. G. (1997). Power at work: A case study of the practice of planning educational programs in a continuing education setting. *The Journal of Continuing Higher Education, 45,* 2–14.

Manglitz, E. (2003). Challenging white privilege in adult education: A critical review of the literature. *Adult Education Quarterly, 53,* 119–134.

Maruatona, T., & Cervero, R. M. (2004). Adult literacy education in Botswana: Planning between reproduction and resistance. *Studies in the Education of Adults, 37,* 235–251.

Mathews, J. (1959). Program planning and development. *Review of Educational Research, 29*(3), 280–285.

Mathison, S. (2000). Deliberation, evaluation, and democracy. In K. E. Ryan & L. DeStefano (Eds.), *Evaluation as a democratic process: Promoting inclusion, dialogue, and deliberation* (pp. 85–89). New Directions for Evaluation, No. 85. San Francisco: Jossey-Bass.

Mattimore-Knudson, R. (1983). The concept of need: Its hedonistic and logical nature. *Adult Education, 33,* 117–124.

Mazmanian, P. (1980). A decision-making approach to needs assessment and objective setting in continuing medical education. *Adult Education, 31,* 3–17.

McClusky, H. (1950). The organization and administration of adult education. *Review of Educational Research, 20*(3), 224–229.

McDonald, B. (1996). Counteracting power relationships when planning environmental education. In R. M. Cervero & A. L. Wilson (Eds.), *What really matters in adult education program planning: Lessons in negotiating power and interests* (pp. 15–26). New Directions for Adult and Continuing Education, No. 69. San Francisco: Jossey-Bass.

Mcquillan, M. (Ed.). (2000). *The narrative reader.* London: Routledge.

Mills, D., Cervero, R. M., Langone, C., & Wilson, A. L. (1995). The impact of interests, power relationships, and organizational structure on program planning practice: A case study. *Adult Education Quarterly, 46,* 1–16.

Mohanty, C. H. (1994). On race and voice: Challenges for liberal education in the 1990s. In H. A. Giroux & P. McLaren (Eds.), *Between borders: Pedagogy and the politics of cultural studies* (pp. 145–166). New York: Routledge.

Monette, M. (1977). The concept of educational need: An analysis of selected literature. *Adult Education, 27,* 116–127.

Monette, M. (1979). Need assessment: A critique of philosophical assumptions. *Adult Education, 29,* 83–95.

Morgan, G. (1986). *Images of organization.* Newbury Park, CA: Sage.

Morgan, G. (1997). *Images of organization* (2nd ed.). Thousand Oaks, CA: Sage.

Munson, L. S. (1992). *How to conduct training seminars* (2nd ed.). New York: McGraw-Hill.

Nadler, L., & Nadler, Z. (1987). *The comprehensive guide to successful conferences and meetings: Detailed instructions and step-by-step checklists.* San Francisco: Jossey-Bass.

Neufeldt, H., & McGee, L. (Eds.). (1990). *Education of the African American adult: An historical overview.* Westport, CT: Greenwood.

Newman, M. (1994). *Defining the enemy: Adult education in social action.* Sydney: Stewart Victor.

Newman, M. (1999). *Maeler's regard: Images of adult learning.* Sydney: Stewart Victor.

Newman, M. (2000). Program development. In G. Foley (Ed.), *Understanding adult education and training.* Sydney: Allen & Unwin.

Nowlen, P. M. (1988). *A new approach to continuing education for business and the professions: The performance model.* New York: Macmillan.

Ottoson, J. M. (2000). Evaluation of continuing professional education: Toward a theory of our own. In V. M. Mott & B. J. Daley (Eds.), *Charting a course for continuing professional education: Reframing professional practice* (pp. 43–53). New Directions for Adult and Continuing Education, No. 86. San Francisco: Jossey-Bass.

Patton, M. Q. (1997). *Utilization-focused evaluation* (3rd ed.). Thousand Oaks, CA: Sage.

Pearce, S. (1998). Determining program needs. In P. Cookson (Ed.), *Program planning for the training and continuing education of adults* (pp. 249–272). Malabar, FL: Krieger.

Pennington, F., & Green, J. (1976). Comparative analysis of program development in six professions. *Adult Education, 27,* 13–23.

Petrina, S. (2004). The politics of curriculum and instructional design/theory/form: Critical problems, projects, units, and modules. *Interchange, 35*(1), 81–126.

Pinar, W. F. (Ed.). (1974). *Heightened consciousness, cultural revolution, and curriculum theory.* Berkeley, CA: McCutchan.

Pinar, W. F., & Bowers, C. A. (1992). Politics of curriculum: Origins, controversies, and significance of critical perspectives. In G. Grant (Ed.), *Review of research in education, 18* (pp. 163–190). Washington, DC: American Educational Research Association.

Pinar, W. F., Reynolds, W., Slattery, P., & Taubman, P. (1995). *Understanding curriculum: An introduction to the study of historical and contemporary curriculum discourses.* New York: Peter Lang.

Prosser, C., & Bass, M. (1930). *Adult education: The evening industrial school.* New York: D. Appleton-Century.

Queeney, D. S. (1995). *Assessing needs in continuing education.* San Francisco: Jossey-Bass.

Rees, E. F., Cervero, R. M., Moshi, L., & Wilson, A. L. (1997). Language, power, and the construction of adult education programs. *Adult Education Quarterly, 47*(2), 63–77.

Reid, W. A. (1979). Practical reasoning and curriculum theory—In search of a new paradigm. *Curriculum Inquiry, 9*(3), 187–207.

Robinson, R. (1970). Toward a conceptualization of leadership for change. *Adult Education, 20*(3), 131–139.

Rogers, P. J., Petrosino, A., Huebner, T. A., & Hacsi, T. A. (2000). Program theory evaluation: Practice, promise, and problems. In T. A. Hacsi (Ed.), *Program theory in evaluation: Challenges and opportunities* (pp. 5–13). San Francisco: Jossey-Bass.

Rossing, B., & Howard, T. (1994). Community leadership and social power structures. In D. J. Blackburn (Ed.), *Extension handbook: Processes and practices* (pp. 79–85). Toronto: Thompson Educational Publishing.

Rothwell, W. J., & Cookson, P. S. (1997). *Beyond instruction: Comprehensive program planning for business and education.* San Francisco: Jossey-Bass.

Russ-Eft, D., & Preskill, H. (2001). *Evaluation in organizations*. Cambridge, MA: Perseus.

Ryan, K. E., & DeStefano, L. (Eds.). (2000). *Evaluation as a democratic process: Promoting inclusion, dialogue, and deliberation*. New Directions for Evaluation, No. 85. San Francisco: Jossey-Bass.

Sandlin, J., & Cervero, R. M. (2003). Contradictions and compromise: The curriculum-in-use as negotiated ideology in two welfare-to-work classes. *International Journal of Lifelong Education, 22*(3), 249–265.

Sandmann, L. R. (1993). Why programs aren't implemented as planned: Toward a flexible planning model. *Journal of Extension, 31,* 18–21.

Schied, F. (1993). *Learning in social context*. DeKalb: Northern Illinois University, LEPS Press.

Schon, D. (1983). *The reflective practitioner*. New York: Basic Books.

Schon, D. (1987). *Educating the reflective practitioner*. San Francisco: Jossey-Bass.

Schubert, W. (1986). *Curriculum: Perspective, paradigm, and possibility*. New York: Macmillan.

Schwab, J. J. (1969). The practical: A language for curriculum. *School Review, 78*(1), 1–23, 586–587.

Scott, S. M., & Schmitt-Boshnick, M. (1996). Collective action by women in community-based program planning. In R. M. Cervero & A. L. Wilson (Eds.), *What really matters in adult education program planning: Lessons in negotiating power and interests* (pp. 69–79). New Directions for Adult and Continuing Education, No. 69. San Francisco: Jossey-Bass.

Seaman, D. F., & Fellenz, R. A. (1989). *Effective strategies for teaching adults*. Columbus, OH: Merrill.

Sessions, K. B., & Cervero, R. M. (2001). Solidarity and power in urban gay communities: Planning HIV prevention education. In R. M. Cervero, A. L. Wilson, & Associates, *Power in practice: Adult education and the struggle for knowledge and power in society* (pp. 247–266). San Francisco: Jossey-Bass.

Shor, I. (1992). *Empowering education: Critical teaching for social change*. Chicago: University of Chicago Press.

Shor, I. (1996). *When students have power: Negotiating authority in a critical pedagogy*. Chicago: University of Chicago Press.

Simerly, R. (1990). *Planning and marketing conferences and workshops: Tips, tools, and techniques*. San Francisco: Jossey-Bass.

Simon, H. A. (1955). A behavioral model of rational choice. *Quarterly Journal of Economics, 61,* 495–521.

Simon, H. A. (1956). Rational choice and the structure of environments. *Psychology Review, 69,* 129–138.

Simon, H. A. (1957). *Models of man*. New York: Wiley.

Sloane-Seal, A. (2001). Program planning in adult education. In D. Poonwassie & A. Poonwassie (Eds.), *Fundamentals of adult education* (pp. 116–132). Toronto: Thompson Educational Publishing.

Smith, D., & Offerman, M. (1989). The management of adult and continuing education. In S. Merriam & P. Cunningham (Eds.), *Handbook of adult and continuing education* (pp. 246–259). San Francisco: Jossey-Bass.

Sork, T. J. (Ed.). (1991). *Mistakes made and lessons learned: Overcoming obstacles to successful program planning*. New Directions for Adult and Continuing Education, No. 49. San Francisco: Jossey-Bass.

Sork, T. J. (1996). Negotiating power and interests in planning: A critical perspective. In R. M. Cervero & A. L. Wilson (Eds.), *What really matters in adult education program planning: Lessons in negotiating power and interests* (pp. 81–99). New Directions for Adult and Continuing Education, No. 69. San Francisco: Jossey-Bass.

Sork, T. J. (1997). Workshop planning—Motivation with a mission understanding. In J. A. Fleming (Ed.), *New perspectives on designing and implementing effective workshops* (pp. 5–17). New Directions for Adult and Continuing Education, No. 76. San Francisco: Jossey-Bass.

Sork, T. J. (1998). Program priorities, purposes, and objectives. In P. S. Cookson (Ed.), *Program planning for the training and continuing education of adults: North American perspectives* (pp. 273–300). Malabar, FL: Krieger.

Sork, T. J. (2000). Planning educational programs. In A. L. Wilson & E. Hayes (Eds.), *Handbook of adult and continuing education: New edition* (pp. 171–190). San Francisco: Jossey-Bass.

Sork, T. J. (2001). Needs assessment. In D. Poonwassie & A. Poonwassie (Eds.), *Fundamentals of adult education* (pp. 100–115). Toronto: Thompson Educational Publishing.

Sork, T. J., & Buskey, J. H. (1986). A descriptive and evaluative analysis of program planning literature, 1950–1983. *Adult Education Quarterly, 36*, 86–96.

Sork, T. J., & Caffarella, R. S. (1989). Planning programs for adults. In S. B. Merriam & P. M. Cunningham (Eds.), *Handbook of adult and continuing education* (pp. 233–245). San Francisco: Jossey-Bass.

Sork, T. J., & Newman, M. (2004). Program development in adult education and training. In G. Foley (Ed.), *Dimensions of adult learning: Adult education and training in the global era* (pp. 96–117). Maidenhead, UK: Open University Press.

Thompson, E. (1963). *The making of the English working class*. New York: Vintage.

Thompson, J. (1997). *Words in edgewise: Radical learning for social change*. Leicester, UK: NIACE.

Tisdell, E. J. (2001). The politics of positionality: Teaching for social change in higher education. In R. M. Cervero, A. L. Wilson, & Associates, *Power in practice: Adult education and the struggle for knowledge and power in society* (pp. 145–163). San Francisco: Jossey-Bass.

Tyler, R. (1949). *Basic principles of curriculum and instruction*. Chicago: University of Chicago Press.

Umble, K. E., Cervero, R. M., & Langone, C. A. (2001). Negotiating about power, frames, and continuing education: A case study in public health. *Adult Education Quarterly, 51*(2), 128–145.

Usher, R., Bryant, I., & Johnston, R. (1997). *Adult education and the postmodern challenge: Learning beyond the limits*. London: Routledge.

Vella, J. (1994). *Learning to listen, learning to teach: The power of dialogue in educating adults*. San Francisco: Jossey-Bass.

Verner, C. (1964). Definition of terms. In G. Jensen, A. A. Liveright, & W. Hallenbeck (Eds.), *Adult education: Outlines of an emerging field of university study* (pp. 27–39). Chicago: Adult Education Association.

Waldron, M. (1994). Management and supervision. In D. J. Blackburn (Ed.), *Extension handbook: Processes and practices* (2nd ed.) (pp. 190–200). Toronto: Thompson Educational Publishing.

Walker, D. F. (1971). A naturalistic model for curriculum development. *School Review, 80*(1), 51–65.

Walker, D. F. (1990). *Fundamentals of curriculum*. New York: Harcourt Brace Jovanovich.

Walker, D. F. (2003). *Fundamentals of curriculum* (2nd ed.). Mahway, NJ: Lawrence Erlbaum.

Walters, S. (1996). Gender and adult education: Training gender-sensitive and feminist adult educators in South Africa—An emerging curriculum. In P. Wangoola & F. Youngman (Eds.), *Towards a transformative political economy of adult education: Theoretical and practical challenges* (pp. 293–319). DeKalb: Northern Illinois University, LEPS Press.

Weiss, C. (1986). The stakeholder approach to evaluation: Origins and promise. In E. R. House (Ed.), *New directions in educational evaluation* (pp. 145–157). Bristol, PA: Falmer.

Welton, M. (Ed.). (1987). *Knowledge for the people: The struggle for adult learning in English-speaking Canada, 1828–1973*. Toronto: OISE Press.

West, C. (1989). *The American evasion of philosophy: A genealogy of pragmatism*. Madison: University of Wisconsin Press.

White, T., & Belt, J. (1980). Leadership. In A. Knox & Associates, *Developing, administering, and evaluating adult education* (pp. 216–248). San Francisco: Jossey-Bass.

Wilson, A. L. (1993). The common concern: Controlling the professionalization of adult education. *Adult Education Quarterly, 44*, 1–16.

Wilson, A. L. (2001). The politics of place. In R. M. Cervero, A. L. Wilson, & Associates, *Power in practice: Adult education and the struggle for knowledge and power in society* (pp. 226–246). San Francisco: Jossey-Bass.

Wilson, A. L. (2005). Program planning. In L. English (Ed.), *International encyclopedia of adult education* (pp. 524–529). London: Palgrave Macmillan.

Wilson, A. L., & Cervero, R. M. (1995). Moving toward a critical pragmatism of teaching program planning in adult education: Linking "how-to" with "what-for." *Review Journal of Philosophy & Social Science, 20*(1&2), 77–100.

Wilson, A. L., & Cervero, R. M. (1996). Who sits at the planning table: Ethics and planning practice. *Adult Learning, 8*(2), 20–22.

Wilson, A. L., & Cervero, R. M. (1997). The song remains the same: The selective tradition of technical rationality in adult education program planning theory. *International Journal of Lifelong Education, 16*(2), 84–108.

Wilson, A. L., & Cervero, R. M. (2001). Power in practice: A new foundation for adult education. In R. M. Cervero, A. L. Wilson, & Associates, *Power in practice: Adult education and the struggle for knowledge and power in society* (pp. 267–287). San Francisco: Jossey-Bass.

Wilson, A. L., & Cervero, R. M. (2002). The question of power and practice. In K. Kunzel (Ed.), *International yearbook of adult education* (pp. 209–226). Cologne: Bohlau-Verlag.

Wilson, A. L., & Cervero, R. M. (2003). A geography of power, identity, and difference in adult education curriculum practice. In R. G. Edwards & R. Usher (Eds.), *Space, curriculum, and learning* (pp. 123–138). Greenwich, CT: Information Age Publishing.

Wilson, A.L., & Hayes, E. (2000). On thought and action in adult and continuing education. In A. L. Wilson & E. R. Hayes (Eds.), *Handbook of adult and continuing education: New edition* (pp. 15–32). San Francisco: Jossey-Bass.

Winter, S. L. (1996). The "power" thing. *Virginia Law Review, 82*(5), 721–835.

Yang, B., & Cervero, R. M. (2001). Power and influence styles in programme planning: Relationship with organizational political contexts. *International Journal of Lifelong Education, 20*(4), 289–296.

Yang, B., Cervero, R. M., Valentine, T., & Benson, J. (1998). Development and validation of an instrument to measure adult educators' power and influence tactics in program planning practice. *Adult Education Quarterly, 48,* 227–244.

Youngman, F. (1996). A transformative political economy of adult education: An introduction. In P. Wangoola & F. Youngman (Eds.), *Towards a transformative political economy of adult education: Theoretical and practical challenges* (pp. 3–32). DeKalb: Northern Illinois University, LEPS Press.

The Authors

Ronald M. Cervero and Arthur L. Wilson have collaborated on research, books, and articles that provide a political perspective and analysis of planning educational programs for adults. Their books include, as authors, *Planning Responsibly for Adult Education: A Guide to Negotiating Power and Interests* (1994), and, as editors, *What Really Matters in Adult Education Program Planning: Lessons in Negotiating Power and Interests* (1996) and *Power in Practice: Adult Education and the Struggle for Knowledge and Power in Society* (2001), which focuses more broadly on the politics of adult education. Cervero's and Wilson's joint research in this area received the 1995 and 1997 Imogene Okes Award for Research from the American Association for Adult and Continuing Education.

Ronald M. Cervero is professor of adult education and head of the Department of Lifelong Education, Administration, and Policy at the University of Georgia. He received his B.A. degree (1973) in psychology from St. Michael's College, Vermont, his M.A. degree (1975) in the social sciences from the University of Chicago, and his Ph.D. degree (1979) in adult education, also from the University of Chicago.

Cervero has published extensively in adult education, with particular emphasis in the areas of power and race, the politics of program planning, and continuing education for the professions. His book *Effective Continuing Education for Professionals* (1988) received the 1989 Cyril O. Houle World Award for Literature in Adult Education and the 1990 Frandson Award for Literature from the National University Continuing Education Association. In addition to his books with Wilson, described above, his other books in this area are *Problems and Prospects in Continuing Professional Education* (1985) and *Visions for the Future of Continuing Professional Education* (1990).

Cervero has served in a variety of leadership positions in adult education. He was on the executive committee for the Adult Education Research Conference (1982, 1983), a cofounder of the Midwest Research-to-Practice Conference in Adult and Continuing Education (1982), a member of the executive committee for the Commission of Professors of Adult Education (1986–1988; 1998–2000), and a coeditor of *Adult Education Quarterly* (1988–1993). He has been a visiting faculty member at Teachers College-Columbia University, the University of Calgary, the University of Tennessee, the University of Wisconsin-Madison, the University of British Columbia, and Pennsylvania State University.

Arthur L. Wilson is professor of adult education and program leader of Adult and Extension Education in the Department of Education at Cornell University. He received his B.A. degree (1972) in sociology from the University of Virginia, his M.S.Ed. degree (1980) in adult and continuing education from Virginia Polytechnic Institute and State University, and his Ed.D. degree (1991) in adult education from the University of Georgia.

Wilson's major research focus is on the politics of adult education, specifically the role of power in shaping educational practices. In addition to his work with Cervero, described above, his interest in adult education foundations has produced a number of historical and philosophical articles and chapters; he received the Graduate Student Research Award (1992) given by the North American Adult Education Research Conference for his graduate study on the epistemological foundations of adult education. Wilson has had extensive editorial experience: as assistant editor of the Virginia

ABE Newsletter (1979–1981), as editor of *Virginia Association for Adult and Continuing Education Newsletter* (1986–1988), and as editorial associate for *Adult Education Quarterly* (1988–1991). He is or has been a consulting editor for *Adult Education Quarterly, International Journal of Lifelong Education, Journal of Adult Basic Education, Canadian Journal for the Study of Adult Education,* and *Studies in the Education of Adults.* He was coeditor of *Adult Education Quarterly* (2000–2003) and *Handbook of Adult and Continuing Education* (2000).

Wilson served on the executive board of the Virginia Association for Adult and Continuing Education (1986–1988) and received its distinguished service award (1987); he also served as the executive secretary for the Indiana Association of Adult and Continuing Education and the Indiana Community Education Association (1992–1995). He has chaired the Imogene Okes Award for Research committee and was on the executive committee of the Commission of Professors of Adult Education (1997–1999). He received a Kellogg Fellowship (1988–1990) to attend the University of Georgia. He has been a visiting faculty member at Old Dominion University, George Mason University, and the University of Alberta, Canada.

Index